Fallacies and Pitfalls
of Language

Fallacies and Pitfalls of Language

THE LANGUAGE TRAP

S. Morris Engel

DOVER PUBLICATIONS, INC.

NEW YORK

Copyright

Bibliographical Note

This Dover edition, first published in 1994, is an unabridged, slightly corrected republication of the work originally published in 1984 by Prentice-Hall, Inc., Englewood Cliffs, N.J., under the title *The Language Trap Or How to Defend Yourself Against the Tyranny of Words*.

Library of Congress Cataloging-in-Publication Data

Engel, S. Morris.
    Fallacies and pitfalls of language : the language trap / S. Morris Engel.
        p.   cm.
    Rev. ed. of: The language trap. c1984
    Includes index.
    ISBN-13: 978-0-486-28274-9
    ISBN-10: 0-486-28274-0
    1. Language and logic. 2. Verbal self-defense. I. Engel, S. Morris. Language Trap. II. Title.
P39.E53 1994
165—dc20   94-19770
                                                  CIP

Manufactured in the United States by Courier Corporation
28274006   2015
www.doverpublications.com

For my colleague
K. T. FANN

Contents

III
THE LURE OF AUTHORITARIANISM

Introduction

Human beings can be defined as talking animals. Talk reveals who and what we are, but talk can also betray us and bring us to grief.

Although language seems the oldest, the easiest, and the most natural of our gifts, it is in reality one of the most difficult, subtle, and treacherous of them. Nothing we do is more complicated than the use we make of language, and nothing else we do reveals so much about us. That language is truly a gift there can be little doubt. If it had not been given to us—if we had not acquired it—we could not have invented it. Those few human beings in whom language was never awakened—feral children, for example—never have in fact succeeded in learning it.

Because our talk is such an intimate and familiar part of us, we let it flow freely from our lips, rarely making a conscious or deliberate attempt to control or guide it. And, on most occasions, when all is well, it needs no such control or guidance. But when things are not well with us—when we are troubled or upset, or even merely preoccupied—our talk is the first to reflect and broadcast this fact. Were we wise, we should be silent at such moments.

What we send out can be absurdly different from what we thought we sent. Yet the responses may turn out to be disquietingly appropriate. A daughter whines pleadingly: "Oh, Mommy, I want you to stop treating me like a child. I'm not a child anymore, you know." And she doesn't understand why her mother continues to treat her that way—nor, perhaps, does the mother. Or someone shouts angrily: "I am not mad! Why do you say I'm mad!" and fails to realize how his tone of voice betrays him. Too late, we may realize what it is we have really communicated, as in the example of the wife who remarked to her husband after looking at some travel folders with him: "Honey, if one of us dies, I think I'll go live in Paris."

Because its roots run so deep, language reveals us to ourselves and to others in profound and crucial ways. And this applies not only to embarrassing "Freudian slips" of the type just noted, but even to such seemingly superficial details of language as errors in spelling and grammar. Often such errors are not accidental but rather indicative of patterns firmly established in us. Similarly, language also pictures our inner qualities. The faults so mirrored may themselves be minor, but what they reveal about us may be far from trivial. The bureaucrat who can't speak in anything but the passive voice (revealing an unwillingness to take responsibility for his or her actions) is displaying not only an irritating linguistic habit but one that is deeply revelatory, psychologically and morally.

The metamessages others send us can therefore be crucial. To ignore them would be foolhardy. Decoding them, however, involves an examination of certain features of language not normally discussed in textbooks on grammar. Nevertheless, we are becoming more and more aware of how very much at the heart of grammar such things indeed lie. And this is true even when no specific grammatical label has yet been devised for the particular lapse that is otherwise psycholinguistically so illuminating.

For example, we have a label for the answer of the little old lady in New York to the fellow who stopped her to ask how he could get to Carnegie Hall: "Practice, practice, my boy." And we can label the reasoning of the man who declared that religion is evil because religion is the worship of the Lord of the land and he had never met a landlord who wasn't evil. But what label exists for the lapse committed by the woman who took her child to a psychiatrist, exclaiming, "I tell her a dozen times a day that I love her, but the brat still hates me. Why doctor?"

Animals are no doubt aware, but only human beings are conscious. And what degree of consciousness, as well as what degree of enlightenment we possess, becomes immediately apparent when we speak. Since a language is also a culture's repository of its accumulated wisdom and values, in speaking it we also cannot help but reveal how we stand within the culture or how alienated we are from it. In our culture someone who is sincerely loved is never referred to as a "brat," and one who is not a crook feels no need to insist, "I am not a crook."

But we need to learn how to protect ourselves not only from ourselves but also—or, perhaps, especially—from others. In Orwell's fantasy about totalitarianism, *1984*, Big Brother plans the gradual replacement of standard English, called *Old*speak, with a thought-control language called *New*speak. In part, this meant that some words would be phased out and other new words phased in. Mostly it meant a continuous conditioning of the public to think of old words in new ways. This massive brainwashing began with Big Brother's three slogans, "War is Peace," "Freedom is Slavery," and "Ignorance is Strength." One does not need to be deeply immersed in the affairs of our own day to recognize that Big Brother has long since arrived on our shores. The only difference is that his slogans are presented to us in somewhat subtler forms than those of Orwell's novel.

But not all that much subtler. Consider, as a case in point, how prone our administration and pentagon officials have been—especially around budget time—to refer to our armed services as "peacekeeping forces." Our armed forces may be many things, but what they primarily are—what all armed services are—are *warmaking* forces. To call them anything else distorts their significance and distances us from the reality of how they are meant to be used.

A defender of euphemistic jargon might argue that this use of the adjective "peacekeeping" really isn't so bad—that it simply refers to an unspoken argument, which states that the mere existence of powerful U.S. armed services will act as a deterrent to foreign aggressors and military adventurers and will thus help to maintain peace. Yet such arguments are much too controversial to be left unstated. Certainly they are too controversial to be offered to us, not as arguments, but as definitions. (Incidentally, one test of the sincerity of this line of argument might be to inquire—since the same dubious logic applies—why we never seem to refer to the massive tank divisions of the Warsaw Pact as "peacekeeping forces.")

Still, if this sly blurring of reality went no further, it might not be intolerably dangerous. In fact, it always does go further. It is all too short a step from calling some military establishment a "peacekeeping force" to defining its essential warmaking activities as "pacifications." That is how we spoke of our savage war against the Viet Cong, and that is how the Russians currently describe their bloody presence in Afghanistan. What begins as a blur somehow ends as a lie, and before we know it—presto!—"War is Peace."

Big Brother's other pernicious slogans insinuate themselves into public debate with equal ease. For example, in the past 20 years how many repressive regimes in, let us say, South or Central America has our government supported on the grounds that the regime represents a bulwark against the spread of Communism? And although we may have been pretty sure that most of the regimes in question could never have survived a free election, some of us might have been able to rationalize away this uncomfortable knowledge by arguing that "the people down there aren't ready for democracy" and that any freedoms they might have gained at the polls would soon have been lost to a Communist takeover anyway. So, in a sense, their freedom would have been their guarantee of slavery . . . wouldn't it? Have the Russians put their case against the Polish Solidarity movement much differently? Score another for Big Brother.

As for "Ignorance is Strength," let us only mention in passing the zeal of some parental and religious groups in cleansing school libraries and reading lists of "smut" and "secular humanism." Let us quickly move on to take note of the sad truth that Big Brother has up his sleeve many more Alice-in-Wonderland slogans than just the three we have mentioned so far.

It is not for some abstract ideal of being "good citizens and intelligent voters" that we have always to be on guard against Big Brother's logical sleights-of-hand. Our immediate personal safety and well-being could very well be at stake. And worst of all is the danger that we might unwittingly become Big Brothers ourselves. It is exceedingly unpleasant to go forth to meet the enemy, only to discover that, in Pogo's words, "they is us."

Although we associate the malignant image of Big Brother with the realm of public policy, there are other areas of life where telling it like it isn't exacts a severe price from all of us. One of these areas is advertising, which has its effects especially on our young people. Their increasing difficulties both in and out of school have been traced by more than one researcher to their early indoctrination by television. To be shown on countless occasions that there are instant simple solutions to all problems is hardly the best preparation for the hard work and frustrations that real life requires of us. Adults may understand that not all—or, indeed, any really important—problems can be solved by Alka Seltzer or Breck shampoo, but children who have been conditioned to think that there are easy remedies for everything are bound to doubt that it is really necessary to devote countless tiresome hours to mastering geometry or algebra. Even if the strength and maturity to submit to such discipline was present in children as part of their natural endowment, those thousands of hours of television would long since have eroded it.

The same, unfortunately, applies to children's physical health: Young children lack the sophistication necessary to deal with the seductive commercials seen daily on television. Where snack consumption is concerned, the hard sell of these ads encourages eating habits that can eventually lead to tooth decay, obesity, diabetes, and heart disease.

The essential point to remember is that advertising is a type of propaganda concerned with the mass selling of a product or a service. Like all propaganda, what it exploits is our human frailties and susceptibilities. None of us wants to offend, and so small fortunes are spent on mouthwashes and deodorants. We all yearn to be popular, so we are easily persuaded that if we can get to look like that model with those Calvin Klein jeans, we couldn't help but be popular. Besides, who are we to question those attractive, appealing, and wordly creatures who come dancing and singing into our living rooms, full of brio, offering to share some of their magic with us? Orson Welles, after all, has been around a good deal; and if he says that a certain wine is never sold before its time, it must be so.

To be sure, this kind of advertising propaganda can be analyzed fairly easily by any adult who is willing to make the effort. Who is recommending the product? What is his or her real motive? Where did he or she get this information? What does it really mean? If we're told that, "Two of three dentists prefer Brand X," let us ask questions. Who chose the dentists? How many were polled? Who did the polling? Might a different group produce different results?

But other kinds of advertising propaganda are not so easy to unravel. For example, National Airline's slogan "Fly me. I'm Joan" helped that firm capture a sizable portion of the passenger traffic. These more subtle appeals exploit a new phenomenon that has swept our time—a phenomenon that, for our present purposes, I shall call "intellectualism." The key characteristic of this typically twentieth-century phenomenon is its absorption with form as such—whether that be the word, the tone, the color, or the symbol. The disciplines of abstract logic, atonal music, nonrepresentational art, as well as much avant garde poetry, are all outgrowths of this intellectual emphasis on form.

Although a great boon to the world of advertising, which has exploited it commercially, this kind of intellectualism has also been responsible for the widespread self-evasion that so many of us are guilty of. Increasingly, we have come to value words above the things they represent. "How to account for all this added heft?" asks a report on obesity. "Adults are obviously not getting appreciably taller, and they usually do not get more muscular. All we can say is that the weight increase we found is due to fat." Superficially these words may sound reasonable, but they merely dance around the point at issue. Would it not have been more honest to have said, "We don't know why people are getting fatter or eating more"? But that is the price we have come to pay for living in the rarefied atmosphere of words. We shall see, in what follows, what havoc abstraction has come to play with the world of fact.

What has fed this tendency toward abstraction, with its attendant increase in self-deception, has been the persistent growth of euphemism in our language. It has not been only the military-industrial complex that has discovered the value of calling warmaking forces "peacekeeping forces" or a refugee camp a "New Life Hamlet." All of us have done so. And thus we have come to use such words as "animal welfare officer" for dogcatcher, "mispeak" for lie, "credibility gap" for deceit. On a somewhat different but no less revealing plane, husbands have become "support persons" and delivery rooms have become "birth suites"—which one gathers, is good news for babies but not such good news for husbands.

Although euphemism may not always be bad, it is obvious that talk of "substandard housing," rather than of rotting slums, has reduced our ability to properly assess the significance of poverty and blunted a good deal of our sensitivity to the suffering endured there. Euphemism is valuable if it doesn't deceive or if we do not use it to deceive ourselves. But we must be careful not to make this a case of the emperor's new clothes, where everybody wants something to work so much that they just believe it does. It might sometimes be necessary and wiser to face up to the fact that some students are not merely "underachievers," but in fact do not have and may never have what it takes to compete with their peers academically. In such cases, it would be kinder to revise the students' goals than to go on mincing words.

By the same token, knowledge of the way a language's structure determines how those who speak it view reality can also help us to better understand the plight of others. If a girl can come to tolerate herself more readily if she thinks of herself as a "swinger" rather than as promiscuous, and if a voyeur can salve his guilt feelings more easily by pretending he is going to see some "adult" rather than porno movie (even perhaps persuading himself he is supporting "freedom of artistic expression" in the process), let us not be too quick to condemn.

The study of such matters can also lead those of us who are parents of young children to become more effective parents. The lesson to be learned here is the same: The reality we live in is largely created by the language with which we describe it. And especially where children are concerned, the value of being able to distinguish between the descriptive and evaluative dimensions of our words can be enormous. Dr. Haim Ginott, the distinguished child psychologist who has earned the gratitude of thousands of parents through his teaching, was the first to apply this classic semantic concept to the raising of children—and with remarkable results. Dr. Ginott has taught parents to steer clear of words like "stupid," "clumsy," "bad," and even words like "beautiful," "good," and "wonderful" that judge a child's character and ability. Instead, he recommends the use of words that describe—describe what the parent sees and feels. The new method has proven to be remarkably effective.

If, for example, a child were to spill a glass of milk, instead of saying, "Stupid! You always spill everything. You'll never learn, will you!" parents have been taught to say, "I see the milk spilled," and then hand the child a sponge. In this way, the blame and verbal abuse is avoided, and the emphasis is put where it belongs—on what needs to be done.

Similarly, if a child's messy room bothers a parent, the parent is taught to feel free to express his genuine feelings—but not with insults and accusations: "Why are you such a slob? You never take care of your things. You've turned this room into a pig sty!" Instead, the parent describes his or her feelings: "When I see how messy this room is, it makes me very angry! I see things lying all over the place, and it makes me furious. I feel like I want to open the window and throw everything out!" There is still yelling here and venting of rage, but there is no name-calling, no berating, and no language that wounds. And the room gets cleaned up just the same.

To realize how people's use of language reveals them is to come to realize for the first time how exposed we all are. Because this has become more and more a world of words, and because a good deal of our life is now led in this more rarefied verbal atmosphere, we owe it to ourselves to learn everything we can about the subtle ways in which language operates. We cannot afford to let our own words betray us. Still less can we afford to let other people's words betray us.

This book is intended to be a kind of "manual of verbal self-defense"—defense against the deceptions that we practice on ourselves and against the deceptions that others try to practice on us, either unwittingly or deliberately. The principles on which this defensive art is based are very ancient—older by far than the precepts of, say, judo, karate, or kung fu. But, as in the martial arts, there are still surprisingly few people who can claim to have achieved the verbal equivalent of a black belt. I say "surprisingly" because verbal self-defense is both much easier to master than physical self-defense and very much more valuable. In fact, if you were to learn no more than the few simple principles set forth in this book, you would—comparatively speaking—probably be well on your way towards qualifying as an expert yourself.

By "expert" I do not, of course, mean someone who cannot be lied to, although verbal self-defense experts are usually much better at detecting outright lies than ordinary people. Rather, the expert is one who cannot be taken in by flim-flam, by misleading propaganda, by short-circuited logic, by proofs that do not prove, by emotion-laden irrelevancies, by specious appeals to authority or principle—in short, by any of the corrupted varieties of intellectual formalism that daily try to divert us from the plain truth.

Such experts can be formidable adversaries in any sort of discussion or controversy, but as a general rule they are not particularly argumentative. They understand mere debater's points too well to be much interested in scoring them. They are far more concerned with keeping themselves and everyone else honest and with making all discussions productive rather than merely competitive.

If I seem to be speaking of verbal self-defense experts as though they were a breed apart, in an all too real sense they are. Even though their stock in trade may seem to amount to little more than an informed clear-headedness, they are a rare and valuable asset to any society. So if this book succeeds in helping even a few people along the path towards acquiring such expertise, it will not only be they who benefit.

1

WORDS

1

The Way Words Work

The first person to recognize the important role of language in our lives was Aristotle, still considered by many the greatest philosopher of all time. The immediate impetus for his study of this topic was a group of highly controversial people called Sophists who held the populace of Athens spellbound with their brilliance and wit. Having mastered the art of winning verbal contests, they offered to teach it to anyone willing to pay their high fees. Athens was a democracy, and knowing how to address a crowd and how to present oneself and one's case in the most appealing light was essential for success. The Sophists, the first to develop and teach the art of persuasion, therefore found no dearth of clients in Athens thirsting for success and willing to pay whatever price was demanded to achieve it. But the Sophists, growing more and more arrogant and radical, pressed their wit too far and eventually began to lose their reputation. In time the very name Sophist came to acquire the meaning it retains to this day. As the dictionary tells us, a sophist is someone who is clever and tricky, who engages in fallacious reasoning, and who tries to outmaneuver and take advantage of an opponent in every possible way.

But when Aristotle first came in contact with the Sophists, in the middle of the fourth century B.C., their reputation, although already in decline, had not yet deteriorated to that degree. Aristotle accompanied Plato, his teacher, as the latter engaged in discussion with them. The young pupil, finding himself baffled and challenged by their ability to outwit and outsmart all comers, decided to examine what it was that enabled these "experts" to accomplish their feats.

The result was a work on logic (one of six he was to devote to the study of thinking) entitled *Of Sophistical Refutations*. The title hints at its content, for Aristotle set out in this manual to expose the strategy and tactics that the Sophists employed in order to gain their verbal victories.

But Aristotle was not the only one to leave us an account of these first "PR men" in the Western world. Plato also devoted a number of his dialogues to them. Probably the most memorable of them, although it is the least subtle and hardly does them justice, is *Euthydemus*.

The dialogue opens with Socrates, who serves as Plato's spokesman, relating his encounter with two recent arrivals in Athens—the Sophists Euthydemus and Dionysodorus. The two have singled out a young boy, Cleinias, and are busy questioning him. Also present is a close friend of Cleinias, Ctesippus, who gets clobbered later when he tries to come to his friend's rescue. The Sophists always attracted a large crowd, and there is one here too.

The questioning begins with Euthydemus asking Cleinias which people learn things best—the wise or the unwise? The boy, understanding the word *wise* to mean "intelligent," naturally replies that it is the wise who learn best and not the unwise. However, by playing fast and loose with the meaning of the word, quickly shifting from one sense of it to another, the Sophist soon gets Cleinias to deny what he has just affirmed, subsequently to affirm it once again, then to deny it, until he is completely befuddled, to the great amusement of the crowd that has gathered to watch the spectacle.

Having finished off Cleinias, the two Sophists turn next to Socrates:

Socrates: Then once more the admirers of the two heroes, in an ecstasy at their wisdom, gave vent to another peal of laughter. Turning to me Dionysodorus said:

Dionysodorus: Reflect Socrates: you may have to deny your words.

Socrates: I have reflected, and I shall never deny my words.

Dionysodorus: Well, and so you say that you wish Cleinias to become wise.

Socrates: Undoubtedly.

Dionysodorus: And he is not wise yet?

Socrates: At least his modesty will not allow him to say that he is.

Dionysodorus: You wish him to become wise and not to be ignorant? You wish him to be what he is not, and no longer to be what he is? . . . You wish him no longer to be what he is? Which can only mean that you wish him to perish! Pretty lovers and friends they must be who want their favorite not to be, that is, to perish!

Socrates: I was thrown into consternation at this and was quite baffled. While in this state, a friend of Cleinias', Ctesippus, intervened and the Sophists turned to him.

Dionysodorus: If you will answer my questions, I will soon extract the same admissions from you, Ctesippus. You say you have a dog.

Ctesippus: Yes, a villain of a one.

Dionysodorus: And he has puppies?

Ctesippus: Yes, and they are very like himself.
Dionysodorus: And the dog is the father of them?
Ctesippus: Yes, I certainly saw him and the mother of the puppies come together.
Dionysodorus: And he is not yours?
Ctesippus: To be sure he is.
Dionysodorus: Then he is a father, and he is yours; ergo, he is your father, and the puppies are your brothers.
Euthydemus: Ctesippus: Let *me* ask you one little question: you beat this dog?
Ctesippus: (Laughing). Indeed I do; and I only wish I could beat you instead of him.
Euthydemus: Then you beat your father!

Plato is in a Neil Simon mood here, engaging in broad comedy. In the course of the dialogue he has them prove, among others things, that it is impossible to tell a lie, since a lie is "that which is not" and thus can have no existence; that good men speak evil, since they would not be good if they did not speak evil of evil things; and that everything visible "has the quality of vision" and hence can see. Not all Sophists were as easy to ridicule, nor were the fallacies committed by them always as easy to track down as those represented here. Nevertheless, this was the task that Plato's able student Aristotle set himself.

Aristotle's little work, *Of Sophistical Refutations,* led to a whole new type of investigation, one that continued to be pursued by other philosophers after him. They recognized, like him, that errors in logic, although often amusing, nevertheless can cause serious problems—for individuals, for groups, and for nations.

In his other logical works, however, Aristotle discovered something else about language and thinking that was to prove of enormous importance. Certainly we can be led astray easily by people like Sophists or by their modern-day counterparts, and a study of their tactics is absolutely essential. But we must also learn to develop a healthy respect for the structures built into our language and even the content packed into our words and idioms. Rules govern the use of language, rules that are binding on all of us and determine what we may or may not say. We violate these only at our peril.

Aristotle went on to show how very limited and bound in fact we are by the way we talk. He demonstrated this by examining the main units of language with which we do most of our thinking—the categorical proposition and the arguments, called syllogisms, that employ those propositions.

By *categorical proposition,* Aristotle meant simply the declarative sentence, the common sentence we all speak: "The table is brown," or "The sky is clear." A *syllogism* is an argument composed of such sentences. Like

Molière's gentleman who didn't realize he had been speaking prose all his life, few of us are aware that most of the reasoning we engage in is syllogistic.

This fact easily escapes us because our reasoning is often highly abbreviated and its formal structure is not always clear to us. Even an epithet like "Liar!" hurled at someone is in essence an argument—and a formally valid one at that. For, unpacked, what it contains is the following reasoning:

> All people who try to deceive others by uttering what they know to be false are liars.
> You are such a person.
> Therefore you are a liar.

Although the categorical proposition is only one way in which we can organize our thought, it is nevertheless the main one, accounting for perhaps as much as 90 percent of our reasoning. Aristotle discovered a surprising thing about it: Although we might believe that the vast number of words in our language would allow us to compose an unlimited number of different propositions and arguments, the fact is that the number of different *types* of propositions we can construct is severely limited, and the combinations of these in possible argument forms can be determined exactly.

Aristotle went on to determine just how many argument forms the various combinations of categorical propositions make possible. He found the number to be exactly 256. So much for freedom of thought! More depressing still was the further discovery that of these 256 argument forms, only some 15 are valid!

Long before Aristotle arrived on the scene people had engaged and reflected on reasoning, but he is considered the founder of logic, and we can see why. He was the first to make a science of it.

Still, although Aristotle singlehandedly founded a new science—one that was considered complete and perfect for over 2,000 years—there was at least one aspect of thinking he did not explore very fully. In fact, that aspect didn't really come to be understood until relatively recent times. Observing the types of propositions we make use of in our thinking, Aristotle decided to investigate the type of thinking made possible by such propositions and their various combinations. And we saw with what results. But in our own day it occurred to some linguists and anthropologists to raise questions about the categorical proposition itself. It became all too apparent that the world's languages were not all the same: Some people spoke languages that were profoundly different in structure from those generally spoken by Aristotle's readers. And the rest of their world also seemed profoundly different from the world familiar to the readers of Aristotle. Could there be a connection, they wondered, between these two facts? Certainly, as Aristotle showed, words have implications and mark off what it is we can or cannot say. But might it not be the case that the sorts of words and structures chosen determine what is even more fundamental, namely, what we can think *to begin with?* For the complete story, then, must we not add to Aristotle's science of thinking a science of what is *thinkable,* and how that too is determined by the structures of language?

The fact that all this was not recognized earlier was due in great part to our strong tendency to believe that thinking is independent of the words that convey it and therefore is not limited in any way by them. The truth is the very opposite: Language is the instrument which makes thought possible in the first place.

In his recent and widely admired book, *Less Than Words Can Say,* Richard Mitchell (the so-called "Underground Grammarian") provides the reader with a striking illustration of how the language we speak colors profoundly the world in which we live. He contrasts two primitive tribes—the Jiukiukwe and the Manhassetites—whose languages differ dramatically in their grammatical structure.

The Jiukiukwe Indians, Mitchell relates, live in swamps near the headwaters of the Orinoco in South America. They are the most primitive people on earth: They do not know the use of fire; they wear no clothing, build no shelters, and use no tools, except for unworked rocks which they bang on trees in order to dislodge the bark and expose the grubs and worms on which they live. Although their technology is limited to the banging of trees with stones, they have numerous words to describe the process. They have separate and unrelated words for flat stones, round stones, big stones, little stones, sharp stones, and so on, but they have no word for "stone." In the case of trees, the vocabulary is even larger, although again they have no word that simply means "tree."

Their vocabulary and grammar of kinship are similarly very large and complex, containing separate words for every possible degree of relationship. There is a special word, for instance, for the oldest son of your mother's next youngest sister, and still another word for him should he have reached that estate through the death of some older brother. However, since all the Jiukiukwe are related to one another in some precisely nameable way, they have no need for words that mean "family" or "relative" and have none. Still, questions of kinship are of supreme importance to them and govern every aspect of their lives, "correct" social behavior being a matter of doing and saying the right thing to the right relative under the right circumstances.

Although the Jiukiukwe have both passive and active forms, they consider it a serious breach of etiquette, amounting almost to sacrilege, to use the active form when speaking of persons. In a child, the use of the active voice in the first person singular is considered less serious, although it is discouraged as a mark of arrogance or aggressiveness. Thus the Jiukiukwe do not say: "I am eating my worm," but rather "With regard to the worm unto me, there is an occasion of eating." Animals and objects, however, are normally the subjects of active verbs. Such sentences as "The sun rises" and "The worm crawls" are quite permissible.

Very different from the Jiukiukwe are the inhabitants of Manhasset, who speak a language in which the typical statement takes the form of a sentence that names a doer and deed. The most common elaboration also names the "object" of the deed. Thus, "I want food" is a typical utterance. The structure of this sentence may be modified and elaborated on in many ways, some of them quite extensive and complicated, but it remains the enduring skeleton of the typical statement: a doer does something, often *to* something or someone. The continuous reappearance of this structure has taught all Manhassetites a particular view of the world and their role in it. They understand the world as a place where doers do things.

And their actions illustrate that understanding, both for good and ill. They possess a relatively advanced technology, which has made possible a more varied and abundant diet, and they are enterprising and vigorous. They are also, however, quarrelsome and quick to anger and belong to a subgroup of a large, warlike tribe whose members are constantly at war with one another.

The continuous reappearance of the type of structure embedded in the language the Jiukiukwe speak, on the other hand, has taught them that doing is properly the business of the things in the world around them. And they do not think of themselves as the "objects" of the things that are done in the world. For the Jiukiukwe, the inanimate or animal doers do deeds as though the tribesmen were, if not always unaffected bystanders, at least no more than accidentally related to what happens. The Jiukiukwe are just there; the world does its things around them, sometimes "in their case."

Since war can arise only from the willed deeds of agents, the Jiukiukwe, unlike the Manhassetites, do not know war and do not engage in it. They are also unburdened with such emotions as hatred, envy, and competitiveness.

Technological change comes about when somebody does things to something, so it is not surprising that life among the Jiukiukwe continues today as it always has. And they will no doubt always live exactly as they do today—unless something occurs to change either their language (which in time will force a change in their technology and therefore mode of life) or their technology directly (which, in turn, will bring concomitant changes in the language). To illustrate the point, Mitchell invites his readers to visualize the following occurrence:

> Imagine that some particularly eccentric or mildly demented Jiukiukwe should develop the rude habit of speaking in the active and saying things

like "I will find worms." He has now announced, to the Jiukiukwe way of thinking, some purported fact about the world and has at the same time subjected himself to considerable social disapproval. If he's to get back into the good graces of his older sister's father-in-law, and of everybody else, he had damn well better come up with the worms, the more the better. Then his arrogant statement might be re-understood and perhaps accepted indeed as a statement of fact about the world. In desperation, he might well discover that you can find more worms by prying off the bark with a sharp-edged stone than by banging the tree till the bark falls off. It might occur to him that some sharp stones are easier to hold and manipulate than others. Remember, he's going to work hard; they're all waiting for him to find worms and thus justify a statement in which he spoke of himself as one might speak of the sun or the moon. That's serious. It won't be long before he finds an obviously broken stone that works very well, and then it will come to him that he might bang some of those less efficient round stones together until *they* break and turn into good worm-diggers. Out of the active voice, a technology will be born. Before long, his relatives, noticing how plump and healthy he looks, will learn to copy both his magic, his verbs as well as his stones, and that will be the end of civilization as the Jiukiukwe know it. [pp. 25–26]

What such anthropological information teaches us is that, immediately and directly, what we know is not "the world itself" but rather an order of things as symbolized and suggested by our language, the structures and vocabularies of which have shaped and formed us into the beings we are. Thus, the greater part of the world in which we live—the one to which we respond and which reacts to us—is in a very real sense a world that we ourselves have fashioned, one that is kept alive by our language and culture. But, of course, it is no less real for all that.

We may well think it only too typical of a primitive and idle people to spend their lives and energies devising and recognizing every imaginable familial relationship, an intricate system of kinship which then comes to govern every aspect of their lives. But they too might find it astonishing that we should have burdened ourselves with the complicated system of social relationships operative in our world. When precisely, they might wonder, to use one of Mitchell's analogies, does a co-worker become a colleague? When does a colleague become an associate? When does an associate become an accomplice? When is an accomplice a partner? When is a partner a sidekick? For the Jiukiukwe to master all this properly, they would need to understand our culture with all its unspoken values and beliefs. (That is why speaking a language—any language—is the most complicated thing a person can do.) And we too would need to learn their culture, with its incredibly complex system of familial relationships, if we wished to avoid betraying our ignorance or severely offending all by, say, referring inadvertently to someone's wife as his whore.

We would not take such an "error" lightly. Nor would they, for slips of the tongue are enormously revelatory about us. They are not simply signs of our failure to master a language; they are signs of our failure as persons. As Mitchell notes:

> If you could ask a Jiukiukwe why he takes such pains to address his mother's only brother's eldest daughter in just that way, he would probably have to say that he does it because it's "right." He's right. That's why we do things like that too. They're right. They are "right," however, entirely in a social sense. Language is arbitrary, but it's not anarchic. Although there's no reason why this or that in a language should be "right" and something else "wrong," it does not follow that you can do whatever you please in it. At some point, of course, when you wander too far from what is "right" you'll cease to be intelligible. But long before you reach that point you will send out the news that you are not a member in good standing around here. [p. 58]

We come, then, as Mitchell realizes only too well, although he does not go on to explore it in his book, to recognize how language can betray us. It does this in different ways. People who can't spell look bad because, as we can correctly assume, that is probably not the only thing they can't do. Besides, bad spelling is obviously a sign of not reading very much, for anyone who reads would have seen the misspelled words written correctly thousands of times. In addition a fluent command of one's language cannot exist as an isolated skill, for people who speak and write their native tongue clearly and precisely do so because of many other skills they possess. So, again, if they don't have this skill, we can assume other skills are also lacking.

One more point seems obvious: If language is not simply the instrument of thought but the mirror of the soul, and if its structures are so deeply rooted as we have seen them to be, then it must be capable of betraying even those of us who are ordinarily quite adept at handling it. For example, the husband, away on a business trip, who sent his wife the postcard with the brief message, "Having a wonderful time. Wish you were her," may not have been as ignorant of the spelling of that last word as we might think. And the wife who said, as she was looking at some travel folders with her husband, "Darling if one of us dies, I think I will go live in Paris" may not have been as innocent of the meaning of her remark as her incorrect usage of language suggests. Language in each case got the better of them, whether they deserved it or not. If we don't always say what we mean, we usually mean what we say.

But poor usage and spelling are only two of several things that can trip up a sentence—and us in the process. There are other ambiguities endemic to sentences as well, and each represents, as we will see in what follows, a special hazard for all of us.

2
Let Me Make
This Perfectly Clear

The man who was always offering to make things perfectly clear and the man of the Watergate tapes whose words were so filled with duplicitous ambiguity were one and the same. Richard Nixon taught us an invaluable lesson about language. Sentences can be filled with linguistic traps, and those who know their way around them can ruthlessly exploit those who do not.

One of the most common of these linguistic traps is called *amphiboly*. The fallacy applies to statements that, because of some ambiguity in them, admit of a double interpretation. The following is a typical example: "With her enormous nose aimed toward the sky, my mother rushed to the plane." Although it is probably clear enough that the enormous nose aimed toward the sky is the plane's and not the mother's, the choice of construction, alluding to a possible resemblance, may have been totally accidental. The same is perhaps true of the advertisement on a roadhouse that announced: "Clean and Decent Dancing Every Night Except Sunday." Although probably not meant to deceive us into thinking that something special in the way of dancing could be expected there on Sundays, the sign may have been designed, subconsciously, of course, to send us a different sort of message about the place. We shall never know for sure.

Not shrouded in mystery, however, are the roots of amphiboly. The ambiguity in sentence displaying the fallacy results from such grammatical lapses as improper punctuation, pronouns having ambiguous antecedents, dangling modifiers, and the like: "It pays to remember your social obligations. If you don't go to other people's funerals, they won't come to yours." (If "they" refers to those already buried, we needn't be overly concerned, of course.) "It all came back to him so plainly: a picture of the loveliest girl he'd ever seen hanging in the Navy locker." (Was it the girl garroted in the Navy locker or her picture?)

Sometimes the error arises from our failure to adjust our words to changing contexts. Failure to clarify the ambiguity by adding an extra word may be humorous, as in the case of the announcement, "Just received a new stock of sports shirts for men with 15 to 19 necks." But sometimes the failure is rather more serious, and perhaps revelatory, as it was in the case of the sign on a drugstore that said, "We Dispense with Accuracy." If the owners don't want us to get the wrong idea, they had better add the word "drugs" after the word "dispense." But then perhaps their carelessness with words is our warning signal.

Another rich source of such revelatory writing is the daily newspaper, especially its advertisement columns. Space is expensive and so shortcuts are taken—often at some risk. A case in point is the man who advertised his dog for sale, saying it "eats anything and is very fond of children." "For sale," another announced, "antique desk suitable for lady with curved legs and large drawers." How innocent of deeper meaning either of these declarations was is difficult to say, but being on guard is never unwise.

Because they must compress as much meaning as possible into few words, newspaper headlines, designed to brighten up our mornings, are also prone to the same kind of errors: "Killer Says Dead Man Was Chasing Him with Drawn Razor" (after he had killed him?); "Dock Workers Set to Walk Out in Atlantic Ports" (on the water?). The same need for compression applies to titles of books and signs in windows, and the same danger exists: *No People Like Show People* (sad to be so disliked!); "Bathing Suits 40% Off" (off the price or the suit?).

Vital statistics, recorded usually when we are under severe emotional pressure, are also a very rich source of such examples. One form that requested the cause of death was filled in with a number of notable replies. Someone said, "Don't know. Died without the aid of a physician." (No doubt they do help sometimes.) Another wrote, "Had never been fatally ill before" (trying to impress with his knowledge of a big word); and still someone else related that the deceased "went to bed feeling well, but woke up dead."

Compare this last example with the following remark by a reviewer of Beverly Sills's performance in Donizetti's opera *Maria Stuarda:* "Going to one's death onstage is nothing new for any opera singer. But Beverly Sills somehow always manages to put new life into it." In context that remark showed that the reviewer, far from being bedeviled by language, rather was able to work its magic.

We should note that a good deal of ambiguous writing is not necessarily revelatory of any special designs that the writers or speakers harbor;

often all it reveals is an author's plain clumsiness or inaneness: "The marriage of Miss Anna Black and Mr. Willis Dash, which was announced in this paper a few weeks ago, was a mistake and we wish to correct it." (What was a mistake?) "Police authorities are finding the solution of murders more and more difficult because the victims are unwilling to cooperate with the police." (What a pity!) "Alderman Sims said the Council ought to be given the whole truth that there was still sufficient coal in the city to last five weeks if nobody used it." (It would last forever under that condition.)

Although amphiboly is generally understood as arising from faulty construction of a single sentence, it can also result from the incongruous juxtaposition of two sentences. A typical example: "Unfortunately the Prime Minister had left before the debate began. Otherwise he would have heard some caustic comments on his absence." Needless to say, if he hadn't left there would have been no reason to complain—and he would have heard nothing! Another example: "Another performance of the pantomime is to be given in the Temple Auditorium. This will give those who missed seeing it, another chance of doing so." This example is perhaps more witty than ambiguous: We put the show on once, the author of the notice may be saying, but you didn't come; we're doing it again, but you turkeys will probably not come again. Finally, there is this testimonial for an insurance company: "My husband took out an accident policy with your company, and in less than a month he was accidentally drowned. I consider it a good investment." This slip-up is gross by any standard.

Amphiboly has sometimes been exploited, however, for humor. The following is a restaurant advertisement: "A Superb and Inexpensive Restaurant. Fine Foods Expertly Served by Waitresses in Appetizing Forms." *They* certainly are trying to make it perfectly clear, however unconsciously.

Belonging to a rather different category is the conscious and intentional use of the device. Of course, deviousness is here as well, but, because we are privy to it, it seems less perverse. An example is the Witch's prophecy in Shakespeare's *Henry VI*, Part II, scene 4. "The Duke yet lives that Henry shall depose," she says, which leaves it unclear whether "Henry shall depose the Duke" or "The Duke shall depose Henry." (She could have made her meaning clear by substituting "who" or "whom" for "that.") A much more interesting Shakespearian example, however, is the Witch's prophecy to Macbeth (Act IV, scene 1):

> Be bloody, bold and resolute; laugh to scorn
> The power of man, for none of woman born
> Shall harm Macbeth.

"None of woman born" turns out to be a bitter deception when Macbeth discovers that his enemy, Macduff, had had an unusual birth, having been "ripped untimely from his mother's womb." Macduff had apparently been born by Caesarian operation and so was not "of woman born" in the usual sense. The Witch was therefore not lying to Macbeth, but she was not exactly telling him the whole truth either.

No doubt the possibility of such ambiguity is why, in taking an oath, we do not swear simply to "tell the truth" (for we could then tell just part of it), nor even to "tell the truth, the whole truth" (for we could then throw in also a few lies, not having sworn not to do so), but rather "to tell the truth, the whole truth, and nothing but the truth." Had the Witch sworn that oath, she could not have used the words she did to Macbeth.

Amphiboly has been used to deceive not only in fiction but in fact as well. The classic example concerns Croesus and the oracle at Delphi. Contemplating war with Persia, Croesus consulted the oracle regarding the outcome. He received the oracular pronouncement that "if he went to war with Cyrus, he would destroy a mighty Kingdom." Delighted with this prediction, Croesus went to war and was swiftly defeated. Upon complaining to the oracle, he received the reply that the pronouncement was correct: In going to war he *had* destroyed a mighty kingdom—his own! The account is given by Herodotus, the first Greek historian, who castigates Croesus for being so dumb:

> But as to the oracle that was given him, Croesus doth not right to complain concerning it.... It behooved him, if he would take right counsel, to send and ask whether the god spoke of Croesus' or of Cyrus' kingdom. But he understood not that which was spoken, nor made further inquiry: wherefore now let him blame himself. [*The Histories,* Book I, Chapter 91]

Besides these ancient or purely literary examples, cases have been recorded of lives and fortunes saved or lost as a result of ambiguities. An interesting and well-known example is the case of the Russian prisoner who sought release from a Siberian prison by appealing to the Czar for a pardon. The Czar returned the unpunctuated reply "Pardon Impossible To Be Executed." He meant for the prisoner to be executed (the period intended after the word impossible), but the jailer in charge read the message to mean, "Pardon. Impossible To Be Executed" and released the prisoner. How the jailer fared subsequently is not related; no doubt when the error was discovered, he was substituted for the prisoner—judging by typical czarist justice.

Amphiboly is also capable of being exploited for purposes of gain. A typical example is the record entitled "Best of the Beatles," which misled many people into buying it, believing they were purchasing a record featuring the best songs of the Beatles. When they played it later at home, they discovered they had purchased a record featuring Mr. Peter Best, who had been a member of the Beatles (their drummer) early in the group's career.

The last example points to the explicit use of the device by people intentionally setting out to exploit language for purpose of deception. But always more interesting, and a good deal more subtle, are those cases in which there is an attempt to deceive but without the perpetrators themselves being totally aware of it—until exposed by language. The unfortunate postcard sent by the husband away on a business trip, and the remark made by the wife as she was looking over some travel folders with her husband are typical cases.

We have only ourselves to blame if in such cases we get the message and overlook the metamessage. If a prosecutor assures us, "The accused will be given a fair trial before he is hanged," we better believe it—and do something quickly.

But not all examples are as clear-cut as this one. Aside from their clumsy attempts at obscurantism and deviousness, what else do the following examples—gleaned from the files of automobile accident claims—reveal about their authors?

1. "An invisible car came out of nowhere, struck my car and vanished."
2. "I was thrown from my car as it left the road. I was later found in a ditch by some stray cows."
3. "My car was legally parked as it backed into the other vehicle."
4. "I pulled away from the side of the road, glanced at my mother-in-law, and headed over the embankment."
5. "The pedestrian had no idea which way to run, so I ran over him."
6. "The indirect cause of the accident was a little guy in a small car with a big mouth."

Perhaps the words tell us something about the real cause of accidents. Hostility may be more at fault than we realize.

3

I Wish You All the
Good Fortune You Deserve

We should listen very carefully to statements such as the one in the title. The tone can be tremendously revealing. If you yourself are ever tempted to say that sort of thing, it would be a good idea to make certain your feelings toward the other person are not somewhat mixed or ambivalent; if they are, it would not be a good idea to risk uttering the words.

Logicians call the linguistic trap to which we are referring *accent*—the fallacy that arises when it is unclear in what tone of voice a certain statement was intended to be uttered or where the stress in it was intended to fall.

A good deal can turn on this type of ambiguity. In one of the transcripts of the Watergate tapes, for instance, John Dean warns Nixon against getting involved in a cover-up, and the President replies: "No—it is wrong, that's for sure." But what inflection was Nixon giving this remark? Was it said in a serious and straightforward tone of voice, or was it said ironically? If it was uttered ironically, the remark would represent additional evidence of his involvement in the Watergate break-in. It is because tone of voice adds a further dimension to language that court clerks usually read testimony aloud in a monotone, trying in this way to keep out any indications of their own feelings about the matter they are reading.

If someone therefore says such things to you as, "I cannot praise this book too highly," "I shall lose no time in reading your paper," or "You never looked better," listen very carefully. On matters of this sort no one, or very few people, will tell you the naked truth. Recognizing the further capacity of spoken language to betray even its most cautious users can sometimes make you privy to facts normally very difficult if not impossible to learn.

24

The question of accent also arises in connection with which word a writer intended to stress. Here again we must recognize that something led the writer to choose a risky form of expression—perhaps honesty or hostility, self-destructiveness, or a growing sense of guilt. It would be a pity if the disclosure now fell on deaf ears, for another such opportunity may not come our way again very soon (at least not from that source).

Our failure to realize how vulnerable we are to this device of language is due perhaps to our not fully appreciating what an important dimension of language stress is. In fact, it is almost as important a part of language as word order. Let us consider, for example, the way the sentence "I hit him in the eye yesterday" changes its meaning as we introduce and move the word *only* around from one place to another in the sentence:

1. *Only* I hit him in the eye yesterday. (I alone did it.)
2. I *only* hit him in the eye yesterday. (I didn't kill him.)
3. I hit *only* him in the eye yesterday. (I hit him and no one else.)
4. I hit him *only* in the eye yesterday. (I hit him there and nowhere else.)
5. I hit him in the *only* eye yesterday. (He was a one-eyed monster, and so I let him have it.)
6. I hit him in the eye *only* yesterday. (It happened only yesterday.)
7. I hit him in the eye yesterday *only*. (It's not something I do every day.)

What is true of word order is true of word emphasis or stress. Thus if someone were to write us that "Jones thinks McIntosh will succeed," we would not necessarily know whether the sentence means that "*Jones* but not Smith thinks so," that "Jones only *thinks* McIntosh will succeed but doesn't really know for sure," or that "Jones thinks that *McIntosh* will succeed (but not, say, Anderson)."

If we find ourselves not caring very much one way or the other, we would probably feel differently were we one day to find the city traffic department putting up signs in our neighborhood reading:

| SLOW SCHOOL | or | SLOW CHILDREN CROSSING |

We would make sure they are quickly removed and replaced with the following designs:

| SLOW SCHOOL | or | SLOW CHILDREN CROSSING |

As with the fallacy of amphiboly, accent can be exploited for humorous purposes as well. A notable example is the poor worker in Charlie Chaplin's film *The Great Dictator* who growled, "This is a fine country to live in" and was promptly arrested by the police. He managed to get himself off, however, by pleading that, after all, all he said was, "This is a fine country to live in"—meaning, that it is a lovely, wonderful place.

Sometimes the humor is not intended. The famous passage in the First Book of Kings (Chapter 13, verse 13) is an example. The passage reads: "And he spake to his sons, saying: Saddle me the ass. And they saddled him."

The ambiguity, however, is not always so innocuous. The command given at the institution of the Eucharist is a case in point. What does the command "Drink ye all of it" mean?

1. "Drink *ye all* of it"—meaning, everyone should drink it?
2. "Drink ye *all of it*"—that is, some of you drink it, but drink it all up?

Doubt regarding its meaning was the cause of a good deal of heated dispute. The modern translation, opting for the former interpretation, is more elegant. It says: "Drink it, all of you."

The ending of the Mass in some versions offers another possible example of accent. The priest says, "The Mass is ended," and the people respond, "Thanks be to God," making it sound as though they are glad it's finally over. To avoid this interpretation, other versions lengthen the priest's speech by adding the words, "Let us go serve the Lord," which does make a difference.

The following two lines from *Macbeth* provide a further example of the kind of problems that accent sometimes poses. The scene (Act I, scene vii) is Macbeth's castle, where a dinner is given for the King and Queen to celebrate the recent military victory. It is the night the Macbeths have arranged to assassinate the King. But Macbeth seems to be having second thoughts, is agitated, and suddenly leaves the table. Lady Macbeth, determined that they should go through with their plot, quickly rises and follows him. Hearing her footsteps behind him, Macbeth turns around and says: "And if we fail?" To this Lady Macbeth replies by using two little words, "We fail." But without more explicit directions, it is really not possible to know what attitude Shakespeare intended Lady Macbeth to adopt here. Did he mean her to adopt a questioning attitude as if to say "We fail? Is that possible?" Or did he mean her to adopt a fatalistic attitude, as if to say: "Then we fail! And that will be that!" Perhaps he meant her simply to adopt an attitude of determination, as if to say: "We fail!? Impossible!!" We shall never know.

Is there any way we can avoid falling into the trap that the device of accent sometimes becomes? Although we obviously cannot always foretell how our words will be used or abused, understood or misunderstood on some future occasion, we can take some precautions. We can provide a background or context that won't leave us so exposed, and it need not be anything very elaborate. The addition of another emphatic word will sometimes do, as in the humorous anecdote about the two miners:

> "What's all this about 'one man, one vote'?" asked the Nottingham miner.
> "Why, one *bloody* man, one bloody vote," Bill replied.
> "Well, why the 'ell can't they say so?"

Sometimes, in order to avoid giving anything away, we need to take care to avoid terms that tend to call too much of the wrong sort of attention to themselves. Consider this newspaper account involving the word *hope*: "They will be married Sunday. Then they will spend a few weeks in a cottage by the sea, and by the time the honeymoon is over the groom hopes to be in the army." The word "expects" would be much more advisable here. A similar misuse can be found in this inscription from a tombstone: "Sacred To The Memory Of . . . . After living with her husband for 55 years she departed in hope of a better life."

The fallacy of accent can be found in still one further form. Sometimes the meaning of a statement or the content of a book, a speech, or a review is distorted by removing or quoting, not merely a word or a phrase, as in the ordinary case of accent, but whole sentences or portions of sentences out of context. This is a favorite device of advertisers, publicists, and journalists. Since very few people ever have or bother to take the time to read everything in their newspapers or other reports, the damage and misinformation conveyed by such dishonest advertising, misleading headlines, and blurbs, to say nothing of out-and-out misquotation, are probably enormous. How many of us have not been misled into buying a certain book or seeing a certain movie as a result of such out-of-context blurbs and misquotations?

Consider a few examples. A drama critic might write that he "liked all of the play, except the lines, the acting, and the scenery"—only to find himself quoted the next morning as saying that he "liked all of the play . . . " Or, to take a sadder example, a schoolteacher might tell her civics class that "communism is the best type of government if you care nothing for your liberty or your material welfare," only to discover that Johnny had quoted her at home as saying that "communism is the best type of government."

There is probably no way to be sure what Johnny will take back from school with him, but responsible writers who pick up a direct quotation should always indicate any omission of words or phrases by the use of ellipses. Not to do so is to tell only half the story and with it only half the truth. In addition, they should make a sincere effort to capture both the tone and flavor of the original in their paraphrase, providing the proper context of the remark in question as well.

A very serious violation of this rule regarding quoting sources with accuracy can be found in Kate Millet's widely read book *Sexual Politics*. One of the themes of Millet's explosive work is the demeaning way in which women are portrayed all-too-often by male novelists. To prove her case, Millet quotes large sections from such writers as Henry Miller, D. H. Lawrence, and Jean Genet. From the quotes she selects, it does indeed seem that these authors have portrayed women in a very shabby way. Millet's quotations aroused Norman Mailer's interest, and he went back to her sources and discovered that in their original contexts these portrayals took on quite a different aspect: Far from being described and portrayed in an insulting, demeaning manner, the female characters very often came off a good deal better than the males with whom their lives and affairs became entangled.

The following, for example, is the way Kate Millet tells her readers what has occurred in a certain place in D. H. Lawrence's novel *Women in Love:*

> Having begun by informing Ursula he will not love her, as he is interested in going beyond love to "something much more impersonal and harder," he goes on to state his terms: "I've seen plenty of women, I'm sick of seeing them. I want a woman I don't see. . . . I don't want your good looks, and I don't want your womanly feelings, and I don't want your thoughts, nor opinions, nor your ideas. [pp. 263–64]

But, as Norman Mailer points out, the scene in the book gives us a quite different impression of what in fact is taking place:

> There was silence for some moments.
> "No," he said. "It isn't that. Only—if we are going to make a relationship, even of friendship, there must be something final and irrevocable about it."
> There was a clang of mistrust and almost anger in his voice. She did not answer. Her heart was too much contracted. She could not have spoken.
> Seeing she was not going to reply, he continued, almost bitterly, giving himself away:
> "I can't say it is love I have to offer—and it isn't love I want. It is something much more impersonal and harder—and rarer."
> There was a silence, out of which she said:
> "You mean you don't love me?"
> She suffered furiously, saying that.
> "Yes, if you like to put it like that. Though perhaps that isn't true. I don't know. At any rate, I don't feel the emotion of love for you—no, and I don't want it, because it gives out in the last." [Lawrence, *Women in Love,* pp. 136–38]

Mailer remarks on how different all this is from Millet's description of it as "going beyond love to 'something much more impersonal and harder.' " Indeed it is. What has happened to the word "rarer" that Lawrence uses? He is obviously thinking of a diamond—something hard and rare; but Millet wants to convey a quite different image—that of steel. Lawrence seems to be emphasizing the feeling that they *are* in love, that the male character is fighting furiously to escape from it.

More striking still is the following example from D. H. Lawrence's *Lady Chatterley's Lover,* considered by many the most erotic novel in the English language. Kate Millet describes that famous episode between Mellors, the gardener, and Lady Chatterley in the following way:

"You lie there," he orders. . . . Mellors concedes one kiss on the navel and then gets to business. [p. 130]

But when we turn to the passage in the novel itself, we find the scene described as follows:

"You lie there," he said softly, and he shut the door, so that it was dark, quite dark. . . . Then with a quiver of exquisite pleasure he touched the warm soft body, and touched her navel for a moment in a kiss. [p. 130]

It is hard to know what precisely irritated Kate Millet so much about this scene that she recollected it in such a distorted version.

Accent can be found in still a further form: when certain remarks or statements are torn not only out of their literary contexts but out of their social or cultural contexts. In the process they are made to carry implications that they did not have in their original setting.

Certain writers have claimed, for example, that this or that great author or artist—say, Shakespeare or Chopin—was homosexual. In support of their claim they quote either from the works of these men or from their personal correspondence. Thus, in Shakespeare's case, the sonnets have been used for this purpose. There are, of course, some very mysterious people in the sonnets, and they are still an enigma to us. There is the fair Young Man whose beauty Shakespeare celebrates in many of the poems (Numbers 1 to 126) and for whom he obviously had a deep affection.

What such critics fail to tell their readers is that, although our present social conventions do not permit men to express such deep affection for other men, the conventions of Shakespeare's day did. Consequently, those love sonnets are no indication at all of Shakespeare's supposed homosexuality. Of course, what they also fail to tell their readers is that the sonnets are full of the poet's love for the Dark Lady (Numbers 127 to 154), with whom he obviously carried on a stormy affair—not being able, as he says in one of the poems, to "shun the heaven that leads men to this hell" (Number 128). Nor do they tell their readers that the Young Man later becomes the poet's rival for the affection of the woman, giving rise to an elegant variation on the traditional triangle.

What has been said here of Shakespeare is true also of Chopin. To quote out-of-context portions of Chopin's letters to his boyhood friend Tytus Woyciechowski is to leave no doubt in the mind of the reader that they had a homosexual relation. But almost in the same breath he begs Tytus to advise him what to do about his yearning for Konstancia Glad-kowska—the girl of his heart at the moment. The critics also fail to mention Chopin's later profound love for Marie Wodzinska. The bundle of letters, found in Chopin's desk after his death, that marked that unhappy love affair was held together by a wrapper on which Chopin had written two sad words, "My Sorrow." (Nor, of course, do they bother to mention Chopin's love affairs with other women.)

Distortion of the meaning of a person's utterances, by ignoring either their literary context or their larger social context, is surely a serious misuse of language about which we should all be wary.

4

Ask Not What

As everyone will immediately recognize and recall with fondness, these are the first three words of John F. Kennedy's famous inaugural appeal to the American people. But in his recent book *Looking Out For #1*, Robert J. Ringer takes President Kennedy to task for the remark and says the following about it and similar sorts of slogans:

> Governments, of course, are the masters of intimidation through slogan, simply because they have the money, the manpower and, if needed, the guns to back them up. My candidate for the most intimidating government slogan ever tossed at the American public was John F. Kennedy's emotion-grabber: "And so, my fellow Americans, ask not what your country can do for you; ask what you can do for your country." The face was handsome, the personality pleasing, the smile captivating, but the words terrified me.
>
> Let's analyze this brilliantly conceived slogan carefully and logically. First of all, what is a country? It's a geographical area composed of—in the case of the United States—over 200 million *individuals*. I've never asked 200 million people to do anything for me, except not to interfere with my right to live a peaceful life. Ask what you can do for your *country?* Does this mean asking each of the more than 200 million individuals what you can do for him?
>
> No, individuals are not what Kennedy or any other politician has ever had in mind when using the word *country*. A country is an abstract entity, but in politicalese, it translates into "those in power." Restated in translated form, then, it becomes: "Ask not what those in power can do for you; ask what you can do for those in power." You wouldn't respond quite so eagerly if it were phrased in its true form, would you? On the contrary, you might laugh in disbelief. [pp. 79–80]

One does not have to sympathize with the philosophy of a work like *Looking Out For # 1* to recognize that what Ringer says about the use of slogans and patriotic terms (such as "country," "freedom," and "law") is both interesting and important. In logic this kind of talk is called *hypostatizing*. To hypostatize is to attribute to things that are not persons (but only ideas or concepts) qualities and properties that only persons can have.

Everyone will remember that delightful encounter between Alice and the cat in Lewis Carroll's *Alice's Adventures in Wonderland*. As Alice takes her leave, the cat begins to vanish slowly, beginning, as Alice tells us, "with the end of the tail, and ending with the grin, which remained some time after the rest of it had gone." Alice is then led to remark in astonishment: "Well! I've often seen a cat without a grin; but a grin without a cat! It's the most curious thing I ever saw in all my life!" (Chapter 6) If we were properly trained in logic, we would feel this same sense of astonishment whenever anyone spoke of such things as "redness," "roundness," "truth," "beauty," and "goodness" as if they could exist by themselves and were not merely abstractions depending on some concrete entity for their being. Imitating Alice, we would express our astonishment by remarking that we have certainly seen "red" *apples* or "round" *balls* and "truthful, beautiful" *people*, but never "roundness" or "redness" or "truth and beauty" *as such*.

A peculiarity of abstract terms, however, is that they can be used without reference to subjects possessing the attributes they designate. That is why it is easy for us to fall prey to the fallacy. Still, we shouldn't be too quick to condemn abstractions, for, after all, they are a tremendously useful feature of language and thought, enabling us to rise above the level of individual concrete things and to discuss ideas like beauty and goodness.

The process at work in hypostatization is similar to personification. To personify is to ascribe to things or animals properties that only human beings possess. It is to speak of things or creatures that are not persons as if they were persons. For example, we personify if we complain of the "cruelty of weasels" because weasels, being innocent creatures, cannot be considered either kind or cruel. To be cruel is to intend and plan some harm, knowing that it will cause pain, and weasels are simply incapable, as far as we know, of entertaining such designs. They are as they are and do as they do. The same applies to expressions such as "the cruel sea." Understood literally, this personification is simply false. To hypostatize is to speak of abstract entities in terms that are similarly appropriate only for persons.

Thus we may say, "The State can do no wrong," "Science makes progress," or "Nature decrees what is right." Since the State, Science, and Nature are incapable of thought or intention, it is absurd to suppose that such abstractions can have the activities attributed to them in such statements. Only persons, not the State, can be said to do right or wrong, only scientists can make progress, and Nature has no voice with which to utter decrees.

To be sure, we do not usually lose sight of reality in most instances when we resort to hypostatization,. When we say that "our budget dictated what we were to do," we are perfectly aware that we mean that our "budgetary considerations"—not some thing called "Budget"—compelled us to do what we did. We also realize that we are speaking metaphorically when we use such similarly innocuous examples of hypostatization as "Love is blind," "Facts call us now to bethink ourselves," or "Actions speak louder than words."

It is less certain, however, that we know what we are about when we say, "The city is aroused," "The State is the march of God through history, or "It is the spirit of the nation that produces its art and literature." In such cases we may have been misled by our capacity for abstraction into thinking that, for example, there actually exists a grand artist at work whom we call the spirit of the nation.

The remark about the state being the march of God in history is a good example of the danger to which this sort of talk is prone. The remark comes from the pen of the great nineteenth century German philosopher Georg Wilhelm Hegel. The world today is what it is largely because of him. Both communism and fascism are generally regarded as having their roots in his ideas.

Hegel was greatly interested in history. It may seem strange to us that there should have been a time when people were not much interested or absorbed in the study of the past. But before Hegel that was generally the case. He started such disciplines as the study of history, the study of the rise and fall of civilizations, and the like. Indeed Oswald Spengler's *Decline of the West,* Arnold Toynbee's *Study of History,* and more recently Charles A. Reich's *The Greening of America* would be inconceivable without Hegel's pioneering efforts in the field of research represented by these later works.

In studying history, Hegel thought he had discovered its key. He thought history was in the process of fulfilling some grand design which he alone had at long last succeeded in unraveling. He thought both the world and all events in it proceeded rationally and were open to our inspection. What was happening was not only inevitable and intelligible to us but also rational and good. There was and is, of course, a good deal of struggle and suffering, war and death in the world. But all of this was both necessary and part of the grand design to achieve the final state that he called the Absolute Idea, a state of affairs in which all contradictions are finally resolved, all oppositions finally reconciled, and everything of value conserved. He tended to believe that such a state of affairs was on the verge of being realized (if not already realized) by the Prussian state of his day—a contention for which he was held in great esteem by the authorities who showered him with many honors.

The ideas that war may be good and that the State is much more important than the individuals in it (who therefore should willingly subordinate their wills and good to it) sound offensive to us. Yet they are, of course, packed into the statement about "the State being the march of God in history." Although this fuller explanation dispels a bit of the profundity and mystery that seem to surround the statement, it does not make it less offensive or, worse still, confirm its truth. It merely opens the statement up for discussion. For we now see more clearly what is implied by it and, therefore, with what sorts of things it ought to be countered.

For what Hegel is essentially expressing is a totalitarian attitude, one that is diametrically opposed to our tradition of liberalism. In communist and fascist systems, the State is all-important, individuals of no matter. Individuals count only insofar as they are part of some greater scheme or plan being busily realized. Liberalism, on the other hand, regards individuals as all-important, and the State as their servant. In our tradition the State ministers to individuals, and not they to it. The State exists only to achieve good for its citizens, and not they for the sake of some greater, higher, mysterious good.

Hegel's writings are as obscure as it is possible for a piece of philosophy to be, and so it is indeed remarkable that they could have seeped down to the proverbial man-on-the-street. The story is told of a student coming to Hegel and asking him to explain a passage in one of Hegel's books. Hegel looked at the statement for some moments and then replied, "When I wrote that, God and I knew what it meant. Now only God knows." And on his deathbed he remarked sadly, "Only one man has understood me." Then after a brief pause, he added: "And even he did not understand me."

No doubt it is the glorification of the State with all its attendant evils that Ringer had in mind in his critique of President Kennedy's appeal.

The danger inherent in hypostatization is real enough, and not just with respect to the State. Consider this example:

> Nature produces improvements in a race by eliminating the unfit and preventing them from polluting the gene pool of the fit. Therefore it is only right for us to eliminate these unfit people.

Nature is especially favored as a subject of hypostatization, perhaps because it is such a complicated abstraction that we have difficulty speaking of it at all without concretizing it. In the preceding statement, nature is endowed with an ability to know what is an "improvement" and what is not, what is "fit" and what is "unfit," although it is unrealistic to impute to nature any humanlike intelligence or intention.

The tendency to hypostatize nature is doubtless related to many people's belief that nature was created by God, and therefore the order of things is divinely ordained. Although ancient, this idea is the source of relatively more recent doctrines such as "natural law." People differ as to whether the word *God* is abstract or concrete, but it is always helpful to know in which of these two senses it is being used on any given occasion. The preceding statement would be significantly altered if the word *God* were substituted for *nature*. If talk of this sort is so harmful, why do we resort to it so frequently? The answer is simply that we get a lot of mileage from such talk. We use it, whether we realize it or not, as a form of verbal magic. Thus the term *science* used in an ad will sell almost anything, as advertisers have come to learn. And doctors, too, have learned that terms like *halitosis* and *pyorrhea* frighten like bogey men, and they use them instead of such more familiar labels as "bad breath," and "gum disease." On the other hand, as psychologist Karl Menninger has pointed out, in his book *The Vital Balance*, "Diagnostic name-calling may be damning. The very word cancer is said to kill some patients who would not have succumbed (so quickly) to the malignancy from which they suffer." We exploit the fallacy, too, of course. For example, we find it much easier to condemn "the Establishment" or "the System" rather than to point out the particular laws or practices that we feel need changing.

But we come to pay a stiff price for this abuse. Take the term *freedom* used so often as a rallying call. We would all gain more were we to pause at such moments and ask ourselves: freedom for whom? freedom from what? freedom to do what? Such questions would save many lives.

We need to remember that terms such as *nature, truth,* and *freedom* are abstractions that do not exist in the real world. To speak of them as we do about existing things is to live in a delusional world, like the insane, who hear voices and see things that aren't there. We can learn to depopulate that sort of world by a process of substitution. Whenever a term appears suspicious, it should be traced back to the thing it seems to signify and a new term should be substituted for the suspicious one. Sometimes the abstraction simply has to be changed from a noun to an adjective. Thus, we can replace "The truth shall make you free" with "Truthful statements shall make you free" and "The State can do no wrong" with "The President (*or* the Congress) can do no wrong." With this kind of analysis, many statements that seem deeply profound often prove not to be profound at all.

Despite what has been said, we ought to remember that not all uses of hypostatization are harmful or dangerous. In the context of poetry or literature this linguistic device is merely a kind of conceit that gives pleasure and harms no one. Here, too, the word *nature* seems to be especially favored. Shakespeare, for example, makes frequent use of it, as in *Julius Caesar,* where he has Antony say of Brutus:

> Nature might stand up
> And say to all the world. "This was a man!"

And so does Alexander Pope in this couplet, written (c. 1730) and intended as an epitaph for Isaac Newton in Westminster Abbey:

> *Nature, and Nature's laws lay hid in night.*
> *God said, "Let Newton be!" and all was light.*

And Robert Burns in his poem "Let Not Women E'er Complain" (1794):

> *Let not woman e'er complain of*
> *Inconstancy in love!*
> *Let not women e'er complain*
> *Fickle man is apt to rove!*
> *Look abroad thro' Nature's range,*
> *Nature's mighty law is change!*
> *Ladies, would it not be strange*
> *Man should then a monster prove?*

And Eddie Cantor, who had a running feud throughout his career with Georgie Jessel, requested that the following inscription be placed on his gravestone when he died:

> *Here in Nature's arms I nestle*
> *Free at last from Georgie Jessel!*

One more, from a tombstone with a rather different sort of inscription, reads:

> *Death is a debt*
> *To Nature due*
> *I have paid mine*
> *And so must you.*

Some people are nasty to the very end.

We must also recognize those cases in which we are not taken in by this form of speech but rather consciously use it with full awareness of what we are about. Christopher Stone's environmentalist work *Do Trees Have Standing?* is an excellent example of this.

For a very long time, as we all know, those who have tried to preserve the environment from abuse have not had an easy time of it—especially not with the arguments with which they have gone to court. Owners of forests and lakes have been able to make short shrift of the standard appeals: We are not to cut down our own forests because once a year you come driving through them? We are not to dispose of our industrial waste in our lakes because you like to fish in them? We need the pulp from those forests to produce the newspapers, magazines, and books which sustain our way of life, and we need our factories and their production to ensure jobs and goods for our people. And besides, the forest is our *property*.

What Stone offers in his little book is a radically different argument—and a far more powerful one. Put very plainly, what he says is this: Do not cut down that tree or pollute that lake, not because your action will spoil the pleasure others take in these beautiful, natural objects, but rather because the tree does not like being cut down or the lake polluted. In short, trees too have rights—and they belong to them because they are beings in their own right and not simply the possessions of possible sources of pleasure for other beings. How egocentric it was of us, Stone argues, to assign to things moral significance purely on the basis of their use to us. We must try to reorient our attitude to nature, cease to view it as our toy or possession to do with whatever we like, and come to regard it as an entity having a value in itself worth protecting.

In his preface to this widely read and admired book, Stone tells the reader that if the view he is advancing (that natural objects have inalienable rights) appears absurd, it will be useful to remember that not very long ago such groups as women, Blacks, and Indians were also denied basic human rights on the ground that they were not quite human. Perhaps in time the argument that trees have rights will not seem as strange as it may at the moment.

What Stone is doing here is inventing a new fiction, pretending that trees are like persons (or, at least, like corporations) and have rights. He is, in short, hypostatizating or personifying natural objects. But, as Garret Hardin, in his foreword to Stone's book, points out, so do the owners of forests and lakes who have claimed those things as their "property":

The most rigid defenders of the momentary legal definition of "property" apparently think "property" refers to something as substantive as atom and mass. But every good lawyer and every good economist knows that "property" is not a thing but merely a verbal announcement that certain traditional powers and privileges of some members of society will be vigorously defended against attack by others. Operationally, the word "property" symbolizes a threat of action; it is a verb-like entity, but (being a noun) the word biases our thought toward the substantive we call *things*. But the permanence enjoyed by property is not the permanence of an atom, but that of a promise (a most unsubstantial thing). Even after we become aware of the misdirection of attention enforced by the noun "property," we may still passively acquiesce to the inaccuracy of its continued use because a degree of social stability is needed to get the day-to-day work accomplished. But when it becomes painfully clear that the continued unthinking use of the word "property" is leading to consequences that are obviously unjust and socially counterproductive, then we must stop short and ask ourselves how we want to re-define the rights of property. [pp. 6–7]*

* Reprinted with permission from Garrett Hardin's Foreword to Christopher D. Stone's *Should Trees Have Standing? Toward Legal Rights for Natural Objects.* Copyright © 1974 by William Kaufmann, Inc., Los Altos, California 94022. All rights reserved.

Unlike Ringer, with whom we began this chapter, Hardin is not necessarily condemning the practice or process of hypostatizing he describes. He is merely urging us to recognize it for what it is. "Property" is a fiction, a notion we have devised or invented. It doesn't stand for some concrete thing we discover that has an existence independent of us or of our wishes. As long as we find the concept useful and helpful we can continue to embrace it; if the notion starts to prove otherwise, let us remember that we ourselves brought it into being (defined it), and nothing therefore should prevent us from banishing it (redefining it) should we decide to do so.

Of course, we are not likely ordinarily to meet the fallacy in this unusually tricky and elegant form. More likely we will find ourselves manipulated by a statement such as, "The world will no longer laugh," never asking ourselves how many of the 4 billion people in the world indeed know us, and of those few who do, how many care one way or another what we do. British admiral Lord Nelson knew the force of such a slogan: Before the Battle of Trafalgar (October 1805) he gave the naval order, "England expects every man to do his duty!" Notice, he did not say *he* expects it (which would have been intimidating enough, for he was an imposing figure) but that *England* does: He meant every Englishman, all English history and tradition, its honor, and so on. Now that should be sufficient to make a man lay down his life!

Even if we are not psychologically subdued or seduced by slogans beginning with "The world" or "People," we may still find ourselves deceived in the manner of the following letter writer:

> What Americans need is patience. A water well goes dry. Nature replenishes it by sending a good rain. Nature shall replenish the great oil reservoirs. Scientists say it takes a few million years. All we need is patience.

"Nature" not being a person, it is doubtful that it is aware that our wells are going dry and need "replenishing," to say nothing of the absurdity of believing we can wait "millions of years" for it to happen.

We must beware of such grand concepts, or we may find ourselves haunted by hypostatized spectres, as is the following writer:

> Because the dumping ground was so far out to sea, the city believed it would never hear from its sludge again, but the city was wrong. The mass of goo slowly grew and sometime around 1970 it began to move, oozing back to haunt New York and the beaches of Long Island.

5

The Miracles of Science

We have arrived at a kind of midpoint in this first part of our journey: We have observed in Chapters 1 and 2 how the structure of the sentences we use can, if we are not careful or if our need is great, betray us. In Chapter 3 which dealt with the content of sentences, we observed how reference of words can become an instrument of domination either for good or ill. We must now go on to trace how the meanings of the words used in our sentences can become sources of confusion.

Of all the intellectual knots represented by the fallacies studied by logicians, one of the most difficult to both spot and untie is *equivocation.* Consider, as a beginning, the following absurd example of this type of error:

> Everything that runs has feet.
> The river runs.
> Therefore the river has feet.

Needless to say the argument is fallacious because, although we do say such things as "the river runs," what we mean is that it flows and not that it runs on feet. The persuasiveness of this very simple example and of even more subtle ones depends on the very same mechanism—a key term switching its meaning at a critical point in an argument.

Consider now the case of the fellow with a Bible tract under his arm who comes knocking at our door and says to us: "If you believe in the miracles of science, how come you don't believe in the miracles of the Bible! You should be consistent!" Of course, what is overlooked here is that the meaning of the word *miracle* in the context of the Bible is quite different from its meaning in connection with science. A miracle in the biblical sense is anything that interrupts or breaks the laws of nature, while the phrase "miracle of science" is really a metaphor that means "the great accomplishments of science." We are therefore not contradicting ourselves or being inconsistent in believing in the one and not in the other. On the contrary, the party at fault here is our missionary friend who is equivocating with the word *miracle*.

Essentially equivocation is a fallacy that arises when a key word in an argument is allowed to shift its meaning in the course of the argument. Should you suspect that this has happened with a particular argument, you can always test to see if it has by watching what happens if you keep the meaning of the argument's key term uniform throughout. Consider this example:

Only man is rational..
No woman is a man.
Therefore no woman is rational.

If the word *man* is being used in the sense of "male," then its first premise states that "only males are rational," which is absurd. If, on the other hand, the word *man* is used in the sense of "human being," then the second premise states that "no woman is a human being," which is again absurd. This argument would be valid if the word *man* had the same meaning each time it occurred, but since it does not, we have an unsound argument and an instance of equivocation.

We can now see more clearly, perhaps, why fallacies of equivocation often appear plausible. Because the propositions out of which they are composed are all unobjectionable when considered individually, any shift in meaning from one statement to another may escape our notice. Both of the statements in the argument we have just looked at are plausible. When they are put together to form an argument, the argument will therefore also seem plausible, unless you recognize that its key term has shifted in meaning as it is used in the first and second propositions.

When the change in meaning of a key word during an argument is especially subtle, the conclusion will seem to follow clearly from the preceding statements, and the argument will appear considerably more sound than it is. Consider this analysis:

The financial page of *The London Times* says that money is more plentiful in London today than it was yesterday. This must be a mistake, for there is no more money in London today than there was yesterday.

In the context of this argument, the terms *plentiful* and *more* at first seem equivalent. On closer examination, however, the first is seen to refer to the distribution of money, the second to the amount.

The fallacy of equivocation is especially easy to commit when a key term in an argument happens to be a figure of speech or a metaphor. By interpreting the metaphor literally, we sometimes persuade ourselves that an argument is sounder than it is. Few are likely to be seriously misled by a figure of speech such as "He has a lean and hungry look," and our language would be poorer without such expressions. But many figurative expressions need to be used with caution, or arguments become confused. For example:

It is the clear duty of the press to publish such news as it shall be in the public interest to have published. There can be no doubt about the public interest taken in the brutal murder of Countess Clamavori and concerning the details of her private life that led up to the murder. The press would have failed in its duty if it had refrained from publishing these matters.

Here the expression "the public interest" means "the public welfare" in the first statement, but it means "what the public is interested in" in the second statement. Thus the argument is fallacious because what the public is interested in is not the same as what is in its best interest.

Equivocation is not confined to figurative expressions, for the vast majority of our words have more than one meaning, any of which can occasion the fallacy. Consider a little word like *some* in the following example:

Some birds are domesticated.
My parrot is domesticated.
My parrot is therefore some bird!

The word *some* here is used both in a quantitative sense in the first statement and in a qualitative sense in the conclusion.

It is useful to remember that at the root of the vast majority of cases of equivocation lies the appeal that we not contradict ourselves, that we be consistent, as in the miracle example. The drive to be consistent can be a trap, however. Consider this example going back several centuries:

There are laws of nature.
Law implies a lawgiver.
Therefore there must be a cosmic lawgiver.

Our reply in this case should be: since *laws* as used in the context of "laws of nature" simply means "set of observations" and *law* as used in the context of "lawgiver" means "set of commands," we are not contradicting ourselves in believing in the one and not in the other.

Similarly instructive is this somewhat longer example:

In our democracy all men are equal. The Declaration of Independence states this clearly and unequivocally. But we tend to forget this great truth. Our society accepts the principle of competition. And competition implies that some men are better than others. But this implication is false. The private is just as good as the general; the file clerk is just as good as the corporation executive; the scholar is no better than the dunce; the philosopher is no better than the fool. We are all born equal.

Our reply: The fact that we believe that all of us have the same *rights* does not mean we must also believe what is obviously false, that all of us have the same *abilities* (and therefore should be treated "equally").

Here is a still trickier example:

> I do not believe in the possibility of eliminating the desire to fight from humankind because an organism without fight is dead or moribund. Life consists of tensions. There must be a balance of opposite polarities to make a personality, a nation, a world, or a cosmic system.

Our reply: Since the phrase "desire to fight" means essentially "violence," and the phrase "without fight" means "will," "drive," or "spirit," it may very well be possible to eliminate the one (violence) without necessarily destroying the other (our spirit).

Finally, consider this example from an editorial:

> I am puzzled by the protest groups that gather in front of prisons when an execution is scheduled. The murderer, who has committed a heinous crime, has been granted all due process of law and is given every opportunity to defend himself—usually with the best available legal minds and often at taxpayers' expense. Yet these same protestors generally favor the execution of millions of innocent babies by abortion.

Our reply: We are not being inconsistent in protesting the *execution* of people found guilty of murder and not the *execution* "of millions of innocent babies by abortion." In the one case it is indeed an "execution" (for the life of a person is definitely involved) but not in the other (for a fetus is arguably not yet a person and perhaps not yet even a "life").

We see from the examples just noted how very intimately the words we use to express ourselves enter into the thinking represented in the arguments. It is as though the words themselves actively lead us astray.

A particularly striking example of the direct influence of language on thinking is the famous fallacy committed by the English philosopher John Stuart Mill in one of his works on ethics. Mill is here dealing with the question of what is the most "desirable" end or aim of human conduct and argues that it is happiness, as utilitarianism teaches. But how can we prove that happiness is indeed the one true ideal that we should desire? To this Mill replies:

> The only proof capable of being given that an object is visible, is that people actually see it. The only proof that a sound is audible, is that people

hear it: and so of the other sources of our experience. In like manner, I apprehend, the sole evidence it is possible to produce that anything is desirable, is that people do actually desire it.

But critics of Mill have pointed out that he had been deceived by his manner of expressing himself. Though the words *desirable, visible,* and *audible* are structurally similar, they are not semantically the same. *Desirable* is not related to *desired* in the same way that *visible* and *audible* are related to *seen* and *heard,* for the first involves a moral distinction that the other two do not. *Visible* means simply that something is "capable of being seen" (and *audible* means something "capable of being heard"), but *desirable* implies that something is "worthy of being desired," that it "ought" to be desired. This being so, it may be quite true that a thing's being seen or heard proves that it is visible or audible, but it does not follow that, because a thing is desired, it is for that reason desirable. Many people may desire dope, but that does not prove that dope is therefore desirable.

Mill had unfortunately been taken in by what we might call a systematically misleading expression. He made the same error involving *desirable* that we would if we were to note that since, say *immaterial* means "nonmaterial" and *insoluble* means "nonsoluble," therefore *inflammable* must mean "nonflammable" (when it means just the opposite of that). Another example of this type of error is that, since *decompress* means to lower or remove compression and *decentralize* means to remove centralization, therefore *delimit* must mean "remove limits" (when, again, it means the very opposite, namely, to "impose limits"). Finally since *manageable* means "capable of being managed" and *breakable* means "capable of being broken," therefore *readable* must mean "legible" (when it really means "good to read"). Obviously, words similar in structure can be very different in meaning.

The notion that language can be systematically misleading is instructive in still another way. What is so very remarkable about logical fallacies, and especially equivocation, is that the same linguistic device that causes us to stumble so that we commit a fallacy is also the device that, if we have our wits about us, we can use to express our sense of humor. Even more strangely, it is what sometimes lies at the foundation of various mental or psychological disturbances.

The humorous correlative of equivocation, for example, is the ordinary pun: To pun is to equivocate and to know it. A well-known example is the famous quip by Benjamin Franklin: "If we don't hang together, we will hang separately." By using the same term, inflexibly and rigidly as in the case of the fallacy, Benjamin Franklin seems to be on the verge of committing the very same fallacy. We smile with relief and pleasure when we realize that, despite the rigid adherence to the term, things turn out not only well, but significantly so. Far from having been exploited by certain hidden tendencies in language and falling victim to them, Benjamin Franklin was, on the contrary, exploiting and working those very same traps of language for his own purposes.

Some further examples: "Good steaks are rare these days, so don't order yours well done!" ... "Diamonds are seldom found in this country, so be careful not to mislay your engagement ring!" ... "Your argument is sound, nothing but sound!" Analyzing such puns is, in fact, rather good preparation for the more difficult task of detecting and avoiding being taken in by appeals that exploit this same linguistic device. And there is no shortage of examples of puns to practice on, for it has become a favorite in advertising appeals: "Milk has something for every body," "Mexico won't leave you cold," or "Datsun: we are driven."

That some fallacies bear a striking resemblance to jokes and witticisms is something everyone must at one time or another have observed and that similarity may not therefore seem surprising. What may seem surprising is the resemblance between these two and various psychological disturbances and interpersonal conflicts.

A typical case is discussed by British psychiatrist R. D. Laing in his book *Interpersonal Perception: A Theory and a Method of Research.* Jack and Jill's marriage is coming apart and they seek help. Each claims not to be loved by the other while insisting that he or she always has and probably always will love the other. How is this possible? When we look into the background of the couple, we find, says Laing, that what lies at the root of their troubles is their differing and contradictory conceptions of "love."

Jack's father treated his mother very differently from the way Jill's father treated her mother. Jack's father was too poor to have brought home enough money to make his family feel secure against the possibility of being evicted or not having enough food. Jack remembers vividly how his mother complained to his father about his inadequate income. From this Jack developed the viewpoint that, if his father had simply made enough money, his mother would have been eternally grateful. Since he is now successful financially, he expects Jill to be eternally grateful to him for providing her with a security that his mother never had.

On the other hand, Jill has come from a wealthy family in which there was never any comparable issue of financial security. In Jill's family, consideration, love, and kindness were expressed through the giving of gifts, the remembering of anniversaries, and so on. She had learned to take it for granted that the man will provide her with an economically secure home. What she looks for are the little niceties that she feels indicate true considerateness, kindness, and love. For Jack these niceties are irrelevant; they are minor details, trivia by comparison to the other things he does for the family.

However, if each can discover his or her own and the other's value system and thereby see the similarities and differences between them, it will become possible for them to explain themselves to each other. It will be feasible, for the first time, for Jack to say: "Well, if it really is that important to you that I remember your birthday, I'll do my darndest to try." It will be possible for Jill to "appreciate" Jack more as a provider in the family. If bitterness and revenge ("I am going to hurt you for the hurt you have done to me") have not intensified too much, it will still be relatively simple for each to satisfy the other's expectations according to his or her idiosyncratic value systems.

Considering the seemingly intimate connections between fallacies, witticisms, and certain psychological disturbances or problems, what is it, then, about language or ourselves that enables us to put the same devices of language to such strangely different uses? What common, inner principle allows our speech to undergo, under the pressure of changing circumstances, such startling transformations?

A clue to the solution to this problem may be found, perhaps, in a justly famous little book on *Laughter* by the great French philosopher, Henri Bergson. Bergson shows in his beautifully written essay that humor results when human beings assume the character of things and respond and act in a mechanical, inflexible, machinelike fashion. That is why we find the stiff and artificial dance of the clown funny, why we laugh at the poor fool who trips over some object in his path that—had he been less absent-minded—he might have avoided, and why we find amusing all sorts of other blunders that result from our not paying attention. As Bergson argues convincingly, what calls forth laughter in all such cases is our absent-mindedness, our lack of suppleness, which makes our activities appear to be mechanical and those who perform them more like things or objects than human beings. Our laughter at such mindlessness, Bergson adds, is a form of social criticism, designed to correct such behavior in order to preserve both life and society.

Bergson's book does not analyze fallacies, but its main thesis fits fallacies extremely well. It is, in fact, surprising how many fallacies illustrate that same inflexible, mechanical, mindlessness which, Bergson has shown, is the source of laughter. But perhaps we should not be so surprised that this is so, for it is just as easy, after all, to trip over a word or concept, if we are distracted and proceed mechanically along the lines laid down by the words spoken, as it is to trip over a log lying in our path.

Of course, in an example such as the one about the miracles of science, the lapse is unintentional; it is also subtle enough for its essential absurdity to escape us. This is not the case, of course, with the example of the river running; the absurdity is plain and so we laugh. In that instance the lapse is, if not entirely deliberate, certainly almost so. And, of course, in the case of Benjamin Franklin's quip about hanging together, we have a true case of a witticism. For Benjamin Franklin set out to exploit the device that in other circumstances often exploits us. We laugh at the pun's cleverness, realizing full well how such things generally master us and not we them.

Wit and equivocation are related not only to one another but to a third commonplace of human existence—mental disturbance. According to Bergson, as we have just seen, what makes us smile in the case of certain amusing anecdotes or laugh at certain jokes is the "mindlessness" exemplified by the subject of the joke or person of the anecdote. Interestingly enough, as Sigmund Freud discovered, it is this same absence of mind, this temporary lack of watchfulness on the part of our consciousness, that allows repressed material from our unconscious to momentarily surface and become the stuff of psychoanalysis.

Such mindlessness is a characteristic not only of those who have gone mad but of all of us in our everyday activities, as Freud shows in *The Psychopathology of Everyday Life*. In this remarkable book, Freud analyzed the unconscious sources of ordinary errors and lapses and demonstrated that such "mistakes" are not accidents but stem rather from disturbances in our personalities, some of which may be buried so deeply that we ourselves are barely aware of them.

A case in point is the common phenomenon of forgetting. As Freud notes, we forget names of people or places, or just ordinary words and phrases, because they become connected in our minds, often in a most superficial way with something painful that we wish to repress or have already repressed. Freud gives an example of a woman who, having been preoccupied with thoughts of no longer being young, could not remember the name of Freud's colleague, the famous psychoanalyst Carl Jung. As in this case, what happens in forgetting is that the disturbing thought ("no longer young") becomes connected with the neutral word ("Jung") by way of a "verbal bridge," as Freud called it, or, from our point of view, by way of equivocation.

There are, of course, other ordinary day-to-day mishaps: slips of the tongue or pen, misreadings, breaking objects, falling and injuring oneself, and so on. In many cases, these are even more revealing than ordinary forgetting, for the repressed things use such moments to break out and reveal themselves—betraying in this way, on occasion, our deepest feelings. Freud gives an example of the disappointed guest who, having expected something more in the way of a repast from his host, remarked in the course of a political conversation (Theodore Roosevelt was then running for president for the second time under the slogan, "He gave us a square deal"), "You may say what you please about Teddy, but there is one thing you can't deny—he gave us a square meal." Of course he had meant to say "square deal." "Deal" and "meal" are not verbally the same words but they are sufficiently similar vocally (as in the recent liquor advertisement "Don't be quart short") for the equivocation to slip through.

Another example mentioned by Freud is the woman who, waiting for Freud to write out her prescription, said to him: "Please, Dr. Freud, don't give me big bills. I can't swallow them."

Our tendency to read into a text what we have an unconscious wish to see there is often similarly amusing and revealing. One of Freud's examples is of a woman who, very anxious to have children, always reads "storks" instead of "stocks." As in ordinary cases of forgetting, here too the most superficial verbal resemblance is obviously used by our unconscious. Needless to say, such errors are not always so irreproachable; in misreading names, as Freud points out, the psychological motive at work may very well be unconscious hostility.

Freud calls such mishaps as dropping and breaking things, mislaying or losing them, and so on, "symptomatic actions." Such actions, in his view, are not only psychically determined but are also revelations arising from the most intimate and deepest parts of our psyche. These mishaps, he argues, are executions of unconscious intentions—intentions, that is, that we have not entirely succeeded in repressing. Although these intentions are, strictly speaking, unknown to consciousness, they are nevertheless "intended" by us, and they are therefore in a very profound sense valid for us. This is true of such an unconscious and seemingly "accidental" (although not uncommon) act as dropping a wedding ring that one has unconsciously removed while distracted in a conversation; and it is true of such "accidents" as breaking some personal (but unconsciously unwanted) possession or even injuring oneself.

Freud sees confirmation of the essential meaningfulness of such errors and symptomatic actions in the fact that such blunders are often met with knowing smiles and laughter, and occasionally with derision. Also revealing is the fact that those who commit these "mistakes" and "accidents" often indignantly deny having done so, and they are intensely offended if one (correctly, of course) insists that they have. Obviously they are ashamed of what they have done, even if they do not consciously know it. And similarly revealing is our own anger at our inability to recall a forgotten word or name. We are not, apparently, in the habit of treating such blunders as mere "mistakes" or "accidents" but, whether bystanders or victims, tend to regard them as deeply motivated, although unwittingly so.

Freud leaves it an open question whether the basically intentional nature of such blunders or mistakes cannot be applied to the more important errors of judgment made by us in our other, more serious, activities. How "accidental," for example, is the unfortunate, but none too rare, administration of the wrong drug to a patient either by the physician or by the nurse? It is not clear whether Freud thinks that all such errors are avoidable, but it is obvious he thinks many are.

In an age of great psychological ferment and interest, as ours is, it is hardly likely that anyone needs to be reminded that the harm others do to us comes nowhere near what we do to ourselves. Although we can prevent a good deal of such harm to ourselves by becoming more "logical" and "rational," we are likely to be more successful in doing this by trying to learn as much as possible about the kinds of tactics and strategies used by the enemy. Such strategies are now often called "games," and the most dangerous are the kind we play with ourselves.

Nor are these games, ironically and perversely, without their amusing aspect. Freud's Rat Man case is typical. The man had many other symptoms and problems in addition to the one that brings him to mind here. One summer, while on holiday in the mountains, this man suddenly got the idea that he was too fat and that he needed to reduce. He subjected himself to the severest regimen: running furiously along the roads in the heat of August, climbing mountainsides, and so on—all in an effort to lose weight. The origin and nature of his compulsion did not become clear until in one session a chain of associations led from the word *dick* (meaning "fat" in German) to the name of the Rat Man's American cousin, Richard, known as Dick. When it emerged that the Rat Man was jealous of this cousin and felt threatened by him because of the attentions he was paying to the girl with whom the Rat Man was in love, it became clear that his furious efforts to get rid of his fat were really a disguised and symbolic way of disposing of his cousin Richard.

The Rat Man was, of course, neither punning (as Benjamin Franklin was) nor equivocating (as the man with his argument about miracles was). The Rat Man was in the grip of a delusion. He had become the slave and tool of a master (his own unconscious) who, as we have seen, makes no distinctions, takes account of no degrees, and for whom the most superficial resemblances suffice to forge binding links.

The striking unity that seems to underlie fallacy, humor, and the operations of the unconscious can on occasion help us unravel and understand somewhat more serious conditions. Consider for a moment the catatonic schizophrenic—the poor wretch who, in a fit of rage, takes, say, the life of his girl friend, or of his wife and children, or perhaps of all of them. Overcome by the horror of the deed, he lapses into madness and for hours or even days stands there in a rigid posture. Why this immobilized posture? If we would see him standing that way on the street corner we would find him amusing. We would laugh at him, probably because, as Bergson has helped us see, he has turned himself into a thing or object. But why? Not, of course, in order to make us laugh but very likely in the hope either of preventing a repetition of the horrible deed or of denying responsibility for it. For if he is a mindless thing he could not possibly have done it, and if he did it, it was not really him but this mindless thing. And so he stands there like a thing. Rigidity and mindlessness—these are the things that make us laugh.

They are also the stuff of equivocation and, at times, the source of that condition we lapse into when that fragile balance called life is upset and we try to set it right.

6

How Can We Love
Our Country and Not Love
Our Countrymen?

The question in the title is from President Ronald Reagan's Inaugural Address and, perhaps inevitably, it now seems more ironic than ever. The answer is, of course, that it's easy, and many millions of Americans have managed it very well.

The error in Reagan's reasoning represented by his question is contained in an even more striking form in the following remarks from an article "The Ban of Saccharine: How? Why?" which appeared on the front page of the Los Angeles *Times*:

> Elusive as the logic of this law may seem to the general public, medical researchers say that the animal experiments upon which such regulatory decisions are based do have a sensible rationale—and that they do have a direct bearing on risk to humans.
>
> It is true, researchers acknowledge, that the rats at the center of this furor consumed each day the saccharine equivalent of roughly 1,000 cans of low-calorie soft drink. But they consider it misleading—if not dishonest— to suggest, as the calorie council has, that this disparity makes the research irrelevant to humans.
>
> People who drink only one can a day of a saccharine soft drink run a comparably lower risk of cancer. But in a population of 213 million people, the collective hazard could still add up to several thousand cases of bladder cancer [March 29, 1977].

The writer of this passage fails to see that, although a large number of the 213 million people in this country drink diet drinks, this fact does not affect the amount each one drinks. Each person still drinks the amount he or she does, an amount remarkably less than the equivalent fed the rats in question.

Logicians call the fallacy exemplified by this example *division*, because it is a matter of *dividing* the property possessed by the whole among the parts or members. Its opposite they have labeled *composition*, because it involves trying to *compose* a whole out of its parts and to attribute to it the properties or qualities possessed by each of the parts. (The whole, however, as the old saying has it, is more than the sum of its parts.)

It is a mistake, logicians remind us, to presume without further evidence that (1) a whole will have the properties possessed by each of its parts or that (2) whatever is true of any member of a group is true of every member. It is equally untrue, as the fallacy of division would have it, that what applies to the whole also applies to its parts or members. Let us consider some obvious examples.

If a person can break one stick, then another one, then still another one, does that mean that individual can break the bundle of sticks as a whole? Probably not.

We can reverse the order of the argument and arrive at the fallacy of division. Thus, if an individual cannot break a bundle of sticks, does that mean he cannot break any one of them individually? Of course not.

What is true here of parts and wholes is also true of groups and their members. Thus, Jones may be the best quarterback in the country, Smith the best halfback, and Davis the best receiver. Yet putting them and other outstanding players together on one team will not (as we have seen only too often) necessarily give us the best team in the country. Or to use another example, the Chicago Symphony Orchestra may be the best orchestra in the country, but that does not necessarily mean that the first violinist in the orchestra is the best violinist in the country.

Why isn't it the case that what is true of the parts is necessarily true of the whole and what is true of the whole is necessarily true of the parts? Or, similarly, why isn't it the case that what is true of the members of some particular group or team is necessarily true of the group or team—and vice versa? The reason is that a whole or a group is something functional and organic and therefore has properties just in virtue of being such a whole or group.

Another example will make this clearer. A woman looks at a flower and says to herself, "Oh, what a very pretty flower!" She does the same with several others. Does this mean that if she gathers them together she will therefore have a pretty bouquet of flowers? Perhaps not, and the reason is that bringing them together gives rise to something new. Will all the different flowers blend properly? That question was not pertinent when each flower was considered by itself. The same would apply to a group of players, to a group of singers, or to any collection of individuals. Although each person, when considered by himself or herself, might be outstanding, whether the group will be outstanding depends on a new factor that arises only with the formation of the group. How well will they work together or how well will their different voices blend together? These are questions that had no meaning when each member of the group was considered individually.

Although composition and division are obviously not very difficult or subtle kinds of fallacies, we tend to commit them rather frequently. Often the reason lies in a confusion of the collective and the distributive sense of certain key terms in arguments. A collective term names a collection or a whole; a distributive term applies only to individuals or parts. The word *all* is probably the best example of a potentially ambiguous term, for it has both senses. When we say, for example, "All donors have contributed $1,000," do we mean that each and every one of them has contributed this amount (using the word *all* distributively) or do we mean that all, taken together, have done so (understanding the word *all* collectively)?

The old riddle "Why do white sheep eat more than black ones?" turns on this confusion of the collective with the distributive. The answer, "Because there are more of them?" treats collectively what seemed to be referred to only distributively in the question.

Another example of an argument involving the same confusion is this one: "Some day man will disappear from the earth, for we know that every man is mortal." In the first part of the argument *man* is used collectively (in the sense of "the human race"), whereas at its second occurrence the term is used distributively (in the sense of "every single person"). From the fact that every single person ("man") is mortal and will therefore die, it does not follow that the human race ("*man*kind") will die. By replenishing itself the race, theoretically, could go on forever. (This argument could also be analyzed in terms of equivocation, if we concentrate on the fact that the word *man* is used ambiguously. Indeed, it may very well have been the equivocal nature of the word that caused the error in the first place.)

Understanding the nature of the fallacies of division and composition enables us to gain another perspective on a number of diverse but all-too-familiar phenomena, such as the behavior of people in crowds, racial prejudice, and even some of our spending habits.

A group of intelligent people does not always act intelligently, nor does a group of civilized people always act in a civilized manner. A mob, as we all know, is not simply a large group of individuals. Something happens to people when they become members of crowds. We do not need the fallacy of composition to remind us of this fact, though the phenomenon of crowd behavior is a typical example of it.

Certain forms of racial (as well as many other kinds of) prejudice also seem to exemplify the fallacy of division. At the root of the problem very often is the attempt to attribute to individuals in a certain group those qualities believed to be possessed by the group. The sad thing is that not only is it unjust and unfair (and logically unsound to suppose) that each member of a group possesses the qualities of the group, but it is often doubtful and sometimes simply false that the group as a group possesses the properties or qualities attributed to it.

And then we have what some have called the spendthrift fallacy: A dollar a week, the advertisement informs us, will bring this TV set into our home; another 50¢ will deliver this freezer, and so on. Of course, $1 a week is not very much, and 50¢ is even less. What the ad fails to remind us of (and hopes we will not realize) is that $1 a week on this, $2 on that, and another 50¢ on that, and pretty soon our paycheck is gone—before we have even had a chance to cash it. To fall for this appeal—and millions do—is to be taken in by the fallacy of composition and to forget that the whole is greater than its parts.

Fallacies, as these last few observations show, have far-reaching implications. Lying at the very root or foundation of our thinking, they determine, in a fundamental way, our very experience of ourselves and the world.

An interesting example is the thought of another great German philosopher of the nineteenth century, Arthur Schopenhauer. It is always tempting to try to account for the deeply pessimistic thought of Schopenhauer by reference to his own sad and gloomy life. We must remember, however, that although Schopenhauer's experiences may explain his pessimism, the validity of his thought can be determined only by reference to his work, not to his own personal history. To evaluate the philosophy of pessimism in any other way in an effort to condemn it would be to commit a fallacy ourselves—one we have not yet discussed but that we will subsequently.

A lot of his own grief Schopenhauer brought on himself. Although remarkably handsome and always impeccably dressed, he neither made friends, nor wanted to. He had a sharp, caustic wit, which he did not fail to use indiscriminately, and he was full of contempt for both his fellow students and faculty. As he wrote later on himself: "From the first dawn of my thought I have felt myself in discord with the world. The more I see of men the less I like them."

Schopenhauer's philosophy stands in stark opposition to Hegel's. For Hegel, as we saw, the world was something totally rational and intelligible, and whatever happened in it was not only inevitable but always for the best. For Schopenhauer the world was totally irrational; it was a frightening and terrible place. His reaction to it was not only pessimistic; it was explosive and violent. On every page of his writing deep gloom is pervasive.

The world, as he explained it in his major work, is the product of a blind and aimless Will. It is the scene of the struggle of innumerable species of things for mere survival. In this struggle the individual counts for nothing, but exists merely for the sake of the species which this Will is anxious at all cost to preserve to all eternity. The struggle produces no heroes and can have no victors. It is a drama in which all the participants are mere puppets, who think they are drawn from in front but are really pushed from behind.

To prove his thesis, Schopenhauer appealed to his readers to observe the world of nature. Consider, he said, the life of nature's creatures. Take the recent report he had just read of the tiny squirrel that was magically drawn by a serpent into its very jaws. After quoting the account at length, Schopenhauer added these comments of his own:

> In this example we see what spirit animates nature. That an animal is surprised and attacked by another is bad; still we can console ourselves for that; but that such a poor innocent squirrel sitting beside its nest with its young is compelled, step by step, reluctantly, battling with itself and lamenting, to approach the wide, open jaws of the serpent and consciously throw itself into them is revolting and atrocious. What monstrous kind of nature is this to which we belong!

Or take, he said, this other shocking incident:

> Yunghahn relates that he saw in Java a plain far as the eye could reach entirely covered with skeletons, and took it for a battlefield; they were, however, merely the skeletons of large turtles, five feet long and three feet broad, and the same height, which come this way out of the sea in order to lay their eggs, and are then attacked by wild dogs, who with their united strength lay them on their backs, strip off their lower armor, that is, the small shell of the stomach, and so devour them alive. But often then a tiger pounces upon the dogs. Now all this misery repeats itself thousands and thousands of times, year out, year in. For this, then, these turtles are born. For whose guilt must they suffer this torment? Wherefore the whole scene of horror?

And again:

> Take, for example, the mole. To dig with all its might with its enormous shovel claws is the occupation of its whole life; constant night surrounds it. But what, now, does it attain by this life, full of trouble and devoid of pleasure? The consciousness of the world of perception gives a certain appearance of objective worth of existence to the life of those animals which can see. But the *blind* mole.

These descriptions and the passion with which they are given are highly characteristic of the kind of writing to be found in the pages of Schopenhauer's works.

It is possible that some readers may find nothing amiss or unusual in this sort of writing—nothing amiss, that is, in ascribing human feelings to animals that cannot have them and of speaking of their situation in such moral categories as "attainment," "consolation," "innocence," "guilt," and so on. The world of literature is, after all, full of such things. On the other hand, having now become alerted to the fallacy of hypostatization or, at least personification, these accounts may seem at least logically curious. In addition, we can now also evaluate them in the light of the fallacies of division and composition. For what Schopenhauer is doing here is, of course, condemning all life, in all its forms, both present and future on the basis of his observation of only some types of life in only some forms in its present state. However full of suffering their life might be, some might find redeeming features in it and be far from willing to see it end.

In fairness to Schopenhauer, however, as far, at least, as the temptation to accuse him of committing the fallacy of hypostatization is concerned, we ought perhaps to caution that in viewing his work in this way, we ourselves do not become guilty of the fallacy of accent. For in their larger context, his talk of the condition of squirrels, turtles, and moles has a point and an appropriateness that is obscured when considered out of context. What Schopenhauer may have been trying to do in giving accounts so full of pathos is not so much to mourn the condition of innocent and helpless creatures as to mourn our own sad and tragic condition. We ourselves are very much a part of that same nature and share in its suffering, he would be quick to point out.

Although as the example of Schopenhauer illustrates, there is a larger sweep to the fallacies of division and composition, defining on occasion whole trends and styles of thinking, we are more apt to meet them in the following somewhat more modest forms:

> It is predicted that the cost-of-living index will rise again next month. Consequently you can expect to pay more for butter and eggs next month.

This argument is an example of the misuse of averages and commits the fallacy of division. The cost-of-living index is something arrived at by averaging out a great number of different items. Since this is so, we cannot tell in advance what the case will be with any specific item. Butter and egg prices may also rise, but then they may stay the same or even go down. Another example of division is the following:

> Since the city revenues have fallen off, I propose a 20-percent across-the-board cut for all city departments. We'll just have to get along with four-fifths of the service we've been used to.

Unfortunately, the results may be quite different. Giving, say, the fire department 20 percent less money than formerly may result not merely in 20 percent less service from it but in no service at all, since that department may not be able to function with such a drastic cut. On the other hand, in other departments no reduction in service may result at all, and in some (perhaps because employees fear loss of their jobs) the public may get better service than ever before.

Committing the fallacy of composition can result in just as faulty analysis. For example:

> It is not going to help the energy crisis to have people ride buses instead of cars. Buses use more gas than cars.

In this case, although each bus uses more gas than each car, there are so many more cars than buses that it would indeed help the energy crisis if more people rode buses. The error lies in failing to see that what is true of *each* bus (as compared to each car) is not true of the *whole* group of buses (as compared to the whole group of cars).

Lastly, consider this example of composition:

> Each manufacturer is perfectly free to set his own price on the product he produces. So there can be nothing wrong with all manufacturers getting together to fix the prices of the articles made by all of them.

Here again, there is nothing wrong with a single manufacturer deciding what price he would like to charge for the item his factory produces; but if all manufacturers decided together on a single price, that would be a case of price *fixing,* not price *setting.* The result would most likely be public harm because competition would have been eliminated and people would be compelled to pay the price demanded.

Much, obviously, can turn on these fallacies of composition and division, innocuous and innocent as they may at first appear.

II
THE MAZE OF INTELLECTUALISM

7

Form and Content

To understand the kind of world we live in today and why we are such easy targets for exploitation because of the kind of world it has become, we have to go back once again to Aristotle and the science he founded.

You may recall that Aristotle was the first to discover what in essence thinking is. It is, he discovered, simply a matter of combining words into sentences and these sentences into longer chains, which he called syllogisms—formulations consisting of a major premise, a minor premise, and a conclusion based on the agreement of the two premises. Aristotle, pursuing this major breakthrough, discovered how predictable and how very limited our thinking is—bound in fact to precisely those 256 structures to which categorical propositions gave rise.

Aristotle's view of our intellectual condition and its possibilities held sway for over 2000 years—in fact, until late in the nineteenth century when logicians began to glimpse other possibilities for thought. Their extensions and discoveries led to a profound revolution in logic which, combined with similar revolutions in such widely different disciplines as art, music, and poetry, changed our whole world.

To understand how a reexamination of such a thing as a syllogism could unleash such global changes, we need to look at its two most powerful properties: truth and validity. These terms are not foreign to us. In fact they are quite common words. They mark a distinction, however, that is not widely understood yet is of utmost importance. For example, people will sometimes be heard to say, "That may be logical all right, but it's just not true"; or they may remark, "The more logical side is not necessarily the right side." Not understanding entirely the distinction that such expressions strive to make, some people have gone on to condemn logic as being somehow opposed to the truth.

A famous example of distrust of logic is this remark from a speech by British Foreign Minister Austen Chamberlain, spoken in Parliament:

> I profoundly distrust logic when applied to politics, and all English history justifies me. Instinct and experience alike teach us that human nature is not logical, that it is unwise to treat political institutions as instruments of logic, and that it is in wisely refraining from pressing conclusions to their logical end that the path of peaceful development and reform is really found.

That is quite a remarkable statement. It was greeted with much applause. Does it mean, though, that truth and logic are in opposition? Chamberlain apparently thought so.

But we ourselves, too, may have been tempted to condemn logic when, in our debates and discussions with our friends, and after giving in on some point without fully realizing its implications, we have suddenly found ourselves committed to accepting some unwelcome (or even *false*) conclusion. Or we may have tried to argue some, to us, obviously true conclusion but without success. Losing an argument and yet being in the right (being right, as we say, for the wrong reasons) is an extremely frustrating experience. But is it proof that logic and truth are indeed in opposition?

Probably not—and the reason is that there is that distinction referred to earlier between validity and truth. That difference must be kept in mind. Truth, or being in the right, has to do with what is the case, with facts. If we say of some statement that it is true, what we mean is that it accords with what the facts in the case are. It accords with the state of affairs as we know it to be. Validity, on the contrary, has to do with the use we make of the facts we have, with our reasoning with the facts, with whether or not we make a proper use of the facts at our disposal. It is therefore possible, and frequently the case, that although we may have our facts all right, we make an improper use of them in our thinking and thus lose an argument. We may even, in such a case, accidentally end up with a true conclusion, but because of the improper (or illogical) way in which we have arrived at that conclusion, those listening to us are not likely to accept it. Consider an example. Suppose we argue:

All cats are animals.
All tigers are animals.
Therefore all tigers are cats.

Now although the conclusion is true—all tigers are indeed cats—we arrived at the conclusion for the wrong reasons. If we could depend upon those reasons to give us a valid conclusion, we would have to accept the conclusion to the following argument as well, for it matches the first one exactly:

All cats are animals.
All pigs are animals.
Therefore all pigs are cats.

In the first case it is simply a lucky accident that we came up with a conclusion that happens to be true: The reasons we used do not logically, or validly, support such a conclusion. We are "in the right" (for tigers *are* cats) "but for the wrong reasons."

We are now perhaps in a better position to see how validity and truth differ and how that difference should not cause us to become alarmed, or, worse, to condemn logic out of hand. Validity has to do with the use of facts—how we set out our premises in an effort to derive a certain conclusion from them. If we put premises together properly, and if they happen to accord with the facts, then the conclusion to such an argument will not only be valid but true as well. But if we put premises together improperly, although we may in such a case accidentally come up with a true conclusion, it will not be a valid one.

What bothered Chamberlain perhaps was the fact that logic could apparently deceive him—that by following logic he could at times come to false conclusions. So he distrusted and dismissed logic. But perhaps you can now see better than he was able to how this could happen. Logic by itself can only guarantee validity; it cannot guarantee truth. To achieve that, you must be certain not only to argue correctly, but to argue correctly *with* true facts. Anyone who argues correctly and still ends up with a false conclusion should, instead of blaming logic, check the facts.

In logic this point is usually made by saying that whether an argument is valid or not depends on the kind of logical "form" it has. We are all familiar with the notion of form, shape, or structure, which we generally distinguish from content, subject matter, or raw material. An argument, just like a jar, also has a certain form or structure. But unlike the form of the jar, the form of an argument can be abstracted from it; it can be "lifted" from it and examined apart from the content. We cannot do that with a jar. Take the form away from a jar and you have nothing left but a plain mess.

Logic is sometimes described, therefore, as a formal science. That definition, like the definition of logic as the study of argument, describes rather well what logicians study—the forms of argument that permit the drawing of valid inferences and those that do not.

Logicians abstract the form from arguments by using symbols. Symbols, like variables used in mathematics, have no meanings in themselves but stand indifferently for any terms assigned to them. By replacing the terms of an argument with such symbols, logicians can make the structure of an argument stand out from its content. Symbols are peculiarly suited for this work. They are used because, unlike ordinary words that are never or almost never precise, symbols are always exact. When a logician uses the symbol *p,* for example, it means the same thing whenever it appears. This cannot be said of natural words, whose meanings tend to shift when their context changes. The tendency of words to change meaning is the reason behind most of the fallacies of ambiguity just discussed. Unlike natural words, however, which tend to arouse all sorts of associations in our minds as a result of their long and peculiar histories, symbols have no such histories and arouse no such interfering associations.

Artificial symbols, furthermore, are superior to natural words not only in being precise but also in being concise. By using symbols, we are able to reduce complicated statements (which previously would have required great mental effort) to such a brief form that we are able to understand them immediately, with little or no effort. Anyone who has dealt with mathematical problems in ordinary language knows the superiority of symbols. Compare, for example, these two formulations, and the difference is immediately clear:

1. Two hundred forty-four divided by four is sixty-one.

2.
$$4\overline{)244}^{\,61}$$

Ordinary language makes such problems seem difficult, even impossible, to understand. Symbols bypass the difficulty because they communicate their meaning or content to us in a direct and immediate way.

Still another advantage of symbols is that, by freeing our mental faculties from deep and involved trains of thought, we can calculate and explore possible inferences almost by simple, mechanical moves. In a sense we might say that symbols do their own thinking. As such they are not only aids to thought, but literally extensions of it. The notable advances achieved as a result of the application of logic's insights in such areas as computer science are a direct result of the development and greater use of symbols.

The increased use of symbols has enabled logicians to see their field of study more clearly: the study of formal structures. That insight has encouraged them to investigate formal structures of all kinds, not just those we happen to make use of in our thinking about things in this world. And this is essentially the difference between traditional, Aristotelian logic and modern, symbolic (or mathematical) logic. Aristotle had confined himself to studying those formal structures that we happen to make use of in our dealings with each other and in our thinking about things in our world. But once logicians came to see that logic is the study of formal structure as such, they asked themselves, late in the nineteenth century, "Why not explore all formal structures, even those that do not happen to apply or could not be conceived applicable to things of this world?" At this point, logic truly became abstract—and very rich in new possibilities.

It is interesting that almost at the same time these developments were taking place in logic, there were very similar developments in several other fields. That is not surprising. Once a new idea appears in one field, it often soon manifests itself in other fields as well. The revolution in logic, then, was only one of a series of similar upheavals in painting, music, poetry, and even the world at large.

Let us consider painting first. For a very long time painters, like logicians, confined their work to things of this world. Their work was representational. They painted trees and lakes, portraits of people, and still lifes. We are all familiar with that kind of painting. We like it; we understand it; many of us think it is great art. But it soon occurred to someone that the purpose of painting may not be to try to reproduce as accurately as possible the forest out there or the nude model posing in a studio; rather its object may be something entirely different—perhaps the exploration of the beauty of shapes or the sense and mystery of light and shadow. If that is indeed so, then why be confined to the shapes and structures of immediate and familiar surroundings? Why not explore shapes and structures of all kinds, regardless whether they will ever actually be encountered? Abstract, nonrepresentational painting thus came into being.

Now abstract painting, unlike traditional art, does not (despite the use of familiar titles as "Nude Descending a Staircase") seem to be about anything in particular. Indeed, strictly speaking, it is not about any *thing*—just as abstract logic is, strictly speaking, not about particular things. Probably that is the reason that both have been disliked and condemned: Their object, meaning, and *raison d'être* having been misunderstood; they have been condemned as absurd. But obviously such works have as sound a justification as the things they have tended to diverge from.

The same is the case with modern, atonal music. It too represents a divorce from everyday. The music we all love and find so familiar is music that has at its core and center of gravity one basic tone. The tonal center makes a piece of music seem right to us, predictable, pleasing, and familiar. Technically, that one tone around which the piece coheres and to which it continually returns is called the *tonic*. For example, if C is our principal tone, then the tones that our ear expects to hear, and feels relieved and pleased if its expectations are fulfilled, are such related and dependent tones as E and G. This expectation is grounded in a physical law in nature that, when any note is sounded (our C, for example), it is not the *only* tone that is being heard at the moment. What we hear, although we may not be completely aware of it, are certain other tones (called *overtones*) sounding at the same time but higher up and fainter. In the case of C, for example, the first overtone that is sounded is, again, C but an octave higher; then G (its second overtone), a fifth higher than the last C; then C again, a fourth higher; than E, a third higher; and so on and on. The notes get progressively closer together, until the human ear can't distinguish them, and so high that it can't detect them. The first few overtones—C, E, G—form a cluster, the "C chord" as it is known, or the tonic in C. (See Figure 7-1.)

Until the early twentieth century all, or practically all, music was written in such a way as to conform to the concept of a strong tonal center in order to satisfy the law or requirement of our nature. We found it pleasing because it satisfied our built-in expectations. Early in the twentieth century, however, the same revolution that took place in logic and painting occurred in music. Composers, like painters and logicians, began to ask themselves why they should confine their creative capacities to exploring or creating works within the confines of tonality. Why not explore new possibilities of richness and a variety of expression by shaking off dependency on the tonic? Such explorations led to atonal or nontonal music—music with no single key base, seemingly weird and incoherent music (music, that is, that does not cohere around some single tone), characterized by great dissonance, unusual rhythms, and abnormally wide leaps and stretches in the melody. That music is based on a radically different "form" from tonal music.

Such music, with its agonized melodies and tension-filled chords, which don't seem to be about anything, is still to many of us rather hard to take—just as abstract painting and abstract logic are. All three are not about anything we are familar with or are attuned to. But that fact does not make them absurd. Music, for example, is not without a certain force and power, regardless of its form. Were we to listen to atonal music long enough, we might even find ourselves quite fascinated with, although perhaps still unmoved by, it—perhaps because the appeal is almost entirely cerebral.

The revolutions in logic, art, and music were duplicated in still another field—poetry. Curiously, although the process of abstraction can be

FIGURE 7.1.

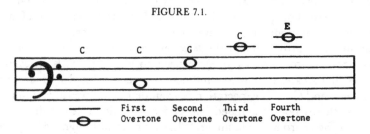

| | First Overtone | Second Overtone | Third Overtone | Fourth Overtone |

FIGURE 7.2

discerned here as well, the new form came to be known as concrete poetry. Although isolated examples of this kind of poetry can be found much earlier, it is a relatively modern phenomenon. In concrete poetry, words cease to be used merely as means for the expression of ideas but are used, explored, and valued in their own right. In the hands of some poets, this may simply be a matter of shaping poems to resemble their subjects, as in the poem shown here by Jiri Kolar called "Brancusi" (Figure 7-2). Other poets

she loves me

she loves me not

she loves

she loves me

she

she loves

she

FIGURE 7.3.

make their writing not only look like their subjects but sound like them as well, as in this verse from a poem by William Carlos Williams, which is about a bellhop dashing down the stairs:

ta tuck a
    ta tuck a
        ta tuck a
            ta tuck a
                ta tuck a

Similarly interesting is this somewhat more complicated but very amusing poem by Edwin Morgan entitled "Siesta of a Hungarian Snake":

s sz sz SZ sz SZ sz ZS zs ZS zs zs z

The words of the title are suggested here by both the shape and combination of letters, as well as by the reversal of the order of the two letters in midline.

Still more complicated is the concrete poem by Emmett Williams, "She loves me, she loves me not," which not only forms the shape of a flower and question mark, but also mimics the familiar action alluded to. (See Figure 7-3.) In the case of more abstract designs, the results can be breathtaking—as in the beautiful love poem by Gerhard Ruhm entitled *"Du,"* meaning "You" (Figure 7-4). The familiar sentiments "You're so different from everyone else" and "you're the center of my world" are made so much fresher by the form they take here.

What is of interest in concrete poetry is the significance of the medium itself—considered not as a means but as an end having a meaning of its own. That is why, like the tones, color, and symbols that are the mediums of modern atonal music, nonrepresentational art, and symbolic logic, the words of concrete poetry come to be valued and explored in their own right, acquiring as a result sometimes an arresting vitality and new significance.

But what has all this got to do with our main topic—the world of words and how we can survive best in it? The answer is: a great deal! The revolutions we have just looked at did not leave the rest of the world we live in unaffected. Those revolutions, or their lessons, were absorbed by others and in some cases came to be subtly exploited by them.

Consider one department of modern life whose influence is both pervasive and persistent and that affects us all—that of advertising. Will Rogers once defined this industry as "the art of persuading people to buy things they don't need with money they ain't got." The way in which the revolutions in logic and the arts prepared the ground for advertisers' messages is almost miraculous. Certainly it must have appeared a godsend to them. A look at the foundations of this great modern industry reveals the connection.

At the heart of all advertising lies the *claim.* Here is where we are told, or rather persuaded, why—lucky us—the product has finally been made available and why we should avail ourselves of it. Since many, perhaps

FIGURE 7.4.

uuuuuuuuuuuuuuuuu
uuuuuuuuuuuuuuuuu
uuuuuuuuuuuuuuuuu
uuuuuuuuuuuuuuuuu
uuuuuuuuduuuuuuuu
uuuuuuuuuuuuuuuuu
uuuuuuuuuuuuuuuuu
uuuuuuuuuuuuuuuuu
uuuuuuuuuuuuuuuuu

most, goods have very little to recommend them and since the vast majority of available brands of the same product do not differ all that much anymore, the art of the modern ad lies in inventing ingenious reasons for, first,
buying the item in question and second, buying one brand rather than another. Advertisers outdo themselves in this area, and the fact that the
claims are often outrageously irrelevant to what is being offered does not
seem to trouble them.

Buying the product, we are told, will make for a happier family
("Wise mothers know that their families need tasty, nourishing food. Be a
wise mother, buy Muggs Lima Beans . . . "). It will make guests happy and
proud of us ("It's hard to forget someone who gives you Crown Royal"). It
will make us proud of ourselves ("Charter 1. The final step up"). It will add
meaning to our lives ("Of course you can live without Chivas Regal. The
question *is* how well?"), or even life to our lives ("Coke adds life"). Certainly we can gain popularity ("Seven out of ten prefer . . . ") and perhaps
even distinction ("VO. What a man serves is often a reflection of the
man"). And it's so easy ("Playing like a winner takes hard work, but looking like one is easy. Just ask for the name, Jantzen").

Many of these claims are irrelevant to the evaluation of the product
advertised. After all, looking like a winner is not going to make us winners
and drinking a certain brand of liquor is hardly the thing that will finally
bring it all together for us. But the claims are also of very low risk to the
advertisers who make them. Copywriters know that in making any *factual*
claim they must be ready and able to back such claims in court should
someone challenge them—as is now, happily, done more and more frequently. To avoid such court battles advertisers resort either to the irrelevant claims, as we have just seen, or to opinion—both masked, of course, so
as to appear factual. The famous actor, actress, or noted personality from
the world of sport, or high finance, or fashion will be offered as an authority
on the qualities of the products being offered. Just as most of us fail to recognize the irrelevance of ads, so do many fail to distinguish an expression of
opinion from a claim of fact.

Just as symbols can be manipulated to extract more profound truth
(in the case of logic) and beauty (in the case of the arts), so we must come to
realize, for our own self-protection and good, that they can also be manipulated commercially for purposes of deception and the encouragement of
the pursuit of false values.

Still the device can be stretched only so far, for people are only so
gullible. We may perhaps accept Dick Van Dyke as something of an authority on photography (as the Kodak ad would have us believe), but we
would hardly accept his word on the value of, say, chemical components in
a detergent. But when the authority of personalities fails to convince, the
authority of science can always be dragged out. For the prestige of science

being what it is, almost anything can be sold if it can be shown to be the latest scientific breakthrough. Of course, the product need not be the latest science has to offer as long as it smacks of that. The result is that what we are now often sold is not "toothpaste" but "dentrifice," which sounds so much more scientific. In Colgate's case, it isn't even dentrifice but MFP, a fluoride ingredient that only the Colgate brand, we're told, contains. Other products contain such exotic, but scientific-sounding, ingredients as Chlorinol, Bio-Enzim, En-Zolve, Gerdal, Dermacil, XK, SL32, and V20. Often, of course, those product additions are merely technically sounding nonsense.

In the case of Colgate's brainstorm, the nonsense we are urged to buy turns out to be somewhat remarkable. MFP, we are led to believe, must stand for some new chemical that Colgate's scientists discovered and were the first to introduce into their product, making it superior to any of its competitors. Unfortunately, that is not the case at all. MFP doesn't stand for anything revolutionary that no other toothpaste yet contains. But the manufacturer needn't fear any court action. If we should try to take them to court on the ground that other toothpastes contain the same ingredient, they can point out that although this is so, they are the only ones who *call* the ingredient "MFP"—and they are the only ones who can do so because they alone own the trademark to that combination of letters! Like concrete poetry, which has affected modern advertising both in obvious and in subtle ways, they are in a sense asking us to value the words or letters for their own sake. Never mind that the letters alone do not prevent tooth decay!

We are by now so accustomed to living in the rarefied atmosphere of words, easily mistaking the word for the thing, that we have become not only easy targets for cunning and subtle advertising but easy prey to our own not so very subtle confusions. "I fail to see why hunting should be considered cruel," we may find ourselves saying, "when it gives tremendous pleasure to many people and employment to even more." In this case, what is wrong is that we have gone from the question of whether hunting is cruel to animals to whether it is cruel to people—deceived perhaps by the fact that the same word is used in both contexts though we are dealing with quite different matters. The question here is not whether people find hunting fun—of course they do—but whether the animals find it so. By concentrating mainly on the words, this may escape us.

In the chapters that follow, we shall examine closely the price we have come to pay for living in the modern world where words can be torn from their context and manipulated. We shall also learn some of the precautions we must take in order to survive in this sort of world. Some of these problems have arisen for us, as we will see, from our failure to bring into harmony the descriptive and the evaluative dimensions of words. A word like *steal*, for instance, doesn't only describe a certain action (the taking of something that doesn't belong to us) but makes a certain, often highly emotional, value judgment about it (namely, that it is wrong to do that). To avoid falling prey to this kind of confusion, we need to ignore the siren call of intellectualization so characteristic of modern life and learn to ground the words we speak in the experience and emotions we have. To learn to do so will not only spare us many confusions and save us much money, but it will also save us much personal anguish. For, as modern psychotherapy has learned, many of our problems arise from our failure to recognize, acknowledge, and come to terms with our feelings and one of the most prevalent ways we manage to disown such feelings is by intellectualizing them. Instead of saying such things as, "Your shouting makes me feel so scared and frightened," we say, instead, in a more detached and philosophical way, "You shouldn't shout. Shouting is so uncivilized." Nathaniel Branden, in his book *The Disowned Self,* describes this all-too-common condition as follows:

> Thinking can become that form of counterfeit reasoning known as "rationalizing"; or it can become "intellectualizing," a flight into abstractions that have no meaningful relevance, or no *experienced* relevance, to the issues one is considering . . . . This is manifested, for instance, in the behavior of the "intellectual" who discusses his personal problems as though they belonged to someone else, in a state of total personal dissociation in which he does not experience the emotional meaning of anything he says or hears; who prefers to talk about psychology in general rather than his agony in particular; . . . . [p. 4]

By such flights into impersonality people often seek escape from themselves and from their pain. The same tendency to over-intellectualize, however, is precisely what others exploit in bringing about the dissociations between the descriptive and evaluative that enables them to perpetrate their deceptions on us—or that we sometimes fall prey to in our own self-deception.

Words are the instruments of deception, but there are also certain things about us—our inflexibility and lack of suppleness—and our carelessness with the world of fact that aid and abet the deception. Enough has already been said in Part I about the former; now we must turn attention to the latter—the way we mishandle facts, or the way others succeed in deceiving us about the world of fact. As we will see from what follows, that is done by simply overlooking important and key facts, by evading them, or, worse still, by distorting them.

8

Shouting at Storks

In that witty collection of tales from fourteenth-century Italy, the *Decameron*, especially memorable is the following story, somewhat abbreviated, concerning the servant boy and the stork:

> A servant who was roasting a stork for his master was prevailed upon by his sweetheart to cut off a leg for her to eat. When the bird came upon the table, the master desired to know what was become of the other leg. The man replied that, "The stork never had but one leg." The master, very angry, but determined to strike the servant dumb before he punished him, took him the next day into the fields, where they saw storks standing each on one leg, as storks do. The servant turned triumphantly to his master, upon which the latter shouted, and the birds put down their other leg and flew away. "Ah, sir," said the servant, "but you did not shout to the stork at dinner yesterday; if you had done so, he would have showed his other leg too."

The story is, of course, amusing (and logically interesting) because it is such a fine illustration of an important point of logic and reasoning generally: Rules are meant to be applied only to those cases that fall under them—not to exceptions. Storks who customarily stand on one leg will put down their other leg when shouted at, but it does not apply in cases of storks who are either one-legged to begin with or roasted.

Understanding such rules and applying them properly is a matter of intelligence. The nature of intelligence, however, is widely misunderstood and needlessly shrouded in mystery. It has also, unfortunately, become an especially delicate subject. Intelligence, however, is in essence nothing more than the ability, which may be learned and which certainly can be greatly improved, to make distinctions—that is, to distinguish between things that seem similar and to discover the similarities in things that seem different.

Intelligence develops as we acquire an ample vocabulary (to mark differences), form the habit of observing the finer and finer distinctions made by words, and gain an eye for those occasions where such knowledge and skill are especially suited.

Two such occasions are the application of general rules and the use of specific cases. Abuse of the former gives rise to what is called in logic the *fallacy of sweeping generalization;* abuse of the latter, to the *fallacy of hasty generalization.*

We probably have all been guilty of making sweeping generalizations at some point in our lives. Consider this example: "Everyone has a right to his own property. Therefore, even though Jones has been declared insane, you had no right to take away his weapon." The first premise in this argument is a general principle that is widely accepted. It does not apply, however, in the specific case of a person who has lost his reason—especially when the piece of property is a weapon.

The source of this fallacy's persuasive power is its resemblance to valid arguments in which individual cases do fall under a general rule. The point to remember is that a generalization is designed to apply only to individual cases that properly fall under it. It is not designed to apply to special cases.

It is certainly valid to argue that, since all men are mortal, Socrates is mortal. But it would be incorrect to argue: "Since horseback riding is healthful exercise, Mary Brown ought to do more of it because it will be good for her heart condition." What is good for someone in normal health does not apply where special health problems exist. The fallacy of sweeping generalization is also referred to as the *fallacy of accident,* to emphasize the irregularity of particular cases to which generalizations do not apply.

Although the examples of sweeping generalization noted thus far are relatively clear-cut, this fallacy can be difficult to untangle when the ideas involved are more complex. Consider this argument:

> I believe in the golden rule as an inherent duty to do unto others as I would have them do unto me. If I were puzzled by a question on an examination, I would want my neighbor to help me. So it is my duty to help the person sitting next to me who has asked me to give him the answer to a question on this exam.

A critical fact has been overlooked here. The purpose of an examination is to find out how much each person knows, and that purpose would be defeated if people helped each other. If that is so, the golden rule does not apply in such circumstances. (In addition, of course, giving someone the answer in a test situation would be harming, not "helping" him.)

An argument of the kind we are examining has two parts to it: a rule and a case. If the argument is invalid, it is because the case to which the rule is being applied is exceptional and therefore does not fall under the given rule. To expose such a fallacy, therefore, all that is needed is to isolate the rule and show that, when properly interpreted, it cannot be applied to the case in question. Reviewing our examples, we might say of them: yes, everyone has a right to his or her own property—if the person has not lost his or her reason; yes, horseback riding is healthful—if one's state of health permits it; yes, we ought to help each other—but not when an examination is involved.

If exceptional circumstances make the rules inapplicable, then what of the popular saying that the exception *proves* the rule? As popularly used and understood, this principle is absurd. For if the word *proves* means "establishes" (or "confirms"), then how is it possible that an exception should be capable of *confirming* a rule? Clearly if the exception is truly an exception, far from confirming the rule it *disconfirms* it. Unfortunately, those who repeat this saying fail to realize that *proves* is used here not in the sense of "confirms" but rather in the now somewhat archaic sense of "tests" (a sense still retained in the phrase "proving grounds"). Understood thus, the principle is not unsound: An exception performs the function of testing our rules to see how adequate they are. Often it proves them to be inadequate.

It should be borne in mind that, although generalizations can be abused, they remain extremely useful. Generalizations allow us to infer universal rules with a reasonable degree of certainty where we could not possibly inspect each and every case. Indeed, to become so technical or precise that we avoid a generalization because we can conceive of an isolated case that might be an exception is to engage in quibbling. Lawyers with a good knowledge of the law and a fine eye for detail will sometimes succeed in having charges dropped against a client on the basis of a technicality—of what in other contexts might be considered pettifogging. But there is some justification to what they do. To fail to recognize mitigating circumstances when judging a person is to serve only the letter of the law, not its spirit. It is, again, to apply the law mechanically while overlooking important facts.

It is because of this that we recognize—although there are times when some of us forget it—that orders are to be followed, but only if they do not violate human rights (the tragic My Lai incident in Vietnam comes to mind here); that laws are to be obeyed, but only if they are just and allow for redress of grievances; and that the press is free, but only, of course, to publish the truth.

A famous and tragic example of the failure to recognize this simple rule—or was it simply the desire not to recognize it?—occurred when American Secretary of State Cordell Hull in Franklin Delano Roosevelt's administration refused to grant asylum to refugees on the ship the *St. Louis*, whose forced return to Nazi Germany meant certain death. He justified his action this way: "I took an oath to protect the flag and obey the laws of my country and you are asking me to break those laws." Hull's reasoning was specious, as he was undoubtedly aware, since the circumstances were special and mitigating. The *St. Louis'* sad mission ended in the ship's return to Europe and subsequently in the death of most of its passengers in Auschwitz, Treblinka, and other death camps.

Precisely the reverse of sweeping generalization is the fallacy of hasty generalization. In hasty generalization, an isolated or exceptional case is used as the basis for a general conclusion that is unwarranted. Consider the following two examples:

1. I had a bad time with my former husband. From that experience I've learned that all men are no good.
2. I know one union representative, and he's a terrible person. I wouldn't trust any of them.

Both arguments are invalid because they assume that what is relatively true under certain conditions is true under all conditions. At most the "evidence" presented here (if one may call it that) warrants only a particular, not a general, conclusion.

Unlike the fallacy of sweeping generalization, which results when a generalization is misapplied, the fallacy of hasty generalization results when a particular case is misused. Here, too, it must be remembered that examining all possible cases is usually impossible—and unnecessary. Unless a sufficient number are tested, however, the conclusion is likely to be too hasty and therefore unreliable.

In some instances, the fallacy of hasty generalization results from resting a conclusion on cases that are exceptional and therefore unrepresentative. Thus we would be guilty of hasty generalization if we were to say, "She speaks so beautifully that anyone can see she must have studied acting," or "This must be good medicine because it tastes awful." In both situations, the particular cases are related to the general rule only in an unessential way. There is no basis for assuming a connection.

The Sherlock Holmes stories by Arthur Conan Doyle abound with illustrations of complicated reasoning by the master detective. Only seconds after being introduced to Dr. Watson, Holmes brilliantly "concludes" that Watson must have been in Afghanistan:

> Here is a gentleman of a medical type, but with the air of a military man. Clearly an army doctor, then. He has just come from the tropics, for his face is dark, and that is not the natural tint of his skin, for his wrists are fair. He has undergone hardship and sickness, as his haggard face says clearly. His left arm has been injured. He holds it in a stiff and unnatural manner. Where in the tropics could an English army doctor have seen much hardship and got his arm wounded? Clearly in Afghanistan. (*A Study in Scarlet,* Part 1, Chapter 2)

Obviously Watson could have had an air of a military man without ever having been in the army; similarly, his face could have been tanned without leaving the British Isles, and so forth. Holmes is guilty of a hasty generalization founded on insufficient evidence.

A famous political example of this failure to make certain that one has not overlooked important facts in the course of reasoning occurred in 1936. A national journal of that day, the *Literary Digest*—as famous in its day as *Time* or *Newsweek* is in ours—attempted to forecast the outcome of the coming presidential election by sending out 2 million sample ballots to voters throughout the United States, asking them which candidate they intended to vote for. The magazine got back about 1 million ballots, most of which favored Alfred Landon, the Republican candidate for President. But Franklin D. Roosevelt won by a landslide. This great fiasco caused the *Literary Digest*, which had become a laughingstock, to go out of business. Whether the magazine deserved that fate or not, it committed a simple and basic error. Wishing to make the job of selecting 2 million names easier, it chose them from telephone directories and from lists of names supplied by car dealerships of people who had recently purchased autos. In 1936 most telephones and automobiles were owned by the well-to-do, and therefore the working people and the poor farmers were almost entirely ignored in the survey.

One variation of hasty generalization involves bringing in evidence to support an argument while ignoring evidence to the contrary. For example:

> Under the capitalist system, many people are poor and there is waste of labor and materials, cutthroat competition, glorification of the acquisitive instinct, depressions on the one hand and inflation on the other. All this proves that the system is thoroughly rotten and ought to be discarded.

Even assuming that all the evidence is this argument is correct, it would not constitute a sufficient basis for the drastic action recommended. To try to correct the abuses by abolishing the system is like throwing the baby out with the bath water. Nor has any attention been given to advantages of the system that may mitigate its disadvantages.

Rather than examining all the evidence, those who make such arguments merely select only what favors their interests (while trying to convey the impression that all the evidence has been presented and that all of it is on their side). Certain politicians thus view all their own actions with pride and all those of the opposition with alarm. Or they appeal for votes on the ground that they will reduce taxes but do not call attention to reductions in government services that will result from such cuts. Loan companies stress how easy loans are to secure and how small monthly payments are, but they do not mention the relatively high interest rates or how difficult some people find it to repay loans. Matters are rarely so simple as these arguments make them seem.

And, of course, the device is rampant in advertising. The following Owens-Corning Fiberglass advertisement is a subtle example: "Fiberglass has helped rocket sales of surfboards 9,900 percent. How much would it boost sales of your product?" The advertiser no doubt hopes his prospect will not realize that the fact that surfboard sales have increased that much may have no effect, or not nearly the same effect on other fiberglass products. The tremendous increase in surfboard sales is due to their popularity, and other products may not enjoy similar demands. More egregious cases of such appeals occur whenever we are told that "9 out of 10 doctors recommend . . . ." with the phrase "that we surveyed" cleverly left out, or that "our cereal contains no sugar" but neglect to tell us that it also contains no vitamins, and so forth.

One place such practices might seem permissible is in a court of law, where it is expected that each side will present its own case in the most favorable light. Even here, however, the principle of cross-examination has evolved in order to ensure that judge and jury attend to all of the evidence and hear the whole truth.

It isn't always merely the fact that some important facts have been slighted; sometimes it is a question of how much weight deserves to be placed on the facts that are cited. An article in the *National Enquirer* is headlined "Women Who Have Had Abortions Have Less Respect for Human Life." What is the evidence in support of that startling revelation? Such women, we are told, have been found to be:

- More in favor of the death penalty, and likelier to volunteer to serve as the executioner.
- More willing to pull the plug on someone surviving on life-support machines.
- Likelier to believe that human life begins at birth and that any fetus surviving an abortion should be killed.
- More in favor of giving homosexuals equal rights.

But couldn't this evidence support a rather different conclusion? Such women may be in favor of the death penalty because they cherish life so much they do not want people running around murdering other people; they are in favor of pulling the plug because they cannot stand to see people suffer, and so on.

But it isn't only such publications as the *National Enquirer* who are guilty of such distortions. An article in *Cosmopolitan Magazine* entitled "Blonde Power" asserts:

Whether platinum or honey, strawberry or ash, a lush mantle of tresses kissed by sunshine promises confidence, allure, a definite edge.

But how much evidence is there in fact to support the conclusion that, because some women board members, executives, and producers are blonde, you must be a blonde to be successful.

Nor does this sort of thinking always spare those who normally know better. The following is a remark once made by Nobel laureate Dr. Linus Pauling about former President Nixon: "For fifteen years I have studied insanity. I saw the eyes on television, and there is madness, paranoia." One would think someone like Pauling would know that it takes more than a certain look in the eyes to establish insanity.

The fallacy of hasty generalization teaches us that we need to exercise some caution before jumping to a conclusion. The fear of committing this fallacy, however, must not make us so cautious that we are too afraid to generalize at all. That would be equally bad, if not worse.

All of us know such overly cautious people—people who never, or hardly ever risk uttering a generalization, as in the story of the two friends who were riding in a train one day when they passed a meadow where some sheep were grazing. Turning to his friend, one man said: "Why those sheep look as if they have been sheared recently." Looking out, his cautious friend replied: "Oh yes, at least on one side."

9

To Be or Not to Be

In the late forties, when the debate about the atomic bomb was raging, the British philosopher Bertrand Russell argued, "Either we must have war against Russia before she has the atomic bomb or we will have to lie down and let them govern us." In the debate some chanted "Better dead than red!" while others replied, "Better red than dead!" Both sides overlooked a third position, "Better pink than extinct!"

Russell and the others who took one side of the argument or the other were guilty of still another fallacy involving the overlooking of important facts—*bifurcation*. Also called the *black-or-white fallacy* and the *either/or fallacy*, it is committed when we presume that a certain distinction proposed is exclusive or exhaustive when other alternatives exist.

Technically speaking, the fallacy works by presenting contraries as if they were contradictories. Two statements are said to be *contraries* when it is impossible for both to be true but possible for both to be false. If we say that Mary Jones may be rich or she may be poor, for example, we mean that she cannot be both at the same time but that she may be neither. Two statements are said to be *contradictories*, on the other hand, when it is impossible for both to be true and also impossible for both to be false. Either a man is alive or he is dead. Either today is your birthday or it isn't. If one contradictory is true, the other must be false, and vice versa. The fallacy of bifurcation arises when an either/or statement that actually contains two contraries is instead put forward as containing two contradictories.

Because our language is full of opposites, the tendency to bifurcate is common. We are prone to people the world with the "haves" and "have-nots," the "good" and the "bad," the "normal" and the "abnormal," "heroes" and "villains"—forgetting that between these extremes lie numerous gradations, any of which could serve as further alternatives to an *either/or* polarity.

Bifurcation is typical of, for example, the busy administrator who cries, "Spare me the details! Is the report good or bad?"—as if it could not be a bit of both. It was typical of those who spoke out strongly against everything Russian during the Cold War, as in the following example from Robert Welch, leader of the John Birch Society:

> Let me give this solemn warning. There can be only one capital, Washington or Moscow. There can be one flag, the Stars and Stripes or the godless hammer and sickle. There can be one national anthem, the "Star-Spangled Banner" or the Communist *Internationale*.

And in a less weighty but equally exasperating vein, it is typical of anyone who counters a complaint in this manner: "So you think the soup is too cold, do you? Well, I suppose you'd like it scalding hot?" What is objectionable about such arguments from a logical point of view is that they force us into a position of choosing between two alternatives when in fact our choices are not so limited.

At one time this fallacy seemed especially appealing to producers (and displayers) of bumper stickers. You may remember such classics as "America: Love It or Leave It" and its answer "America: Change It or Lose It." The one seen on an Indian reservation was even more memorable: "America: Love It or Give It Back."

Thinking in extremes can be appealing, unfortunately, for not only does it attract attention but it also requires less mental energy than exploring all aspects of a problem. That is perhaps why for some people if two things do not differ in kind but only in degree, they do not see them as different. In the eyes of some people, for example, if you're not for capitalism, you must be a communist. Socialism, differing from communism only in degree, is overlooked or not recognized by them. Similarly, with arguments regarding foreign policy, other nations are either our friends or our enemies—as if such a complicated thing as the relations of one country to another could be dealt with adequately in such a simplistic fashion.

In the 1970s, we heard the fallacy repeated in arguments about energy policy and pollution. The following are two typical examples:

We can become independent of Arab oil only by ruining our environment.

But are these indeed the only possibilities? Safeguards to protect our natural resources can be found; and we are not necessarily bound to deal only with Arab states. In addition, new reserves keep being discovered, and the world supply appears to be greater than first believed.

And somewhat more long-winded:

> The peoples of the world necessarily face widespread and horrible death within the next century. If enough food is produced to feed the expanding world population, then water and air will be polluted beyond tolerable limit by the amount of fertilizers and insecticides that are required. So people will die of water and air poisoning. If these fertilizers and insecticides are not used, not enough food will be able to be produced on the land available, and people will starve.

Is it not possible, however, that a safe amount of insecticides could be used so that widespread hunger would not occur? Limiting the use of insecticides to either too much or none at all makes our situation appear more desperate than it is.

Advertisers, knowing our weakness for oversimplification, exploit this tactic to sell products: The strategy is to cut off our critical thinking about a product by creating an either/or view that suits their aim. "When you're out of Schlitz," the jingle lets us know, "you're out of beer." This well-known commercial is very catchy. Needless to say, however, other beers may be just as preferable, if not more so. (Schlitz is the beer, as the reader may remember that was once advertised as "washed with live steam"—a slogan that led the public to believe it was the only beer to be so treated, enriching the company enormously as a result. In fact, this was, as some later learned, standard procedure in the beer industry.)

Of course, Schlitz isn't the only offender. The following are a random selection of current favorites:

1. If you know about BMW, you either own one or you want one.
2. People either ask for Beefeater, or they ask for gin.
3. Either you drive a Jaguar, or you don't drive at all.
4. All my men wear English Leather or they wear nothing at all.
5. Coffee, Tea, or Vivarin?
6. With all the talk about smoking I decided I'd either quit or smoke True.
7. Volvo: the car for people who think.
8. Grand Marnier Liqueur. Either have an extra bottle in reserve or an eloquent apology.

This sort of thinking characterizes many clichés: "Now or Never" (but tomorrow might be better); "Better safe than sorry" (what about, though, "Nothing ventured, nothing gained"?); "A miss is as good as a mile" (but isn't coming close sometimes good enough?); "All that is good in the world is either illegal, immoral, or fattening" (that seems to have the ring of truth to it).

You also find this sort of reasoning represented in remarks by the famous:

1. George Orwell: "Life is like that, take it or leave it." (Why not try to change life or, failing that, change oneself?)
2. Nietzsche: "What does not destroy me, makes me stronger." (Is that always so? Often enough it embitters people and diminishes them. Here F. Scott Fitzgerald's remark seems truer to life. He said: "A man does not recover from such jolts—he becomes a different person and eventually, the new person finds new things to care about.")
3. Patrick Henry: "Give me liberty or give me death." (It may sometimes be more courageous to try to survive and fight another day.)

In some instances of the fallacy of bifurcation, two terms are made to seem contradictory when they are not even contrary. Again consider this example, which might be heard on the political stump:

> We must choose between safety and freedom. And it is in the nature of good Americans to take the risk of freedom.

Safety and freedom are not necessarily incompatible. By implying that they are, this argument commits a fallacy, for it invites us, once more, to overlook facts that bear on the argument.

> If we are going to buy a car, we have to buy either a good one or a cheap one. We can't afford a good one, and we don't want a cheap one; so we'll just have to do without a car.

The terms *good* and *cheap* are not necessarily incompatible here either. It is entirely possible to find a cheap car that is good—that is, that functions well, does not cost much to maintain or operate, and has other desirable characteristics. The speaker implies that the terms are contradictory (that it is impossible for both to be true and also impossible for both to be false) when in fact they are not.

Some examples of the fallacy are simply humorous, although not always intended as such. For example, Senator Richard Russell was once quoted as saying, "If we have to start over again with another Adam and Eve, I want them to be Americans and not Russian."

Less humorous are the occasions when we commit the fallacy from prejudice or bigotry, with a need for a scapegoat or villain to vent our rage at our own inadequacies, failings, or deprivations. Villains have for a very long time been a support of the film industry, although (because of the opposition from Blacks, Jews, Indians, and other minorities to this exploitation) Hollywood has begun to run out of villains and more recently has had to turn to such nonhuman hate objects as sharks, natural disasters (fires, earthquakes, etc.), and alien phenomena.

But long before Hollywood discovered how profitable it could be to exploit hatred for a villain, it had been exploited by literature and the legitimate theatre. Some think that Shakespeare's *Merchant of Venice* is a classic example. Shylock is now, of course, a universal symbol. It is not a compliment to be called a Shylock, and Jews have suffered much as a result of the characterization. It is understandable, therefore, that whenever the *Merchant of Venice* is produced, many Jews are upset and wonder about the motives of those responsible for presenting it. Many Jews even had mixed feelings about Shakespeare himself for having created such a character (or fiend, as they regard him) in the first place.

But both they and those who take delight in seeing the image of Shylock kept alive are sadly deceived about Shakespeare and the play he created. Both have fallen into the pattern of thinking that the *Merchant of Venice* is a play about heroes and villains, about good guys and bad guys—about how a villain (Shylock) tries to outsmart some good, innocent citizens of Venice only to be outsmarted in the end by them. But to see or think of this play in these simplistic terms is not only to fall victim to the fallacy of bifurcation but to do violence to Shakespeare's play. For in reality the play is noticeably devoid of good guys.

The plot turns on Bassanio's need for money in order to outfit himself, make himself appear rich, and thus win the hand of the wealthy Portia—hardly a noble purpose. He convinces his friend Antonio to make a loan from Shylock, who, we are informed, has been ill treated by Antonio on numerous occasions. Shylock agrees to the loan on the condition that, if the money is not repaid on the agreed-upon date, Antonio will forfeit a pound of his own flesh. Shylock is certainly no saint, but then neither are the other characters that surround him. Even Portia, whose speech on the quality of mercy has become a classic, shows not one iota of mercy herself when she proceeds, through the sham of a court proceeding, to deprive Shylock of both his money and his religion.

Besides revealing the darker side of all the principals, Shakespeare further prevents us from a too simplistic reading of the character of Shylock by giving him some of the most unforgettable speeches in literature. They can be read as a defense not only of himself but of any minority that is cruelly and viciously mistreated by a hate-filled and vindictive majority. The most famous, undoubtedly, is the one where he defends the harsh terms of his loan to Antonio:

> He hath disgraced me, and hindered me half a million; laught at my losses, mockt at my gains, scorn'd my nation, thwarted my bargains, cooled my friends, heated mine enemies: and what's his reason? I am a Jew. Hath not a Jew eyes? hath not a Jew hands, organs, dimensions, senses, affections, passions? fed with the same food, hurt with the same weapons, subject to the same diseases, heal'd by the same means, warm'd and cool'd by the

same winter and summer, as a Christian is? If you prick us, do we not bleed? if you tickle us, do we not laugh? if you poison us, do we not die? and if you wrong us, shall we not revenge? if we are like you in the rest, we will resemble you in that. If a Jew wrong a Christian, what is his humility? revenge: if a Christian wrong a Jew, what should his sufferance be by Christian example? why, revenge. The villainy you teach me, I will execute; and it shall go hard but I will better the instruction.

It does not take much experience of the world to realize that there is often much villainy in our heroes and much heroism in our villains.

10

When Many People Are Out of Work, Unemployment Results

We chuckle over this explanation of unemployment offered by President Calvin Coolidge and are inclined to respond with, "No kidding." Sad to say, however, very similar "explanations" often carry a great deal of weight with us.

Logicians call the fallacy committed by Coolidge *begging the question*—a logical lapse committed when, instead of offering proof for its conclusion, an argument simply reasserts the conclusion in another form. Such arguments invite us to assume that something has been confirmed when in fact it has only been affirmed or reaffirmed.

Thus were we to argue that "the belief in God is universal because everybody believes in God," we would be guilty of the fallacy, since "universal" means something applicable to "everybody." In effect, such an argument lacks premises and is therefore not an argument at all, for all we have done is repeat the very point with which we began. That is, such things as "Honesty is praiseworthy because it deserves the approval of all" or "Miracles are impossible because they cannot happen" is really to say nothing.

Such "arguments"—merely explaining as they do, their own terms—are unsound because to explain terms is not to establish their truth or validity. As in Molière's famous play where a physician explains the soporific effect of opium by citing its sleep-producing properties, it is a matter of explaining a thing by the very thing that needs explaining.

The following are further examples:

1. Tom committed suicide because he had a death wish.
2. Bodies fall because they have a downward tendency.

Since *death wish* is another term for suicide, and *downward tendency* another term for *fall*, these are not even explanations of the things in question—let alone confirmations of them. At most what we succeed in accomplishing in speaking in this way is to point to a further name of the event or phenomenon.

Mayor Richard Daley of Chicago employed the fallacy for humor—and perhaps to evade the facts—when a reporter asked him why Senator Hubert Humphrey had failed to carry Illinois in the election of 1968. Humphrey lost the state, replied Daley, because "he didn't get enough votes." The question really was: Why did he not get enough votes?

Fallacy and wit have much in common, though they are not the same. Mayor Daley's reply was meant to be amusing, which is why it is not a fallacy: To feign an error is not to commit it. And the same is probably true of the answer that Joseph P. Kennedy, father of the noted political clan, gave to a long, involved questionnaire attempting to probe the personality characteristics of the rich. He returned the questionnaire unanswered with a note stating, "I am rich because I have a lot of money."

The mechanism Mayor Daley exploited can be found in numerous witty remarks: "I don't want to be a millionaire," Joe E. Lewis once quipped, "I just want to live like one." "I can resist everything," Oscar Wilde acknowledged, "except temptation." And when asked why he robbed banks, Willie Sutton replied, "Because that's where the money is." On occasion, however, the laugh is on the speaker, for this very same device, by exposing ignorance or deliberate blindness, may cause embarrassment. The man who said he wasn't jealous, though he didn't like the idea of his wife talking to other people, is a case in point. This is not unlike the remark made by Tallulah Bankhead: "Cocaine isn't habit-forming. I should know—I've been using it for years."

But the genius of language, or those who use it, is such that the same devices that yield fallacy can come to have stunning effects. Shakespeare's *King Lear* is a good example. The plot hinges on the decision of Lear, having grown old and somewhat foolish, to divide his kingdom among his three daughters. He accedes to the flattery of two of them, and the third daughter, Cordelia, who is really devoted to him, is forced to flee. Left in the hands of his evil daughters, Lear begins to descend into insanity (though Shakespeare implies that he has also paradoxically become much more clear-headed than ever). When Cordelia comes to rescue him, he is overcome with both joy and anguish. Not daring to believe that it is truly Cordelia, that he could be forgiven, or that she could shed tears for him, he raises his trembling hand to her cheek and, with a voice barely audible now, says: "Your tears are wet."

How moving and pathetic those four words are in context, and how dramatically right. Yet from a strictly logical point of view the remark could be ranked with the others as an example of an absurdly vacuous statement (for what else could tears be?). But of course it is not. One person's fallacy is another's profundity. Here as elsewhere the extremes have a tendency to meet.

Flagrant examples of this fallacy escape easy detection if the statements involved are somewhat drawn out, in which case our memories may fail to spot the repetition. Consider this example in a political argument:

> Free trade will be good for this country. The reason is patently clear. Isn't it obvious that unrestricted commercial relations will bestow on all sections of this nation the benefits that result when there is an unimpeded flow of goods between countries?

Because "unrestricted commercial relations" is just a more verbose way of saying "free trade," and since the wordy conclusion of the argument is merely another way of saying "good for this country," the argument says, in effect, that free trade will be good for the country because free trade will be good for the country.

Here is another such example, which a "gifted" political orator might try to pull off:

> To allow every person an unbounded freedom of speech must always be, on the whole, advantageous to the state. You ask why? Well, it is highly conducive to the interests of the community that each individual should enjoy a liberty, perfectly unlimited, of expressing his sentiments.

Here again "a liberty, perfectly unlimited, of expressing his sentiments" is simply a more drawn out way of saying "freedom of speech." And "highly conducive to the interests of the community" is another way of saying "advantageous to the state." What we are told here, therefore, is that "to allow every person unbounded freedom of speech is advantageous to the state because it is advantageous to the state to allow every person an unbounded freedom of speech"!

The world of advertising has not overlooked the potential for evasion made possible by this sort of appeal. An ad reads: "Macaroni and Cheese in Tomato Sauce. Containing Tomato Sauce, Macaroni and Cheese." The space taken up by the silly repetition might have been used to inform the buyer about the ingredients' nutritional contents. "Our low prices are the direct result of our lowered price policy," another advertisement announces, trying to make us believe we now know the reason behind the price reductions. What, however, is the real reason for the price reductions? Is the store trying to undercut a nearby competitor? Has business been poor? And, finally, more subtle still is the following advertisement: "Rally Car Wax. It shines better because it cleans better."

Arguments that beg the question are circular arguments. They make use of the capacity of our language to say a thing in many different ways, ending where they began and beginning where they end. They are like the proverbial three morons, each of whom tied his horse to another's horse, thinking that he had in this way secured his own horse. Naturally, all three horses wandered away because they were anchored to nothing but each other.

The circle that is involved in such arguments can be appreciated in this scene, which takes place in a loan company office.

Manager: And how does our loan company know that you are reliable and honest, Mr. Smith?
Smith: Well, I think Mr. Jones will give me a good reference.
Manager: Good. But can my company trust the word of Mr. Jones?
Smith: Indeed it can, Sir! I vouch for the word of Mr. Jones myself!

If Jones is to vouch for Smith and Smith for Jones, we are no further ahead than we were at the outset. This is not unlike the remark to the clerk at a motel: "Certainly she's my wife. I'm her husband." He would be her husband if she were indeed her wife, but how do we know she really is his wife? *Husband* and *wife* being correlative terms, one is dependent on the other.

Circular arguments reason that *A* is so because of *B*. But *B* turns out to be true only if *A* is true. The question, "Is *A* true?" remains unanswered. The question is begged. Here is a familiar example.

God exists!
How do you know?
The Bible says so.
How do I know that what the Bible says is true?
Because the Bible is the word of God!

Such arguments are sometimes called *vicious*—as in the familiar phrase, "vicious circle"—to indicate that whenever we try to break through them we are forced back again.

In that charming book by Antoine de Saint Exupery called *The Little Prince*, read and admired by millions, the little prince, in his search for another home on another planet, runs into a typical case of just such a vicious circle. Meeting with all kind of adventure, he lands on an asteroid inhabited by a single being, a tippler.

> "What are you doing here?" he said to the tippler, whom he found settled down in silence before a collection of empty bottles and also a collection of full bottles.
> "I am drinking," replied the tippler, with a lugubrious air.
> "Why are you drinking?"...
> "So that I may forget,".....
> "Forget what?" inquired the little prince, ...
> "Forget that I am ashamed,"....
> "Ashamed of what?" insisted the little prince, who wanted to help him.
> "Ashamed of drinking!" The tippler brought his speech to an end, and shut himself up in an impregnable silence.
> And the little prince went away, puzzled.

On the psychological plane, circular reasoning very often manifests itself in precisely such ruts.

To see more clearly, however, why such arguments are fallacious, we might note a further form in which they sometimes appear. People occasionally try to establish a particular proposition by subsuming it under a generalization. If the generalization itself is questionable, however, then the argument is fallacious. Consider the following argument: "Clearly Professor Jones is an atheist; he's a philosopher, isn't he?" Here the conclusion ("Professor Jones is an atheist") is made to rest on a general assumption (that all philosophers are atheists), which is much wider and much more questionable than the conclusion itself.

This form of begging the question is sometimes used in arguments about criminal responsibility. Some argue that a particular crime is the result of childhood environment because all such crime is rooted in childhood experiences. Such an argument is circular because the generalization on which the particular is based is one whose truth is not accepted by opponents of the position. People who make this argument, however, might maintain that their reasoning is perfectly sound because, after all, they are merely drawing out implications contained within the given premises. For if it is true that all such crimes are rooted in childhood, then it follows that this crime too must be similarly rooted. If to argue so is fallacious because it is circular, then perhaps all arguments are fallacious.

There is some point to this observation. All arguments, attempting as they do to draw out implications contained in their premises, are in a sense circular. There are two respects, however, in which sound arguments differ from those that we condemn because of their circularity.

First, a sound argument contains premises that assert information not contained in the conclusion. That is, the premises provide evidence for the conclusion rather than simply restating assertions made in the conclusion, as circular arguments do. Second, a sound argument contains obviously true premises rather than premises that are open to question. An obviously true premise, for example, would be that someone cannot be in two places at the same time; anyone using this premise in an argument would have to be granted it without having to demonstrate it. Circular arguments, on the other hand, are attempts to persuade us of a doubtful conclusion by presenting us with evidence that is equally suspicious.

It is useful to remember that the fallacy of begging the question, like all fallacies, is most easily detected when we examine the argument from the standpoint of what we are rationally obliged to grant within the structure of a given argument, or what our rights are where such things are concerned. We will learn to exercise those rights more frequently and more effectively once we achieve a deeper understanding of the devices that deceive and bedevil us.

We are on our way to doing so when we not only chuckle at but also find Coolidge's remark about unemployment fatuous, when we find refreshing the patient's reply to the doctor who had told her "You know none of us is getting younger"—"I don't care about not getting younger; I just don't want to get older," and when we find rather mean the wife's reply in this interchange:

Husband: Dear, where are my cuff links?
Wife: Where you left them!

Appreciation of those different forms of the fallacy is excellent preparation for defending against such "arguments" as the following, which are their correlatives:

1. School isn't worthwhile because book learning doesn't pay off.
2. Death for traitors is justified, because it is right to put to death those who betray our country.
3. "He that hath wife and children hath given hostages to fortune; for they are impediments to great enterprise, either of virtue or mischief."

All of these statements have the same form: *A* because of *B* where *B* is simply the same as *A*. Recognizing this, we should be able to respond by saying:

1. Since "book learning" is the same as "school," and "doesn't pay off" the same as "isn't worthwhile," all we are told here is that "school isn't worthwhile because school isn't worthwhile."

2. Since "right to put to death" is the same as "justified," and "those who betray our country" the same as "traitors," all we are told here is that "Death for traitors is justified because death for traitors is justified."

3. Since "they" here refers back to "wife and children," and "impediments to great enterprises" is just another way of saying "hostages to fortune," all that this famous aphorism of Francis Bacon asserts is that, to put it in current English, "He who marries and has children throws away his chances of making it big, because he who marries and has children throws away his chances of making it big!"

Having mastered the fallacy in this form, we may then be in a position to recognize and deal with it when it takes the form of A because of B where B is not, strictly speaking, the *same* as A, but *dependent* on it. Here are some examples:

1. He talks with angels.
How do you know?
He said he did.
But suppose he lied?
O, perish the thought! How could any man lie who is capable of talking with angels!

2. What makes you think Lefty is a crook?
Well, look at the crooks he associates with!
How do you know they are crooks?
Well, anyone who'd associate with a crook like Lefty . . .

3. *Bill:* I enjoy only good books.
Tom: How do you know when they're good?
Bill: If they're not good, I don't enjoy them.

Our response here should be that:

1. Since "he talks with angels" (A) is made to depend on the fact that "he said he did" (B), the person making the claim cannot turn around and make (B) depend on (A) without also going around in a circle.

2. Since the fact that "Lefty is a crook" (A) is made to depend on the fact that "his friends are crooks" (B), it cannot therefore be proven that those friends (B) are really crooks because Lefty (A) is one.

3. If the fact that "books are good" (A) is made dependent on the fact that "Tom enjoys them" (B), the claim that he enjoys them (B) cannot be taken as proof that they are good (A) without going around in a circle.

And having arrived that far in our ability to defend ourselves against such deceptions, we might then come to recognize the fallacy in one further form. In this very subtle manifestation of begging the question, A is made to follow from B where B is even more suspect than A. Here are two examples:

1. Suicide is a crime because it is a crime to commit murder.
2. Moral beliefs are unjustified because they are not verifiable in sense experience.

We are not logically obligated to accept the conclusion in either of these arguments. For in the first case we are asked to assume that taking one's own life is the same as taking someone else's life, and in the second that only things verifiable in experience are justified—and no evidence is provided for making either assumption.

Such self-training would make it immediately obvious why such a typical outburst by the Rev. Jerry Falwell, prophet of the so-called Moral Majority, is a classic example of begging the question:

> Abortion stands as an indictment of murder against America for killing unwanted babies. America has the blood of all those babies on her hands.

Rev. Falwell may believe he knows when life begins, but many of the rest of us are not so sure.

It is comforting to know, however, that the ability to distinguish between proving something and simply assuming it is not always absent from those who represent or speak for us. An interesting example of the recognition on the part of a court and jury of this distinction—in which a great deal of money was at stake—involved a prospector named James Kidd. Kidd vanished in Arizona, leaving a handwritten will (Figure 10-1) directing that his fortune ($230,000) go toward research to prove scientifically that a soul leaves the human body at death. One hundred and thirty individuals and institutions filed for Kidd's estate, including Dr. Richard Spurney, a junior college teacher. Spurney submitted to the court a foot-thick pile of "evidence" that included three unpublished books. He had fifty "proofs" of the existence of the soul. Spurney summarized his main proof as follows:

> Death is decomposition. Hence, what cannot decompose cannot die. But decomposition requires divisibility into parts. Thus what is not divisible into parts cannot die. But divisibility into parts requires matter. Hence what has no matter in it is not divisible into parts and so cannot decompose, and so is necessarily immortal.

After hearing testimony for thirteen weeks, the court decided against Spurney and awarded the estate to the Barrow Neurological Institute of Phoenix, Arizona.

The court was right in rejecting Dr. Spurney's argument, for the man had simply presupposed just what he was supposed to prove—that a human soul exists. The fatal error occurs at the point in Spurney's summary where he says "what has no matter in it . . . ." Where is his proof that such a matterless thing exists? Certainly if such a matterless thing—a soul—existed, then it would not be divisible and hence not decomposable and hence imperishable. Yet whether such a thing exists is the point of the whole question and therefore must not be begged.

FIGURE 10.1.

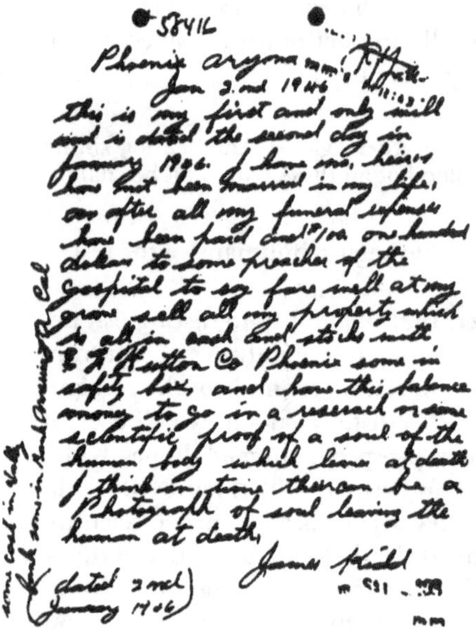

Phoenix Arizona
Jan 2.nd 1946
this is my first and only will
and is dated the second day in
January 1946. I have no. heir's
have not been married in my life,
an after all my funeral expenses
have been paid and $100. one hundred
dollars to some preacher of the
gospital to say farewell at my
grave sell all my property which
is all in cash and stocks with
E F Hutton Co Phoenix some in
safety box, and have this balance
money to go in a research or some
scientific proof of a soul of the
human body which leaves at death
I think in time their can be a
Photograph of soul leaving the
human at death,
                                James Kidd

(dated 2nd
 January 1946)

some cash in Valley
bank some in Bank America LA Cal

11

The Scoundrel Hounded
His Wife to the Grave

To assume the point in dispute is, as we have seen, to beg the question. Sometimes it is possible to do so with just a single word or phrase suggesting that a point at issue has already been settled when in fact it is still in question. Since many of our words possess both a descriptive and an evaluative dimension, the possibilities for using *question-begging epithets*, as such words are called, are endless.

Since another term that we may use for "descriptive" is *factual,* and another term for "evaluative" is *judgmental,* what we really want to consider here is something very simple but crucial—the difference between stating a fact and making a judgment about it. Thus to say something like "The scoundrel hounded his wife to the grave" or "This criminal is charged with the most vicious crime known to man" is not only to describe what happened but to make a judgment about it. In the latter case, the simple statement "This man is charged with homicide" would have done just as well. And, as far as the former is concerned, if all someone did was try to reach his wife by calling or writing to her a number of times, that would hardly make him a "scoundrel" who "hounded" his wife to the grave.

In the same way, to call a certain act "stealing" is not merely to describe but to make a judgment about it as well, for the term suggests that the action is wrong. In the case, say, of a woman "stealing" food in order to prevent her children from starving to death, the use of such a word would beg the question, since in light of the circumstances her action would probably be considered appropriate.

This linguistic device is so widespread that it has come to be known by a variety of labels: "mud slinging," "name calling," using "loaded words" and "controversial phrases," "verbal suggestion," and "emotive language." Marshall McLuhan called this tendency to dismiss an idea by the expedience of naming it "libel by label"—or the "label-libel" gambit. Consider these examples from the political arena:

1. A man should find it degrading to live on a dole or any payments made to him without his being required to render some service in return. But how many of them do feel degraded by it? From an economic standpoint, such loafers are simply parasites and should be dealt with accordingly.
2. The councilman's shocking proposal is calculated to subvert the just aspirations of hard-working men and women.
3. No right-thinking American could support this measure—a cunning plot hatched in the smoke-filled rooms where bossism rules.

The question-begging epithets used in these arguments are logically objectionable because they assume attitudes of approval or disapproval without providing evidence that such attitudes are justified. To call someone a "loafer" or a "hard-working citizen" is not to establish that the name fits; nor does calling a certain measure a "cunning plot" or "shocking" make it so.

As these examples indicate, people can beg the question not only with uncomplimentary epithets but with complimentary ones as well. An interesting form of the latter is found in history books, where the word *Reformation* is used to refer to the breakup of Christianity in the sixteenth century. The appellation is question-begging since the word "reform" means not simply a change but a change for the better.

One of the most famous instances of the uncomplimentary form of this fallacy was Vice President Spiro Agnew's remark, "A spirit of national masochism prevails, encouraged by an effete corps of impudent snobs who characterize themselves as intellectuals." Cartoonist Al Capp improvised a similarly unkind epithet for students walking out in protest from a lecture he was delivering in Hartford: "Hey! Don't go. I need an animal act."

Question-begging epithets are objectionable because they serve only to arouse passions and prejudices through the use of emotionally charged language. By overstatement, ridicule, flattery, abuse, and the like, users of such epithets often seek to evade the facts.

Sometimes, the fallacy is commmitted unknowingly or innocently, owing to a failure to distinguish the descriptive and evaluative dimensions of words. The following example, taken from general semanticist S. I. Hayakawa's book *Language in Thought and Action,* is an amusing example of this confusion:

Witness:	That dirty double-crosser Jacobs ratted on me.
Defense Attorney:	Your honor, I object.
Judge:	Objection sustained. (Witness's remark is stricken from the record.) Now, try to tell the court exactly what happened.
Witness:	He double-crossed me, the dirty, lying rat!
Defense Attorney:	Your honor, I object!
Judge:	Objection sustained. (Witness's remark is again stricken from the record.) Will the witness try to stick to the facts.
Witness:	But I'm telling you the facts, your honor. He did double-cross me.

Unless the cross-examiner exercises some ingenuity in order to get at the facts behind the judgment, the process could continue forever. To the witness it is a *fact* that he was "double-crossed" and that the other man is a "dirty, lying rat."

But the fallacy is not always committed innocently and is not confined to the uneducated or ignorant. Nor is the failure to distinguish the evaluative from the descriptive a cause of bitterness and misunderstanding only among individuals; it is also one of the major causes of misunderstanding among nations. The misunderstanding that the Western world has had with the Soviet Union is a classic case.

At one time, for example, both the Russians and the Western nations seemed to agree on the meaning of the word *totalitarian*. But in fact, to us the word carried with it an element of disapproval, whereas to the Russians it had no such implications. To them it was simply a neutral, descriptive term. Their failure to feel moral indignation at being accused of "totalitarianism" was therefore not a sign (as we were tempted to interpret it) of moral depravity.

Another similar case concerned the charge of aggression in the early days of the Cold War. While both sides seemed to agree regarding the evaluative meaning of the word—it was a "bad" word for both—they did not seem to agree regarding its descriptive meaning. Thus for them, aggression apparently did not include propaganda, sending military equipment or intelligence into another country, providing foreign armies with a body of instructing officers, and so on. For us, however, at least then, all such acts were regarded as acts of "aggression." Thus to have accused the Russians, as we were inclined to, of hypocrisy when they denied being guilty of "aggression" was to be blind to the underlying semantic problems that were at the root of this linguistic misunderstanding.

More revealing still are the confusion and irritation that continue to underlie use of the term *democracy* by the communists. Many regard the communists' claim that their system is democratic as either comical or perverse. But, to be fair, the descriptive content of that word is simply different for them and us. In calling their state "democratic," they have in mind such things as the elimination of class antagonism, the removal of economic classes, and universal education. In short, for them democracy is chiefly a social ideal whose value can be judged by the ends achieved, not by the means used to achieve them. For us, on the other hand, it has always been a political ideal, standing for a certain form of government and a certain way of arriving at political decisions. Without freedom of speech, parliamentary procedures, majority vote, and civil liberties, there is no "democracy," we have tended to think. Since the term is used by both sides to stand for such vastly different things, it is little wonder that each has come to accuse the other of bad faith.

We must remember, however, that realizing how the Russians use the term is not somehow magically to change the things referred to so that we might all agree that the Russians do have democracy. Obviously, despite such clarification, the communist system is still what it is, and ours is what it is. What such clarification does achieve is a clearing of the air, better understanding, and more tolerance.

When the confusion between the evaluative and descriptive ends in accusations, much bitterness can result—a dangerous development in the international arena but equally explosive in personal relations. How can such apparent attacks be dealt with? A very effective way is what is sometimes called *clouding* in assertiveness training. Without denying what has been asserted or becoming defensive or responding in kind, you cloud the issue somewhat by calmly acknowledging that there may be some truth in what has been said and go on to state what that is by replacing the uncomplimentary terms with more neutral or even laudatory ones. The following are some examples from a course manual by Dick Sutphen on assertiveness training:

Boss: Diane, sometimes you seem to take twice as long as other times to get your work done.

Diane: It does seem that I am more productive on some days than I am on others.

Boss: Maybe you should be paying a little more attention to your duties.

Diane: I'm sure there are times I should be a little more attentive.

Boss: Maybe you aren't getting enough rest, and shouldn't stay out so late on a week night.

Diane: You could be right. If I feel the need for more sleep, I'll get in earlier.

A little humor doesn't hurt either:

In-Law: My daughter deserves a husband who is more ambitious.

Paul: I probably could be more ambitious than I am.

In-Law: I don't know what she ever saw in you, anyway.
Paul: I don't know what she sees in me either but I'm glad she does.

Nor does a bit of foggy generalizing:

In-Law: Sometimes just your presence irritates me.
Paul: People often irritate other people.

And gentle self-deprecation:

In-Law: Don't you have anything more to say?
Paul: I guess I haven't had a lot to say, have I?*

The purpose of such substitutions, of course, is not to irritate or frustrate an opponent but to defuse the emotional charge their words carry.

It would be much more effective if instead of resorting to name calling, we shared with others our mutual feelings about behavior that we consider offensive. That is particularly good advice in child rearing. Instead of telling a child, for example, "You're bad" or "rotten," it would be much better—and much more effective in changing the child's behavior—to say instead, "What you're doing makes me feel very bad." With attention thus focused on the action rather than on the doer—and the doer no longer feeling on the defensive—such an approach can lead to surprising results (to say nothing of it's being logically more defensible).

* *Assertiveness Training Course Manual* (Malibu, CA: Valley of the Sun Publishing Co., 1978), pp. 31–32.

12

When Should You Buy Your First Cadillac?

It is told of King Charles II of England that he once asked members of the Royal Society to determine why, if you place a dead fish in a bowl full of water, it makes the water overflow, while a live one does not. Some of the members thought about this a very long time and offered ingenious but unconvincing explanations. Finally, one of them decided to test the question. He discovered, of course, that it did not make a bit of difference whether one placed a dead fish or a live one in a bowl of water.

Whether the story is true or not, it holds an important lesson. Before rushing to answer a question, it is best to question the question, for every question necessarily brings with it a set of assumptions that determine the lines along which it is to be answered. Sometimes those assumptions may render the argument fallacious.

We are familiar with this type of question in the form of the prosecutor's query, "Have you stopped beating your wife?" You simply can't answer a question like that without incriminating yourself. But such *complex questions*, as they are called, are not limited to the courtroom. Consider these examples that are representative of the kind of arguments heard in bull sessions or on the media:

1. Why is it that women are more interested in religion than are men?
2. Why is private enterprise so much more efficient than any government control of industry?

In each of these questions there lies an assumed answer to a previous question. The first assumes that women are more interested in religion than men (and often no evidence of this is ever offered). Similarly, the second assumes that private enterprise is more efficient than any government control of industry, and again, when the question is debated, little or no evidence generally is offered to support this assumption.

Like question-begging epithets, to which it is related, the fallacy of complex questions goes under a variety of names. "Loaded questions," "trick questions," "leading questions," "fallacy of the false question," and "fallacy of many questions" are a few of them.

We can sometimes deal with such questions by "dividing" them—that is, separating the part we want to answer with a yes from the part we want to answer with a no, as is done in the following:

Interviewer: Is this policy going to lead to ruinous inflation?
Official: The policy is designed to lead to inflation but not a ruinous one.

A complex question may often appear in combination with a question-begging epithet:

> Are potential school dropouts to continue to be allowed to endanger, disrupt, and destroy the academic opportunities of the serious students who desire to learn the requirements of our complicated technological and multifaceted culture?

Before an argument such as this one can be dealt with properly, the complex question in which it is couched must not only be divided into prior and subsequent questions but also into descriptive and evaluative elements. In this case we should ask, first, whether it is true that some students are "endangering," "disrupting," and "destroying" the academic opportunities of the other ("serious") students. If that is so, then we should ask to what degree such highly emotional and explosive terms as "dropouts," "endangering," "disrupting," and so on are accurate descriptions of the students and the behavior referred to?

Complex questions can take the form of asking for an explanation for "facts" that are either untrue or not yet established. Here are some typical examples:

1. Why is a ton of lead heavier than a ton of feathers?
2. What time was it before time began?
3. What is the explanation of flying saucers?
4. Can we know our past lives? (Rosicrucian ad)

By focusing our attention on explaining the "facts," such questions divert attention from the fallaciousness of the questions themselves:

1. The first example is, of course, an old riddle, and its solution is that if each weighs a ton, there is no difference in weight.
2. The second is more difficult. Like the first, however, its solution lies in attending to the form of the question: If there was no time before time began (as the question assumes) then there couldn't have been a time in which it began. But surely, someone will be tempted to reply, it must have begun at some time? Yes, our answer will be, but only if (as *this* question now assumes) time did not always exist.
3. The assumption here is that there are such things as flying saucers (with everything that implies).
4. This ad assumes that we have had a past existence—a large leap indeed!

The study of complex questions teaches that questions should be asked one at a time and that no attempt should be made to answer a question until the one on which it depends has been settled. This principle is acknowledged in legal and parliamentary procedure, where the rules allow for a motion "to divide the question." This procedure provides for the fact that questions may be so complex that they should be considered only when separated.

Unfortunately, however, this procedure doesn't always govern our ordinary dealings with one another, and we violate it only too often. A husband, beer can in hand, furiously opening drawer after drawer and irritable after a hard day at work, shouts at his wife: "Where did you *hide* the can opener?" A parent, worried his son is turning into a professional student, explodes with the question: "How much longer are you going to waste your time in school when you might be doing a man's work in the world and contributing to society?" And an interviewer asks his distinguished guest: "Senator, why is it so hard for you to come to a conclusion?"

The prevalence of the use of this form of question, and our growing tolerance for it, has made us especially vulnerable to its exploitation by advertisers and salespeople. Since advertisers must be careful about making explicit claims (for someone may then challenge them to back these claims in court), the discovery of the device of asking a question that only suggests or assumes something to be the case but doesn't explicitly state it to be so has been a gold mine to advertisers.

One device used by advertisers is to assume, on our behalf, the positive merits of the product advertised and then to narrow the argument to the less weighty question of when we will avail ourselves of the item. For example, one advertisement for Bohemia beer asked the question, "If you had to name the three finest beers in the world, what would the other two be?" Here the advertiser didn't need to claim explicitly to be among the best; letting the customer make the inference is so much more subtle (and safer). And similarly clever is the advertisement for mascara, "Are your lashes as beautiful as they used to be?" It is designed to lead women to believe that using the product will make their lashes beautiful once again (when in fact they may not have been beautiful in the first place and the product may not improve them at all).

More devious still is the following advertisement for a fountain pen: "How many other lifetime investments cost as little as $13.50?" Here the advertiser does not come right out and say the fountain pen will last a lifetime; more safely, the assumption that it will is made from the way the question is posed.

And perhaps even more subtle is the General Motors' advertisement: "When should you buy your first Cadillac?" This ad tries to make Americans feel that the purchase of the car represents one of those important milestones in life—like a first date, graduation, or a first job. It also makes people feel that its purchase means having finally arrived.

But surely most devious of all is the sugar advertisement "If sugar is so fattening, how come so many kids are thin?" It is no doubt true that kids eat a lot of sweets and yet stay thin. What the advertisement hopes we will fail to see is that, unlike us, kids lead an active life and work off the calories. Adults who lead a much more sedentary existence can expect the intake of sweets to have visible results.

If such forms of persuasion are found somewhat wanting in achieving the desired results, there is always the use of fear to persuade us to part with our hard-earned money. And so sometimes we are confronted by such loaded questions as: "Is your car entirely safe? Install Sure-Grip Tires today!" (which is designed to lead us to do exactly that even when quite unnecessary). "Would your wife and children have security if you died today? If not, shouldn't you buy more insurance?" (even when you have sufficient coverage already). And so on.

Ads are the modern-day equivalents of old-fashioned pitches made by salespeople. People in sales are just as well trained as ad men in the art of posing complex questions. Here are some questions—all familiar to us— that salespeople are trained to ask us in order to "close the deal," long before we have even made up our mind whether we want the item:

1. Will you be paying by check, cash, or credit card?
2. Would you like me to make this contract out for 12 or 18 months?
3. We make our own deliveries. What days would be best to deliver this item to you?
4. What kind of accessories would you like with your new vacuum cleaner?

Learning how to detect such questions and to deal with them can save us a good deal of money.

13

My Son's a Don Juan—
She's a Tramp

People who think they are special tend to apply a standard to themselves and their doings that is somewhat more generous than the standard they are inclined to apply to others and their doings. I once heard someone say, for example, "I know how to be thrifty, but Larry is simply a tightwad." Both *thrifty* and *tightwad* describe the same characteristic, but the term the speaker used for himself was positive, whereas the one he applied to his acquaintance was negative. Logicians have a name for this fallacy: They call it *special pleading*.

When we engage in special pleading, we favor ourselves and are prejudiced against others. As in the case of question-begging epithets, we imply—and hope others will believe—that our labeling correctly describes reality when in fact it merely reflects our prejudice.

Like all fallacies, this one can be exploited for its humorous effects. When asked her opinion of on-stage nudity, the actress Shelley Winters (then age 46) replied: "I think it is disgusting, shameful, and damaging to all things American. But if I were 22 with a great body, it would be artistic, tasteful, patriotic, and a progressive, religious experience."

To engage in special pleading is to be partial and inconsistent. It is to regard our own situation as privileged while failing to apply to others the standard we set for ourselves (or, conversely, to fail to apply to ourselves those standards we apply to others). It is to speak, for example, of the "heroism" of our troops, their "devotion," and "self-sacrifice" in battle, while describing the enemy as "savage" and "fanatical." Consider the following remark from an editorial: "The ruthless tactics of the enemy, his fanatical, suicidal attacks, have been foiled by the stern measures of our commanders and the devoted self-sacrifice of our troops." Do "self-sacrifice" and "suicide" describe different events? Obviously they do not, but such use of language hopes to persuade others that the difference in labels reflects a difference in the quality of the events in question.

Another typical but even more serious example of this tactic is the following statement by Andrei Vishinsky when he was the Soviet ambassador to the United Nations:

> While in those countries which have entered the North Atlantic alliance a mad armaments race is taking place and an unbridled war propaganda is being broadcast, and while the war psychosis is being incited more and more, the Soviet Union is the scene of peaceful, creative work. All the forces of our country are directed to the fostering of our national economy and to improving the standard of living and the welfare of the Soviet people.

We in the West are thus described as engaged in a mad armaments race, incited by war psychosis and propaganda while the people of the Soviet Union (that workers' paradise) are occupied with peaceful, creative work. Doing what? No doubt reading their bibles, writing poems, and things like that.

What is sad about all of this is that often, not recognizing how language is used here to deceive, we believe and are persuaded by what the speaker says when we ought really to be insulted by it. Someone trying to play that kind of number on us cannot have a very high opinion of our intelligence.

Without using the label of "special pleading" to identify the device, Edwin Newman, in his book *Strictly Speaking,* provides a striking and illuminating example of this tactic from the Vietnam era:

> The war in Indochina produced a host of terms that media folks accepted at their peril: protective reaction strike, surgical bombing, free-fire zone, interdiction, contingency capability, New Life Hamlet—which in sterner days was a refugee camp—and many more. Money paid to the family of a South Vietnamese civilian killed by mistake was a condolence award.
> In February, 1971, South Vietnamese forces, with American air support, moved into Laos. Rarely had the importance the government attached to language been made so clear. An incursion, Washington called it, and there were official objections to our calling it an invasion, evidently in the belief that incursion implied something softer than invasion did, and that an incursion was permissible where perhaps an invasion was not. . . .
> [But] the distinction between incursion and invasion was a distinction without a difference, in grammar and in fact. The incursion into, or invasion of, Cambodia in 1970 enormously increased death and destruction there, and the incursion into, or invasion of, Laos increased death and destruction there.

As the example indicates, special pleading makes use of a feature of language we have explored in connection with question-begging epithets: the ability of our words to both describe and evaluate. The existence in our language of a large body of paired terms such as "incursion/invasion" makes it all too easy to engage in special pleading.

Norman Mailer made the point well in a recent interview, in which he was asked whether, after publication of a second work by him on Marilyn Monroe, he might consider the actress an obsession of his. He replied:

> If John Updike writes about something twice, he's got a theme. If I write about something twice, it's an obsession. Let's say Marilyn Monroe is one of my themes.

Mailer was quite correctly pointing out that a double standard was being applied to his work and that of others.

Feminists have been quick to point out how well our language lends itself to special pleading in the form of the double standard: a man is "attentive," a woman "possessive"; a male executive is a "take-charge guy," a female a "domineering old bag"; my son's a "Don Juan," but your daughter's a "tramp." The consequences of such a double standard can be quite far-reaching—impeding women's progress on the job and limiting men's emotional life.

Though not unrelated to it, what we are dealing with here is much more serious than the device known as *euphemism*. Euphemism ("telling it like it isn't") is substituting a new and seemingly more pleasant term for one that has become too threatening, familiar, or common. When we wish to avoid mentioning death, for example, we resort to euphemisms like "passed on," "departed this life," or "went to her reward," trying thereby to transform the event, perhaps even to deny it.

Euphemisms are also used to glorify the commonplace. We call "third class" today "tourist class," and what used to be called a "traveling salesman" is now a "field representative." We use euphemisms as well to cover our embarrassment about bodily functions. Our linguistic ancestors, the Anglo-Saxons, were blunt: They called the place you "go to" the "gong." Our sensibilities are more delicate: It would be hard for the foreign tourist to discern what the "powder room" might be used for—and she might have trouble finding it even if she did know, given the extremes to which modern architects seem to go in concealing the place.

What we are dealing with here, though, under the heading of special pleading is much closer to what is known as *General Semantics* than to euphemism. General Semantics, unlike ordinary semantics, is not the study of the meanings contained in words but rather the study of attitudes and prejudices that come to be enshrined in words. It is the study of the way we organize the world by way of language and how these organizations control us.

General Semantics was founded by an American of Polish origin, Count Alfred Korzybski. Like so many other great achievements, at the core of General Semantics there lies something very simple, even obvious. It occurred to Korzybski that language plays a much greater role in human life than has been properly acknowledged or understood. He thought that if people did come to see the sort of profound influence that words have on their lives, they could correct much that is wrong with them and their society. Korzybski explored this idea in great detail and with much care in *Manhood of Humanity, Science and Sanity,* and other works. Unfortunately for the young science of General Semantics, Korzybski tended to claim too much for it. He thought it could or would cure more than seemed to many people possible or reasonable.

The person who probably did the most to popularize General Semantics was not Korzybski but rather an early disciple of his—S. I. Hayakawa, former Sen. Hayakawa of California. Hayakawa incorporated the findings of Korzybski and others in a book that was a best seller and widely regarded—*Language in Thought and Action.* He also founded a journal devoted to research in General Semantics entitled *Etc.* This was an especially suitable title, for it is one of the tenets of General Semantics that words can never say all there is to say about anything and facts are never all in. All our sentences should therefore end with the word "etc." In time Hayakawa and Korzybski had a falling out—over "words," as the former once explained it.

Describing what General Semantics is about is difficult. Mainly, however, it tries to refute the limerick that all of us as children were quoted whenever we returned home in tears because someone called us a bad name: "Sticks and stones may break your bones, but names will never hurt you." That is all wrong, semanticists say, because a stone thrown at you may make a wound that in time will heal and then be completely forgotten, but a name hurled at you may stick in your mind forever, so that you will never be rid of it. And this is true of good names as well as bad ones, so that, as far as General Semantics is concerned, Juliet was certainly mistaken in thinking that "a rose by any other name would smell as sweet." In all likehood, it would not.

Semantics is a discipline more closely related to psychology than to grammar. It is the study of how words, with various attitudes and evaluations built into them, affect and influence those to whom they are directed as well as those who direct them. As Hayakawa once put it: "Human beings are the only ones who can talk themselves into trouble; and semantics is concerned with how to avoid doing so."

Thanks indeed to General Semantics, we have become a good deal more sensitive to language and a good deal more knowledgeable about the kind of influence it exerts on our thought and behavior. Medical institutions are no longer called "hospitals for incurable diseases," for example, for we now realize that to be wheeled into a place with that sort of name is not to be inspired with any great hope. You might as well be wheeled directly to the cemetery. Also such a name, aside from its psychological insensitivity, is out of keeping with the spirit of science: diseases that are not curable today may find their cure tomorrow.

We also realize that to call someone "culturally backward" is not only to describe that person's condition but to condemn and blame him or her for it. Our more current phrase—"culturally deprived"—tends to shift responsibility to where it probably belongs—to ourselves—and to encourage us to do something about it.

Tagging some people with the term "half-breed" presents a similar problem. Far from being simply a descriptive term, it is one that carries feelings of arrogance, superiority, and contempt. It is just another way of saying that someone is subhuman. Anyone who believes that certain people are subhuman will find it easy to treat them as subhuman. The end result can be mountains of baby shoes in storehouses, lamp shades made from human skin, and soap made from human fat.

In addition to sensitizing us to words, General Semantics has helped us understand a related phenomenon: When we predict that something will happen, the prediction itself contributes to making it happen. The tendency is known as a *self-fulfilling prophecy*. When we call someone a "no good bum," for example, adding that the individual will probably never amount to anything, we are almost certainly guaranteeing that the observation will come true. Not only do our words discourage the person from trying to improve; they also convince *us* that efforts on our part to help him or her are futile and not worth making. And so the individual remains a bum—and years later we have the satisfaction of saying: "Well, didn't I tell you he'd never amount to anything!"

We have it in our power either to enhance and beautify our world or to degrade it and ourselves by the way we use language and by such devices as special pleading or self-fulfilling prophecies. The tools we use to put others down can be used to build them up. If by thinking worse of people we make them worse, perhaps by thinking well of them we will make them better.

I like to think of this device as the "Dulcinea effect" after Cervantes' classic *Don Quixote* (1605)—a work revived in our day in the stage musical *Man of La Mancha*. The story, as retold in the stage version, is about a man, Don Quixote, who leads a drab, mean, and poor existence until he decides to live out a fantasy of himself as a dauntless knight in the glorious days of chivalry. Since every knight must have his lady, Don Quixote chooses as his object of veneration a common prostitute, whom our hero sees as the flower of virtue. He calls her not by her real name, Aldonza, but by a name he fancies as much more suitable, Dulcinea. The lady, of course, thinks him crazy but is gradually won over by his vision of reality. His faith in her transforms her into the person of beauty she held within herself in spite of the external conditions of her life.

It would be a mistake to confuse the Dulcinea effect with being sentimental. On the contrary, it is a matter of being very realistic. Far from being merely wishful thinking, the effect derives its power from the belief that we can make things happen, bring something into existence by sheer force of will and by controlling our response to what does happen—even if initially we have to fake it! A Hassidic master once responded smartly when one of his followers came to complain about another disciple who was passing himself off as a saint. Someone who pretends to be a saint, he said, has a severe punishment coming—if he keeps it up long enough, he may become one.

Max Beerbohm, the British essayist and humorist, wrote a charming story called "The Happy Hypocrite" that illustrates the point of this famous Hassidic remark beautifully. A man who had led a dissolute life went one day to the theatre, where he saw and promptly fell in love with a beautiful young actress. He went backstage and proposed to her. But she took one look at him and said: "You have the face of a dissolute man. I could love only a man with the face of an angel." Undaunted, the man went off to a maker of masks and had a mask fashioned that gave him an angelic appearance. When he returned to the theatre wearing the mask, the young actress took one look at him and fell in love. They married and went off and lived happily in a cottage in the woods. After some years the man was traced down by a discarded mistress, who threatened that if he did not return to her she would expose him before his wife. The threat was eventually carried out, but when the man was unmasked, lo and behold, his face had grown to resemble the mask.

The principle behind self-fulfilling prophecies and the Dulcinea effect has been well understood by science for a very long time. Whenever a doctor offers a patient a placebo, he is invoking that principle.

The device has also been well understood by the business world, which prides itself on selling not products but dreams. Unfortunately, the principle is not always as well understood by the rest of us in our personal lives. How many parents, for example, are consciously aware of the messages they are indoctrinating their offspring with in giving them such names as John Jr. (to follow in daddy's footsteps) and Gigi (expected to be sexy and seductive)? Such names are frequently labels and advertisements.

14

Archimedes:
World's First Streaker

In this chapter (and the next two), we consider how to recognize messages that contain a significant distortion of facts. We have noted throughout our discussion how important it is to develop the ability to see differences and recognize similarities—that, in fact, the essence of intelligence lies in being able to do precisely that sort of thing. There is, however, a certain technique of reasoning, called *analogy*, which is occupied specifically with the drawing of likenesses. Because it is easily abused, it deserves special attention.

When we reason by analogy, we liken something that is obscure or difficult to something else that is already known and understood. This is a valid way of arguing so long as the two things being compared resemble each other in important respects and differ only in trifling ways. However, if they are alike only in unimportant ways and different in important ways, then the analogy doesn't hold. The fallacy of false analogy that results is a distortion of facts. Merely to seize upon some slight similarity as a basis for concluding that what is true of one is also true of the other is to be seriously misleading.

Consider this argument, which has been advocated by diverse groups throughout history;

> It is necessary to force other people to accept our religious beliefs about an afterlife for their own good, just as force must be used to prevent a delirious person from leaping over the edge of a steep cliff.

Even if we were to grant that our religious beliefs are superior to others, this argument would remain unsound because of the false analogy employed. For in the one case it is a matter of saving a delirious person from committing suicide, while in the other case the persons involved are presumably not delirious. Thus it would not follow that, just as force is necessary in the case of the delirious person concerning this life, so force is necessary in the case of other people concerning an afterlife. If someone should say in reply that surely anyone who did not believe in our religion must be mentally incompetent and thus "delirious," he would commit the fallacy of begging the question. (The mere fact that an individual claims that someone is delirious is no proof that he or she is.)

To expose a false analogy—or, as it is also called, an *imperfect analogy*—all that is necessary is to show the significant differences or the insignificant similarities. The technique is especially useful in analyzing political arguments. For example, supporters of nuclear reactors sometimes make the argument that an atomic power plant is infinitely safer than eating since some 300 people choke to death on food every year, whereas far fewer people die as a result of exposure to radiation. This is not a very meaningful comparison, however. When 300 people die from choking accidents, only they die. Yet in the case of nuclear power plant accidents, not only will countless numbers of people suffer immediately from the disaster, but the environment wil be adversely affected for thousands of years and generations of people may well suffer. Furthermore, just because there have been more choking accidents than nuclear power plant accidents does not mean that such a situation will continue into the future. The chances are that, as more nuclear power plants are built, the likelihood that an accident will eventually occur increases.

Arguments in the political arena that turn on a false analogy are not new phenomena. There have been examples throughout history, some of them by people who, we might be tempted to say, "should have known better." Consider this argument from the great sixteenth-century philosopher, Francis Bacon, in support of war:

> No body can be healthful without exercise, neither natural body nor politic; and, certainly, to a kingdom, or estate, a just and honorable war is the true exercise. A civil war, indeed, is like the heat of a fever; but a foreign war is like the heat of exercise, and serveth to keep the body in health; for in a slothful peace, both courages will effeminate and manners corrupt. [*Of the True Greatness of Kingdoms*]

Bacon is trying to persuade his readers that a "war exercise" is like physical exercise. What he fails to note is that nations are not analogous to persons.

Furthermore, unlike the exercises individuals do, war exercises take their toll on other people.

Note that not every analogy is an argument by analogy. Often analogies are constructed not with the purpose of advancing an argument or proving a thesis, but merely for illustrative purposes or to lend color to a position supported in other ways. Such analogies may still mislead, of course, but no more weight should be placed on them than their authors intended them to carry. The following passage from Karl Marx is a case in point:

> As the heavenly bodies, once thrown into a certain definite motion, always repeat this, so it is with social production as soon as it is once thrown into this movement of alternate expansion and contraction.

The cyclic or periodic behavior of the heavenly bodies is used here merely as an illustration of economic cycles and not as the reason for their occurrence. The purpose of analogies such as these is not to establish a conclusion but rather to gain attention, to make their meaning clearer by providing us with a striking mental picture, to move us, and so on.

Far different is this economic argument against government regulation from the contemporary philosopher Ayn Rand:

> By what conceivable standard can the policy of price-fixing be a crime, when practiced by businessmen, but a public benefit, when practiced by the government? There are many industries in peacetime—trucking, for instance—whose prices are fixed by the government. If price-fixing is harmful to competition, to industry, to production, to consumers, to the whole economy, and to the "public interest"—as the advocates of the anti-trust laws have claimed—then how can that same harmful policy become beneficial in the hands of the government? [*Capitalism: The Unknown Ideal*]

Rand's analogy of price fixing by government and price fixing by private firms is clearly misleading. When the government fixes prices, it tries to make them as fair as possible to producer and consumer alike. But individual businesspeople, whose private interests are involved, would naturally try to make as much profit as possible without regard for the public welfare. Private business, unlike government, is not a disinterested third party.

It is not just political and economic arguments but sometimes moral ones as well that turn on an unjustifiable analogy. One of our greatest Supreme Court justices, Oliver Wendell Holmes once made the following astonishing argument in favor of eugenics:

> We have seen more than once that the public welfare may call upon the best citizens for their lives. It would be strange if it could not call upon those who already sap the strength of the State for these sacrifices, often

not felt to be such by those concerned, in order to prevent our being swamped with incompetence. It is better for all the world, if instead of waiting to execute degenerate offspring for crime, or let them starve for their imbecility, society can prevent those who are manifestly unfit from continuing their kind. The principle that sustains compulsory vaccination is broad enough to cover cutting of the Fallopian tubes.

The analogy between vaccination and forced sterilization is a dangerous one. Compulsory vaccination, we all agree, protects us against disease, but to use "preventive medicine" to stop the "unfit" from having children is pernicious. Since we are not all agreed as to what or who is to be regarded as "fit" or "unfit," compulsory sterilization could easily be turned into an instrument of repression of minorities.

A more recent example of a deceptive analogy to justify a questionable moral position was a statement by the Mexican Bishop of Montevideo, Andrés Rubio. In defending the survivors of an airplane crash in the Andes who resorted to eating human flesh to sustain themselves while waiting for rescue, the Bishop said:

> You cannot condemn what they did when it was the only possibility of survival. . . . Eating someone who has died in order to survive is incorporating their substance, and it is quite possible to compare this with a graft. Flesh survives when assimilated by someone in extreme need, just as it does when an eye or heart of a dead man is grafted onto a living man. [Quoted in Piers Paul Read, *Alive: The Story of the Andes Survivors*]

While it is true that in both grafting and cannibalism there is "assimilation" of someone else's flesh or organ into one's own body, there are important differences. One of the main ones is that in the case of grafting, the organ in question continues to function as it had and is not transformed into energy and waste matter. In addition, of course, in the case of grafting the donor has given his or her consent, which is not generally so in the case of cannibalism.

In reasoning, analogies tend to confuse rather than illuminate. While we may admire the skill with which some of the analogies discussed here were constructed, we must never mistake metaphorical meaning for logical meaning. To do so is to invite foggy thinking. Pseudosciences like astrology thrive on such thinking. Consider this argument for the validity of astrology:

> People who dislike astrology will sometimes say, out of malice, that the stars' distances are sufficient to make the effects of their vibrations negligible. This is easily refuted. First, the space between earth and the stars is nearly a vacuum, empty enough to let vibrations pass almost undiminished in vigor. Second, the Chicago exposition in 1933 was opened by a ray of light from the star Arcturus hitting a photoelectric cell. If a star as re-

mote as Arcturus can open a fair in Illinois, it is very careless to argue that the stars are too far away to affect our lives.

The author of this analogy has unfortunately failed to see that, while photoelectric cells are things designed to receive or respond to light waves or vibrations (however faint or distant they may be), we are not such cells and therefore are not "affected" by such phenomena.

So attached are we to the use of analogy that it frequently happens that we adopt an analogy and continue to use it in ways that make no sense at all—in fact, in ways that are simply absurd. Take the statement, "The razor edge of his intellect will be blunted by constant use." The comparison of a person's mental ability to a sharp razor is certainly striking and perhaps even illuminating—illustrating how the minds of very intelligent people work (their ability to "cut" through a mass of detail, going straight to the "heart" of a problem, etc.). But it is absurd to extend the analogy by implying that, just as a razor will be blunted by constant use, so will our minds if used often. Far from deteriorating from too much use, the mind is improved by it. Of course, people may become tired from overwork, but that is a different matter. Once they have rested, they will find that their minds have become sharper, not duller, as a result of the exertion. But we have become so attached to the comparison of the mind with a razor that we do not realize how absurd some of its further uses are.

On occasion, nevertheless, reasoning by analogy can be instructive. Such a case was the famous discovery of the Greek mathematician Archimedes that a body immersed in fluid loses in weight an amount equal to the weight of the fluid displaced. Archimedes is said to have made this discovery while attempting to solve a problem for King Hieron, who wished to know what metals had been used in his crown but did not wish to destroy the crown by melting it down. Archimedes solved the problem by observing the water in his bath rose as his body displaced it. He reasoned by analogy that a certain weight of gold would displace less water than the same weight of silver because it was smaller in volume. Dripping wet, he ran out in the street shouting, "*Eureka! Eureka!*" It was a double first—a great scientific discovery by the world's first streaker!

The great Renaissance astronomer Copernicus is said to have made his revolutionary discovery using the same reasoning process. While drifting in his boat near a river bank, he had the illusion that the bank was moving while his boat remained stationary. It suddenly struck the astronomer that the same illusion might be the cause of the belief that the earth remains still while the sun moves around it. The analogy turned our view of the universe upside down and was the basis for modern astronomy.

More often, however, discoveries are made by testing analogies carefully, for many of those used in argument will be found to be fallacious. We smile today at our forebears who delegated the sowing of crops to women who had borne many children, on the assumption that human fertility was somehow analogous to a rich harvest. We wonder how a superstition could arise that led people, when wishing to injure an enemy, to make an image of the enemy and then destroy it. But we moderns are misled by analogies every day. The best defense against this distortion of facts is always to sort out those aspects of the analogy that are relevant to an argument and those that are not.

15

Playing Something Badly
Every Night
Before Going to Bed

We come now to a form of distortion in our reasoning that, although still tempting and prevalent, has slipped somewhat in prominence as a result of the spread of science. I mean our confusion over causes. This is not to say that we are no longer inclined to commit it; we are, of course, but the tendency to do so does not reveal itself any longer in the crude forms in which it once did. The early Greeks, for example, believed that night is the cause of the extinction of the sun, for, as evening came on, shadows arose that seemed to blot out sunlight. We now know that the Greeks had reversed cause and effect: It is the sun setting that causes the shadows and not the shadows that cause the sun to be obscured. Still that realization doesn't stop students from arguing, in a way similar to the Greeks, that since those who get A's study hard, the best way to get *them* to study hard is to give them A's.

Or again, we tend to chuckle at the drunk who reasons: "Last week I got smashed from drinking whiskey and soda, and this week the same thing happened with scotch and soda—I gotta stop drinking that soda." Still, many take seriously the suggestion that, since every major war in which we have taken part during the last few generations has happened when we had a Democractic president, we ought therefore to think twice before voting for a Democrat in this presidential election.

As one final example, we often find persuasive the following argument:

> More and more the government is originating welfare legislation designed to alleviate our citizens from the slavery of economic necessity. At the same time, however, we are seeing an increase in immorality, alcoholism, and

suicide, among our citizens. This makes it clear that, to get rid of this upsurge in immorality, alcoholism, and suicide, we must stop the government from instituting welfare measures.

This argument, however, should be compared with the one below that, although it is almost an exact match, is patently absurd:

> More and more young people are attending high schools and colleges than ever before. Yet there is more juvenile delinquency and more alienation among the young. This makes it clear that these young people are being corrupted by their education.

The *fallacy of false cause*, as it is called, can assume many different forms, but its most common form is the mistaken belief that, because something occurred just prior to something else, it was therefore its cause. Probably the most famous literary exemplification of this error is Chanticleer—the rooster in Chaucer's *Canterbury Tales* who thinks that if he doesn't cock-a-doodle-do in the morning, the sun won't come up.

Like Chanticleer, many humans fail to see that sequence alone is no proof of consequence. A multitude of events occur the second before a given event, any one of which can very well be the cause. Much more knowledge is therefore required in order to be able to identify its cause. Failure to recognize this is what has led many into egregious errors. Consider this argument about the "cause" of crime:

> If strong law enforcement really prevented crime, then those areas where police patrols are most frequent would be the safest and best protected. Actually, the very reverse is true, for in such areas even one's life is in danger, and crimes of all kinds are more common than in other areas where police patrols are infrequent.

The writer believes strong law enforcement actually causes crime because police patrols are most frequent in areas with a high crime rate. But the cause-effect relationship has been reversed in the argument. The high crime rate is the cause or reason for the frequent police patrols, not the other way around. If the police stay there long enough, no doubt the crime rate will go down.

Besides mistaking sequence for cause and consequence, those who commit the fallacy of false cause are also usually guilty of oversimplification: They assume that *A* is the direct, immediate, sole cause of *B* when the situation is generally much more complicated than that. Consider this argument:

> In the years prior to the outbreak of recent wars, there has always occurred an increase of armaments among the belligerents. It is obvious, therefore, that increased armaments is the cause of war.

Obviously the investigation of causes here has failed to proceed far enough. Before concluding that the increase of armaments is the cause of war, we should need to know what caused the increase of armaments. When dealing with a phenomenon such as a war, no one thing can be singled out as *the* cause. There are probably numerous factors involved.

Businesspeople who argue on the basis of increased sales that an advertising campaign has been successful are guilty of the same sort of oversimplification. Other factors, such as improved economic conditions or the season of the year, may have been responsible for the sales increase.

It is good to remember in such cases that two events may be related even though neither is the cause of the other. In such instances, both are effects of a third event, which is the cause of each of them. An interesting historical example concerns the ibis, a bird sacred to ancient Egypt. Egyptians worshipped the ibis because each year, shortly after flocks of ibis had migrated to the banks of the Nile River, the river overflowed its banks and irrigated the land. The birds were credited with causing the precious flood waters when in fact both their migration and the river's overflow were effects of a common cause, the change of season.

Let us consider another, somewhat more difficult example of this type:

> Twenty-five years after graduation, alumni of Harvard college have an average income five times that of men of the same age who have no college education. If a person wants to be wealthy, he or she should enroll at Harvard.

Here, too, the investigation of causes has failed to proceed far enough. Although attending a school such as Harvard no doubt contributes to the kind of income someone is likely to make, it is well to remember that Harvard attracts and accepts only outstanding students, or students who come from a background of affluence. Harvard alumni, therefore, would probably achieve high income regardless of which college they attended—perhaps whether they attended college at all.

If an event's coming immediately before another is an insufficient basis for establishing causal connection, it goes without saying that events even more remote from one another give still less warrant for assuming causality. Thus the fact that *homo sapiens* follows the ape in the succession of primates is no proof that we are descended from the ape; nor is the fact that the Roman Empire declined after the appearance of Christianity proof that Christianity was the cause of its decline.

Like all fallacies, this one has been exploited for its humorous possibilities. The following exchange between Glendower and Hotspur in Shakespeare's *Henry IV* is a funny and famous example:

Glendower: At my nativity
The front of heaven was full of fiery shapes,
Of burning cressets: and at my birth
The frame and huge foundation of the earth
Shaked like a coward.

Hotspur: Why so it would have done at the same season if your mother's cat
had but kittened, though yourself had never been born [Part I, act 3,
sc. 1].

Similarly amusing is the following passage from Mark Twain's *Adventures of
Huckleberry Finn,* which also illustrates the fallacy:

> I've always reckoned that looking at the new moon over your left shoulder
> is one of the carlessest and foolishest things a body can do. Old Hank Bun-
> ker done it once, and bragged about it: and in less than two years he got
> drunk and fell off of the shot-tower and spread himself out so that he was
> just kind of a layer, as you may say; and they slid him edgeways between
> two barn doors for a coffin, and buried him so, so they say, but I didn't see
> it. Pap told me. But anyway it all come of looking at the moon that way,
> like a fool [Ch. 10].

Less broadly funny but nevertheless an example of the use of the fallacy for
the expression of wit is the following letter, written by George Bernard
Shaw, after hearing Jascha Heifetz (then 19) play:

> My dear Heifetz:
>
> Your recital has filled me and my wife with anxiety. If you provoke a jeal-
> ous God by playing with such superhuman perfection, you will die young.
> I earnestly advise you to play something badly every night before going to
> bed, instead of saying your prayers. No mortal should presume to play so
> faultlessly.
>
> G. Bernard Shaw

Although this is a beautiful way of paying someone a compliment, we must
realize that great artists are sometimes tragically struck down at the height
of their careers, not because of envious gods but for various physiological
reasons.

We began our discussion of this particular distortion by noting that
we do not any longer tend to commit it in the absurd forms in which people
of the past did. The notion, for example, that nature acts with a purpose is
slowly becoming a thing of the past. It would be a rare person who would
argue that it will be a hard winter because hollyberries (which nature provides for birds in hard weather) are abundant this year.

Nevertheless, we occasionally run across contemporary statements
that sound very much in their reasoning like something out of the past. For
example, in 1973 a local Louisville preacher was quoted as denouncing

area productions of the rock musicals *Hair* and *Jesus Christ Superstar* after a tornado ripped through portions of Louisville. He warned people to mend their evil ways or expect another devastating storm. His remarks were almost exactly parallel to those of a certain Thomas White, who, in 1577, preached a sermon to his London congregation in which he said:

> I understand [that plays] are now forbidden bycause of the plague. I like the pollicye well if it hold still, for a disease is but bodged or patched up that is not cured in the cause, and the cause of plagues is sinne, if you looke to it well: and the cause of sinne are playes: therefore the cause of plagues are playes.

Most would agree today that both men were guilty of ignoring the natural or physical causes of the catastrophes that struck their communities in order to forward their own private world views.

But although in general we are growing more sophisticated in our reasoning about natural or physical causes, this is not so true of our reasoning about psychological causes. Many people still seem to believe, for example, that merely saying an event will happen helps make it happen. A good case can be made for this form of the self-fulfilling prophecy, as we have seen, but on psychological rather than magical grounds. What actually happens is that, for example, fearing others will be unfriendly to us, we act in an unfriendly manner that frequently makes them unfriendly in return. Or, expecting a friendly welcome, we greet others warmly and they respond in kind.

The belief in bad luck or a "jinx" is similar. What actually happens is that people who believe they have been "jinxed" are likely to falter in ways that will work against them. They may, on the other hand, take special pains to function well, in which case they are likely to experience good fortune. Causes are at work here, but they are often causes other than those we think.

A well-known example of the belief in jinxes has to do with the fears that some stars or athletes have of appearing on the cover of a national magazine. Some insist that it leads to disaster. An amusing incident illustrating the prevalence of the fear involved Secretariat who was featured on the cover of *Time* magazine the week before running for the Triple Crown at Belmont. The following week *Time* published one of the letters that had been received. It said that the letter would be sent before the running of the Belmont and that Secretariat would lose, the writer was sorry to say, because the horse had just appeared on the cover of *Time*. *Time*'s reply to this was: "*Ha!*" Secretariat, of course, had won.

Then, of course, horses don't read *Time* magazine.

16

Why Does O. J. Carry The Ball So Often?

Of all the forms of distortion examined thus far, none is potentially more deceptive—or for that matter, more interesting—than the one we are going to explore now, called *irrelevant thesis.* A thesis is a position that one advances by means of an argument—as in a master's thesis, in which a particular view on a subject is set forth with supporting evidence. In logic, a thesis is the same as a conclusion. The fallacy of irrelevant thesis is therefore an argument in which an attempt is made to prove a conclusion that is not the one at issue. Often it takes the form of disorting an opponent's argument and then attacking this distorted version.

The ploy goes by a variety of other names: "irrelevant conclusion," "ignoring the issues," "befogging the issue," "diversion," and "red herring." Red Herring may seem a puzzling name. It derives from the fact that escapees sometimes smear themselves with a herring (which turns brown or red when it spoils) in order to throw dogs off their track. To sway a red herring in an argument is to try to throw the audience off the right track onto something not relevant to the issue at hand.

The fallacy derives its persuasive power from the fact that it often does prove a conclusion or thesis (though not the one at issue). An example makes this clear.

> The advocates of conservation contend that, if we adopt their principles, we will be better off than if we do not adopt them. They are mistaken, for it is easy to show that conservation will not produce an Eden on earth.

Two quite different questions are clearly at issue here: (1) whether conservation is the best available measure, and (2) whether conservation will produce a Garden of Eden on earth. By refuting the second argument rather than the first, the argument commits the fallacy of irrelevant thesis. The argument seems persuasive, at first, because it points out what we feel must be true: No conservation measures can assure us of an Eden. We may therefore be tempted to reject out of hand any suggestion that conservation is worthwhile. But this would be a mistake, for all that is at issue is whether conservation is our best alternative.

The famous philosophical novel *Candide* by the eighteenth-century French thinker Voltaire yields another example of irrelevant thesis. Voltaire invented the character Dr. Pangloss, who is tutor to the hero Candide, to represent Leibniz, a philosopher with whose optimism Voltaire disagreed.

> Dr. Pangloss contends that this world is the best of all possible worlds which God could have made. What a ridiculous assertion! As if everything in this world were as good as it could be!

Here too, by misrepresenting the point at issue, the refutation seems to appear cogent. That it is not at all cogent becomes obvious when we realize that Leibniz did not say that everything in this world is as good as it can be, but only that this world is better than some other worlds God could have made. (God, Leibniz would have argued, could have made a world that would have been free of, say, earthquakes, but then something else would have had to be wrong with it, something worse than earthquakes. All things considered, Leibniz maintained, this is the best "possible" world God could have made.)

Voltaire's employment of this device is perhaps forgivable since, as a form of satire, its main intent is not so much to distort but rather to exaggerate in the hope of alerting fellow citizens to potential dangers or abuses. Political cartoonists often use the same device, as when they exaggerate the physical features of people in public office. Reagan's predilection for western dress, his hand ready for the draw, is the latest example of such distortion.

When the fallacy shows up outside of satirical works, the main purpose is generally to impute to adversaries opinions a good deal more extreme than those they have set out and are willing to defend. Distorting a position in this way makes it appear ridiculous and thus easily overthrown. If the adversaries are tricked into defending a position that is more extreme than their original one, they are in all likelihood destined to fail. Although this is a popular trick in debating, it is a dishonest one.

Not all fallacies of irrelevant thesis stem from a conscious effort to distort, however. Pressed for time, or in need of a polite way of refusing, we may regard certain facts as relevant that we would otherwise recognize as beside the point. The letter writer who answers a charitable solicitation by saying he cannot possibly respond to all the charitable appeals made to him provides an example. The refusal is a polite one, but it does not speak directly to the appeal. The writer, after all, was asked to give to only one charity, not to all.

There are other reasons as well for the appearance of the fallacy. Just as some people faced with a problem simply get up and run away, so in argument some people faced with a difficult or unpleasant line of reasoning simply take cover under some piece of irrelevance. Typical is the reply Nancy Reagan once gave to the question, "What is your personal stand on the Equal Rights Amendment?" The First Lady said, "I am for equal rights for everyone, not just women. I'm for equal opportunity and equal pay if both men and women are equally qualified."

The ploy is especially common in arguments over political and social issues. For example, in a debate on prison reform, one of the participants argued:

> My opponent in this debate has said that our prisons turn out more hardened criminals than enter them. He recommends emphasizing rehabilitative possibilities. He has mentioned job training, psychological therapy, and other education programs. Well, I certainly don't like all the prison riots and so forth that we've recently had, but I don't think we should change prisons into schools and hospitals. After all, criminals are in jail because they broke the law. They should pay the penalties.

The arguer is guilty of constructing a straw man. The suggestion was not to change prisons into schools and hospitals. Rather it was to train prisoners in skills and provide those who may need it with psychotherapy so that, when finally released, they will be able to find a place for themselves in society and not resort to crime.

Perhaps more subtle is the following letter to the editor on the issue of an oil tax:

> I completely disagree with Smith's assertion that to really conserve gasoline we need to "tax the hell" out of it. Increasing the cost of gasoline and diesel fuel will only set off another round of price-wage increases, which will pound another nail in the coffin of the American free enterprise system. More taxes on petroleum products, whether they are directly on the oil companies—the so-called windfall profits tax—or charged to the consumer at the pump, will not produce one more barrel of oil.

Did Smith propose that high taxes on gas will produce more oil? No, his argument was merely that they will cut down the amount used so that we would not need to import as much.

In learning to deal with this kind of argument, we need to keep in mind that it is logically irrelevant that certain undesirable consequences might derive from the rejection of a thesis or certain benefits accrue from its acceptance. Consider in this connection the argument discussed earlier concerning hunting. The argument was: "I fail to see why hunting should be considered cruel when it gives tremendous pleasure to many people and employment to even more." We remarked that whether hunting gives employment or pleasure to people is irrelevant to whether it is cruel to animals; thus, the argument that hunting is cruel has yet to be challenged. But there is an additional point: The fact that certain benefits will result from accepting a certain proposal (pleasure and employment from hunting) is no proof of the proposal's correctness, validity, or truth. The popular maxim that the end does not justify the means gives expression to the same notion.

It is, perhaps, easy to see and accept this type of reasoning and criticism in a case such as the above, for the irrelevance of the proof becomes obvious after a moment's reflection. But in other cases this may not be as clear from the start. Practice in this sort of analysis is needed.

Consider the *consequences* appealed to in the following examples:

1. The United States had justice on its side in waging this war. To question this would give comfort to our enemies and would therefore be unpatriotic.
2. I do not permit questions in my class, because if I allow one student to ask a question, then everyone starts asking questions and the first thing you know, there is no time for the lecture.
3. Vegetarianism is an injurious and unhealthy practice. For if all people were vegetarians, the economy would be seriously affected and many people would be thrown out of work.

All these are examples of the fallacy of irrelevance although the irrelevance is somewhat more subtle and more difficult to expose. In the first case, we can agree that to question whether the United States was right to do what it did may give comfort to our enemies, but that is irrelevant to the question of whether the criticism of the country's involvement is in fact justified. The United States may still have been wrong in entering the war. In the second example, the teacher should state why he or she refuses to answer the question asked, not those that might be asked. If the question is a proper one, it should be answered; if it gives rise to other questions, these can be dealt with as they arise or deferred until after the lecture. In the last example, it needs to be pointed out that it is logically irrelevant that certain undesirable consequences (a crippled economy) might result from the acceptance of a certain proposal (vegetarianism). The question at issue, after all, is whether vegetarianism is healthy for vegetarians, not for the economy.

Because nothing is so effective in relaxing people's attention as laughter, it is not surprising that fallacies of irrelevant thesis can be amusing, as in this tale about the theft of a pig:

> "Well now, Patrick," said the judge. "When you are brought face to face with Widow Maloney and her pig on Judgment Day, what account will you be able to give of yourself when she accuses you of stealing the little animal?" "You say the pig will be there, Sir?" said Pat. "Then I'll say: 'Mrs. Maloney, there's your pig!' "

This argument has no other point but humor. But sometimes humor can be used to divert attention from a quite serious point—and that can be dangerous. This excerpt from a British parliamentary debate over the exportation of guns, cited by Susan Stebbing, provides an example:

> *Sir Philip:* You do not think that your wares are any more dangerous or obnoxious than boxes of chocolates or sugar candy?
>
> *Sir Charles:* No, or novels.
>
> *Sir Philip:* You don't think it more dangerous to export these fancy goods to foreign countries than, say, children's [fire] crackers?
>
> *Sir Charles:* Well, I nearly lost an eye with a Christmas [fire] cracker, but never with a gun. [*Thinking to Some Purpose*]

As Stebbing points out, Sir Charles's response diverts attention away from the point of the dangers of guns by comparing them to firecrackers. But though firecrackers may injure, they are not, like armaments, made solely for the purpose of killing and wounding people and destroying buildings. And the point of the debate is armaments, after all.

A very similar argument about guns was made recently in the following letter to the editor:

> My gun has protected me, and my son's gun taught him safety and responsibility long before he got hold of a far more lethal weapon—the family car. Cigarettes kill many times more people yearly than guns and, unlike guns, have absolutely no redeeming qualities. If John Lennon had died a long, painful and expensive death from lung cancer, would you have devoted a page to a harangue against the product of some of your biggest advertisers—the cigarette companies?

Gun control, the writer argues here, should not be touted if some other lethal substances, like cigarettes, are not denounced. However, the fact that smoking is dangerous yet not prohibited by law is irrelevant to whether or not *guns* should be prohibited. Both, no doubt, are dangerous: Nevertheless, in deciding whether to control handguns, we should not be considering whether other harmful things are restricted by law. They have no bearing on the arguments concerning gun control.

All such befogging of the issue is best rebutted by the simple statement: "True, perhaps, but irrelevant." With presence of mind, a simple, incisive retort such as this will bring an audience back to the issue and may even succeed in demolishing the offender. The story is often told of an actor, playing the role of Shakespeare's King Richard III, who had just done his best with the line: "A horse! A horse! My kingdom for a horse!" "Will an ass do?" came a shout from the gallery. "Certainly," the actor shouted back. "Come on down." The shift of attention that lies at the heart of the fallacy of irrelevant thesis can be used effectively to demolish the fallacy.

Needless to say, the same device can be used to avoid a question we do not, for one reason or another, wish to answer. Coach John Mackay of the USC Trojans avoided a reporter's embarrassing question as to why O. J. Simpson carried the ball so often, with the reply, "Why not? It isn't very heavy."

This way of dodging questions is apparently a favorite of politicians. Juan Peron, dictator of Argentina, took a 13-year-old mistress after his wife Eva Peron died. Later he dismissed criticism of the affair with the remark that he was not superstitious.

No doubt there are appropriate times for dodging a question. What we are faulting here is not the witty use of befogging the issue, but the deliberate manipulation of the fallacy in situations where serious argumentation should be expected. By diverting attention, the fallacy of irrelevant thesis can be used either to *distort* the position of an opponent, thereby facilitating an attack, or to *exaggerate* it, thus making it appear ludicrous.

But this ploy can be put to still another use that we ought to look at. This is a matter of using it to wound or hurt another. A child asks her mother, "Mommy, do you love me?" Instead of reassuring the child, for that is really what is behind the question, the mother, becoming suddenly philosophical, replies: "What is love?" As in other examples that we have seen, the answer is to a different question than was asked. In addition, the answer here is far beyond the capacities of the child to deal with, and it may even give the child the message that perhaps she really is not loved.

The emotional use of the fallacy not to wound or hurt, but to divert attention is still another possibility. Indeed, an appeal to emotion can be just as effective as humor in dodging an issue. Consider this example:

> The president's decision to veto the tax bill was a wise one. Never has a man taken office under such difficult conditions. The nation's economy, dislocated by a long and costly war, its nerves stretched to the snapping point by the threat of another, is in desperate need of stewardship. The president has made this decision faced with revolt within his own party and with a torrent of abuse from a hostile press.

This argument attempts to divert attention away from the issue—whether the president's veto of the tax bill was wise—by playing on our sympathies.

It is similar to the famous editorial reply to the letter written by a little girl called Virginia asking whether there was a Santa Claus. The editorial reply in the *New York Sun* of 1897 was:

> Yes, Virginia, there is a Santa Claus. Alas! How dreary would be the world if there were no Santa Claus! It would be as dreary as if there were no Virginias.

No doubt the reply has poetic charm that cannot be ignored. But, to play Scrooge for the moment, from a purely logical point of view, the fact that the world would be a very dreary place if there were no Santa Claus is irrelevant to the question of whether there is a Santa Claus.

But these last examples, although they can be dealt with as types of irrelevant theses, border on a group of ploys and dodges that form their own peculiar set. They will be discussed next.

III
THE LURE OF
AUTHORITARIANISM

17

The Depressing World
of Stanley Milgram

In the early 1960s a young social psychologist at Yale University named Stanley Milgram conducted an experiment whose disturbing results reverberate to this day. In terms of conception and execution, to say nothing of its chilling disclosures, the experiment must rank as one of the half dozen most significant in our century. Milgram was led to the experiment by the unspeakable horrors of the Holocaust. This mass slaughter of Jews was carried out by a people who were as civilized as any in the world. How was it possible, he wondered, for the Germans to act so cruelly? Did their behavior reveal a potential that is present in all of us? As a social psychologist whose job it is to look into the why and how of human behavior, he decided to explore the response of ordinary people to immoral orders.

Milgram started by placing an advertisement inviting applicants to participate in a study of learning. Upon arriving, an applicant was greeted by a man in a gray technician's coat (a symbol of authority) who introduced the volunteer to a second "participant." He then told the two they were about to take part in a scientific experiment to test whether the use of punishment improves the ability to learn. Next, lots were drawn to see who would be the teacher and who the learner, with the newly arrived applicant always turning out to be the teacher and the other person (really the technician's stooge) the "learner."

After watching the learner being strapped into place, the new volunteer was taken into the main experimental room and seated before an impressive-looking shock generator. Its main feature was a horizontal line of thirty switches, ranging from 15 to 450 volts, in 15-volt increments. It also had labels that ranged from "slight shock" to "DANGER—SEVERE SHOCK."

The teacher would be told that he or she was to adminster the learning test (a simple word-pair test) to the person in the other room. When the learner responded correctly, the teacher was to move on to the next item; if the person gave an incorrect answer, the teacher was to administer an electric shock starting at the lowest level (15 volts) and increasing one step each time an error was made. The point was to determine how far volunteers would proceed on the shock generator before they refused to go on.

Before carrying out the experiment Milgram asked various people how they thought they would behave in this situation. He posed the question to several groups—psychiatrists, psychologists, and ordinary people. All said virtually the same thing: Almost no one would continue the experiment to the end if they could see they were inflicting pain.

But the results were in fact very different. At 75 volts, the "learner" was instructed to grunt, and, although the teachers usually indicated mild surprise, they ordinarily went on. At 120 volts, the learner would complain verbally, but as a rule the teachers, with some assurance from the technician, proceeded. At 150 volts, the learner would demand to be released from the experiment. As the shocks escalated, the learner's protests would grow increasingly vehement and emotional—turning eventually into agonized screamings. Yet with the continued encouragement of the technician, the teachers usually continued to administer the shocks till, in many cases, the learner "expired."

The results surprised and dismayed Milgram. Writing in his book *Obedience to Authority,* he said:

> The results, as seen and felt in the laboratory, are to this author disturbing. They raise the possibility that human nature, or—more specifically—the kind of character produced in American democratic society, cannot be counted on to insulate its citizens from brutality and inhumane treatment at the direction of malevolent authority. A substantial proportion of people do what they are told to do, irrespective of the content of the act and without limitations of conscience, so long as they perceive that the command comes from a legitimate authority. [p. 189]

The results must be disturbing to all of us. What, indeed, is there about the nature of obedience to authority that can result in a situation where one person can command another to harm, even destroy, another innocent party and have those commands carried out impassively, submissively, routinely? As Milgram put it:

> Ordinary people, simply doing their jobs, and without any particular hostility on their part, can become agents in a terrible destructive process. Moreover, even when the destructive effects of their work become patently clear, and they are asked to carry out actions incompatible with fundamental standards of morality, relatively few people have the resources needed to resist authority. [p. 6]

Certainly for those of us who believe in the primacy of democratic, human-itarian values, Milgram's findings are enormously disillusioning. We can-not, of course, have a society without some structure of authority, and every society must inculcate a habit of obedience in its citizens. No doubt some societies overdo it. Some go on to produce citizens whose depleted moral resources and lack of self-esteem make them prime targets for mass manip-ulation. Such people thirst to replace the vacuum within themselves by espousing a "great cause." In the last generation it was the ideal of fascism; in our time we are seeing the rise of fundamentalism—whether of the sort advocated by the Moral Majority in our own country or of the Islamic type in the Middle East. That is all the more reason why the rest of us need to struggle hard to hold onto our individuality and selfhood, not allowing ourselves to merge into the larger institutional structure. In part, that task requires us to understand and learn how to fight off the authoritarian and manipulative devices that will be explored in the chapters that follow.

So far we have been examining the life of the mind at the level of language and thought, and we now turn to consider its nature and vulnera-bility at the level of emotion and feeling. The six main types of vulnerabil-ity discussed in what follows—all of which make us such easy victims to authoritarianism—cover a wide spectrum of emotion: our susceptibility to prejudice, to flattery and envy, to pity and vanity, to pride and intimida-tion. The fact that we have such susceptibilities is not a new discovery. They have always been with us, and their formal discussion goes back at least to Greek and Roman times. We continue to use the ancient terms to identify many of the devices and ploys, in order to pay respect to those who were first to formally alert us to their ever-present danger.

Just as language can be used to build as well as to destroy, so too can feelings. Not every feeling, nor every form of authority, nor every kind of appeal should be regarded with suspicion. The true test is always the in-tention behind the appeal: Is it to build confidence or destroy it, to benefit you or them, to enhance life or demean it?

And we must always respect a thin line between manipulation and what we might call "engineering." The latter is finely illustrated by a story that circulated during the Mideast Peace Accord discussions in Israel con-cerning the source of Kissinger's success. On one of his last visits to Israel, the story goes, the Secretary of State spoke with one of the young Israeli guards assigned to his protection.

> "How are you, young man?" he said.
> "Fine."
> "And how is your wife?"
> "I'm not married."
> "Oh, a nice young man like you should be married."
> "No. I'm not really ready for marriage."

"But I have a girl for you!"

"Thank you, but I'm really not ready."

"This is a very special girl!"

"Who?" the young man finally asked.

"How about the daughter of Baron Rothschild?" Kissinger replied.

"Well, of course, if it's the daughter of Baron Rothschild . . ." the young man responded with surprise.

Kissinger said he would get back to him and then flew to Paris to see the Baron.

"Baron, how are you?"

"Fine."

"How is your daughter."

"Fine."

"How is her husband?"

"She's not married."

"She must have a husband."

"No, she is too young."

"I tell you she should be married. I've got just the boy for her!"

"Really, I'm not interested."

"But he is a very special young man."

"Who, for example?" Baron Rothschild asked.

"Well, what would you say to the assistant director of the World Bank?"

The Baron said: "Assistant director of the World Bank? I will consider."

Kissinger said he would be back to him and then flew to Geneva to see MacNamara.

"Mac, you've got to have an assistant director."

"I'm doing just fine," MacNamara said.

"Ah, but I have a special young man."

MacNamara said "Who could be so special?"

And Kissinger replied: "What would you say to the son-in-law of Baron Rothschild."

That is "engineering" things.

If the ploys you are to read about shortly smack of similar sorts of engineering, they differ and are manipulative because they are directed by a will that is far from benevolent.

18

He Who Slings Mud
Loses Ground

The notion that mudslingers ultimately undermine their own forward progress is attributed to American diplomat Adlai Stevenson. Unfortunately, that is not always the case. Mud thrown at an opponent can be very effective—which is why so much of it is thrown. Someone smeared in this way needs to spend a good deal of time removing the dirt and has little left to present his or her case to the public.

The many different mudslinging tactics and strategies—all designed to divert attention from the question being argued by focusing instead on those arguing it—speak of human inventiveness and subtlety. We will explore five specific ones which are especially favored.

The first of these, called the *genetic fallacy* by logicians, is mudslinging that, curiously enough, contains no explicit abuse. What the genetic fallacy tries to do is to prove a contention false or unsound by condemning its source or genesis. Arguments that rely on this technique are, of course, fallacious, for the origin or source of a view, or what led someone to it, is entirely irrelevant to whether or not the view is true. Thus it would be fallacious to argue that since chemical elements are involved in all life processes, life is therefore nothing more than a chemical process; or that, since the early forms of religion were matters of magic, religion is nothing but magic. Were we to put our trust in arguments of this sort, we would have to believe that, since we are all descendants of immigrants, all of us are therefore foreigners.

Accounts of the way in which ideas originated may very well be true or even illuminating, but they are nevertheless irrelevant to whether the ideas themselves are true. The truth of the account of an idea does not and cannot make the idea false. For even if it were the case that religion, for example, did begin in the way described, this does not mean that religion is conceived and understood that way today.

With the growth in popularity of the psychoanalytic method in recent years, the genetic fallacy has proliferated. Instead of meeting someone's argument with evidence, for example, an opponent will seek to psychoanalyze him or her. If a politician says that a strong government is desirable, he is said to be seeking a substitute for a father image. If he thinks a weak government is desirable, then he is in revolt against his father image. This sort of unfavorable psychological account of how or why the advocate of a certain view came to hold it can eventually be used to undermine any argument whatsoever. But although it may be true that someone's motives may weaken his or her credibility, motives are irrelevant to the credibility of an argument itself. Arguments are sound not because of who proposes them but by virtue of their internal merit. If the premises of an argument prove its conclusion, they do so no matter who happens to formulate the argument. If they do not, the greatest logician cannot make them sound.

The following is a typical example of a psychoanalytical attack that depends on the genetic fallacy:

> We must take Schopenhauer's famous essay denouncing women with a grain of salt. Any psychiatrist would at once explain this essay by reference to the strained relationship between Schopenhauer and his mother.

It is, of course, true that Schopenhauer's relationship with his mother was a "strained" one, and it may even have been true that what led him to adopt his negative attitude to women was that poor relationship. But surely that could not have been Schopenhauer's justification for the view he adopted in his essay. The essay, if it hopes to persuade *us*, had to contain arguments in defense of a negative view of women, and those arguments certainly could not be boiled down to the contention that women are reprehensible because the philosopher's mother was reprehensible.

And that, perhaps, is what is fundamentally wrong with this type of attack: It tries to make us believe that the origin or cause of a certain person's belief or view is that person's only justification for holding it.

If the historical origins of a view are irrelevant to its validity, why do we nevertheless tend to place such emphasis and importance on history? Studying the history of an idea or hypothesis is enormously important in making it clearer to ourselves. Seeing how a great mind hit upon a certain idea and going through the same steps he or she took in arriving at it very often helps us grasp it much more easily and understand it better. What such an analysis does not and cannot do is validate or invalidate the idea.

In addition, it often is very useful and even sobering to realize that great things and ideas frequently have very humble origins and that the source of the greatness of a work is to be looked for elsewhere. It is useful to remember in this connection the remark made by the sculptor Rodin to the man who served as his model for his famous work, *The Thinker*. After completing it, Rodin turned to the model and said, "O.K., stupid. You can come down now."

A variant of the genetic fallacy is what logicians call the *abusive ad hominem argument,* which, in addition to drawing attention to the source of an idea, goes on to shower that source with insult or abuse. Consider the following example:

> It must be false that in a capitalistic economy small business tends to disappear, because this is said in the *Communist Manifesto,* and the only person I have ever heard affirm this was a communist.

Since many still regard calling someone a communist as a form of abuse, we have here an obvious attempt to cast aspersions on the source. By reducing the person's social acceptability, his or her arguments are less likely to be taken seriously.

Turning attention away from the facts in arguments to the people participating in them is characteristic not only of everyday discussions but of many of our political debates as well. Rather than discuss political issues soberly, rivals may find it easier to discuss personalities and engage in character assassination. This tactic can be effective because, once a suspicion is raised, it is difficult to put it to rest. Not surprisingly, therefore, this sort of argument is all too common in debates among people seeking office. When feelings run high—or, by contrast, when people simply do not care enough about an issue to give it close scrutiny—abusive tactics can persuade.

The stakes may be political office or they may involve a controversial issue. One such issue that gave rise to extensive name calling was the validity of the Warren Commission Report on President Kennedy's assassination. Many critics of that report argued at length, among other things, that Oswald could not have been the sole assassin of Kennedy because he did not have the time or ability to fire the required number of shots. Supporters of the Warren Report often answered by accusing the critics of being publicity hounds, of exploiting the assassination of Kennedy for personal gain, of giving the country a bad name, and so on. In the heat of the fray, however, it was all too often forgotten that, even if all these accusations were true, the logical merit of the critics' arguments would be totally unaffected.

Not all abusive *ad hominem* arguments are, however, irrelevant. In a court of law, for example, it would not be irrelevant to point out that a witness is a perjurer or a chronic liar. On the other hand, although the accusation would tend to reduce the credibility of the witness' testimony, it would not in itself prove that testimony false, for even chronic liars have been known to tell the truth. On the contrary, we ourselves would be guilty of a breach of logic were we to argue that what a person says is a lie because he or she is a liar.

Calling a person a liar or making some other unpleasant accusation is not the only way to undermine an opponent's credibility. That can also be done by making him or her appear ridiculous, as in the following example:

> We shall reject Mr. Jones' suggestion for increasing the efficiency of our colleges. As a manufacturer, he cannot be expected to realize that our aim is to educate our youth, not to make a profit.

By suggesting that Jones is interested only in making money and that, as far as education is concerned, he is a complete ignoramus, the speaker succeeds in turning him into a figure of ridicule whom no one can take seriously.

Less obviously offensive is the speaker who cracks a joke at an opponent's expense. The purpose is the same, though—to demolish the opponent's arguments by making him or her appear silly.

There is, in addition, still another favorite way to abuse a person in argument—namely, to accuse him or her of being inconsistent and erratic. Consider these examples:

1. This birth control proposal is contrary to your religious principles; you should be the first one to reject, not support it.
2. In reply to the gentleman's argument, I need only say that two years ago he advocated the very measure that he now opposes.

In the first example, the person is accused of committing a straight inconsistency (which casts suspicion on his or her judgment). In the second, the person is accused of being changeable and erratic (which is also a cause for mistrust).

In the case of such attacks it is sometimes useful to remember three things. First, if there is a true inconsistency, then one of the views must be incorrect (for two contradictory views cannot both be true). But simply to charge someone with an inconsistency is not to say which of the two views is the true one. Obviously, it need not be the one upheld by an opponent. Second, it does not necessarily follow that if someone's stand is inconsistent with a previous stand, both are therefore suspect and should be rejected. That would still need to be shown to be the case. In this sense the charge of inconsistency should by itself not be allowed to carry much weight with us. Finally, we should not be intimidated by the charge of someone having a change of mind. The implication is, of course, that the person who does this is erratic. But this implication should be challenged. Why not think of such a person as flexible and perhaps even courageous—for having the courage to admit having been mistaken and the flexibility to perceive and to do something about it?

Occasionally instead of engaging in direct abuse, an opponent will try to undercut a position by suggesting that the views being advanced merely serve the advocate's own interests. Logicians call this the "circumstantial" form of the *ad hominem* argument. Consider this exchange:

Smith: Of course you would be in favor of reduced real estate taxes because you would benefit personally by such a reduction.
Jones: Of course you are against such a reduction because you own no real estate.

Each accuses the other of taking a position on the tax issue from motives of personal gain and not because of any objective reasons they may have for doing so. But we cannot know this to be so until we examine the reasons that each one maintains his or her position.

Although to charge an opponent with having certain vested interests in a matter may be regarded as a kind of reproach or abuse, such an argument differs from the ordinary abusive *ad hominem* in that the abuse is only incidental and not central. The following is another typical example of such an argument:

Congress shouldn't bother to consult the Joint Chiefs of Staff about military appropriations. As members of the armed forces, they will naturally want as much money for military purposes as they think they can get.

This argument does look as if it could easily fit under the category of the abusive *ad hominem*, for there is a certain amount of abuse implied by it: It suggests that the people in question are self-interested, perhaps even greedy, and certainly irresponsible. On the other hand, being able to identify it as a case of circumstantial *ad hominem* is to see more clearly the tactic exploited and thus to be in a better position to deal with it. In this case, the defense against the argument is quite simple: Who else could really tell the nation so well what its military needs are than the people charged with meeting them?

We have now observed three of the main tactics used to destroy a person's credibility. It is sometimes done, as we saw, by way of deflation (the genetic fallacy), straight-out insult (the abusive *ad hominem*), or insinuation (the circumstantial *ad hominem*). There are, in addition, two further ways that are somewhat more complicated.

The first of these tactics goes by the quaint Latin name *tu quoque*, which does not have a very clear or simple English translation. The two

Latin words mean "you too," but a more colloquial translation would be, "Hey! Look who's talking!" as in the following interchange:

> "Smoking is unhealthy. You should quit!"
> "Hey! Look who's talking! You smoke!"

In the *tu quoque* fallacy, then, an opponent's argument is said to be worthless because the opponent has failed to follow his or her own advice. Our reply, however, should be that two wrongs do not make a right: Though it may weaken its moral force, the fact that the suggestion to quit smoking comes from a fellow smoker does not undermine the argument. The assertion that smoking is unhealthy may still be true whether the person who makes it smokes or not.

We have a natural tendency to want others to "practice what they preach." But practice is irrelevant to the merits of an argument. The following retort seems reasonable enough at first glance, but it has no place in logical discourse.

> If you think socialized medicine is such a great idea, why don't you move to Sweden?

Obviously, socialized medicine may have merit even though the person advocating it is not willing to emigrate to enjoy its benefits. Those who resort to this kind of attack often draw courage from another cliché: that people in glass houses should not throw stones. There is no reason, however, why a stone thrown from a glass house cannot find its mark.

Besides *attacking* others for acting in a manner that contradicts the very position they are taking, the fallacy sometimes also takes the form of *defending* oneself for engaging in a particular activity by arguing that others engage in it too. Here is an example:

> My client did not act improperly in using an official car for commuting between his home and his office. Even the mayor does this from time to time.

The fact the mayor does it, of course, does not justify anyone else doing it. Two wrongs do not make a right: If the mayor does it, then he or she too is doing something that should be condemned.

A similar reply could be made to the Soviet official who defended his own country's stand on human rights by saying:

> What moral right do the Americans have to act as preachers of freedom and democracy, especially in light of events which occurred in recent years in America itself?

The official pointed to Watergate and Wounded Knee as examples of what he was talking about. But violations of rights in one country can hardly excuse violations in another.

Benjamin Franklin provides us with an amusing example from his own life of the strong tendency we all have to invoke this kind of appeal. He writes in his *Autobiography:*

> I believe I have omitted mentioning that in my first voyage from Boston to Philadelphia, being becalmed off Block Island, our crew employed themselves catching cod and hauled up a great number. 'Till then I had stuck to my resolution to eat nothing that had had life; and on this occasion I considered, according to my Master Tryon, the taking every fish as a kind of provoked murder, since none of them had or ever could do us any injury that might justify this massacre. All this seemed very reasonable. But I had formerly been a great lover of fish, and when this came hot out of the frying pan, it smelled admirably well. I balanced some time between principle and inclination till I recollected that when the fish were opened, I saw smaller fish taken out of their stomachs. "Then," thought I, "if you eat one another, I don't see why we mayn't eat you." So I dined upon cod very heartily and have since continued to eat as other people, returning only now and then occasionally to a vegetable diet. So convenient a thing it is to be a *reasonable creature,* since it enables one to find or make a reason for everything one has a mind to do.

The point here is that, although fish survive by eating other fish, that is no reason for eating them ourselves. After all, members of certain African tribes practice cannibalism, but we do not use this fact as a justification for our eating human flesh. Because they do so does not mean that we should. Franklin tries to remind us here of how easily we rationalize when our interests are at stake.

It is only a step from an argument charging "You do it too!" to one that charges, "You would do the same thing given the chance." Notice this shift between the next two arguments:

1. Far too much fuss has been made over our Central Intelligence Agency's espionage abroad. Other countries are just as deeply engaged in spying as we are.
2. It may be true that Kuwait hasn't yet carried out any espionage activities in the States, but it would if it had the chance. Let's beat Kuwait to it, I say.

The fallacy is fundamentally the same in each case. Whether someone else is already acting in a manner counter to the conclusion at issue—or whether someone else would act in such a manner if the opportunity arose—has no bearing on the rightness or wrongness of the conclusion. As in all fallacies based on personal attack, any consideration of those who hold a position or who originated a position or who are opposed to a position must be viewed as an irrelevance.

The final fallacy of this sort that we will consider is called *poisoning the well,* as illustrated in the following example:

> Don't listen to him; he's a liar!

This may seem at first simply a case of the abusive *ad hominem,* for the term *liar* is a term of abuse. But the fallacy is a little more complicated than that, for it involves not merely putting an opponent down but making it impossible for him or her to offer a defense. A position is assumed so that nothing can count as evidence against it. Having already assured everyone that an individual is a liar, there is nothing that person can possibly do in self-defense, for every attempt will be discredited in advance as a further case of lying.

The expression "poisoning the well" goes back to the Middle Ages, when waves of anti-Jewish prejudice and persecution were common. If a plague struck a community, the people blamed it on the Jews, whom they accused of poisoning the wells.

Examples of poisoning the well are not hard to find. Hungarian actress Zsa Zsa Gabor once provided an interesting illustration on late-night TV. According to reports of the incident, comedian Peter Cook once told Ms. Gabor in front of millions of television viewers that she was "vain, untalented, and a complete nonevent." She replied:

> You cannot be very talented yourself, otherwise you would recognize talent in others and you would not have said I was untalented.

Zsa Zsa poisoned the well: She placed Cook in the position of being either a liar or a fraud. If he now claims she is talented he affirms he lied, and if he continues to aver that she is untalented, he proves himself to be a fraud (for only talented people can recognize others similarly gifted). In either case, she wins.

Attempts to rebut arguments that poison the well by further logical arguments are futile, since anything said only seems to strengthen the accusation. The very attempt to reply succeeds only in placing someone in an even more impossible position. It is as if, being accused of talking too much, you cannot argue against the accusation without condemning yourself; the more you talk, the more you help establish the truth of the accusation. And that is what such unfair tactics are ultimately designed to do: By discrediting in advance the only source from which evidence either for or against a particular position can arise, they seek to avoid opposition by closing off discussion.

In the context of political debate, a speaker sometimes makes use of this sort of dodge, by saying to the audience:

Any man who rejects my conclusion is either an insane bigot who claims my pity, or a foul-mouthed slanderer who has my contempt.

There is one defense against such a blatantly unfair means of intimidating an audience—exposing to everyone's sight the ploy used by the speaker. If someone merely stood up and said, "At the risk of being declared an 'insane bigot' or a 'foul-mouthed slanderer' by that *bigot* and *slanderer* up there . . ." the speaker's tactic would be unveiled for all to see.

Although from a logical point of view, poisoning the well is an absurdly simple knot to untie, frequently it is severely debilitating psychologically. An interesting example is the account of a case treated by famed British psychiatrist R. D. Laing, concerning a person he calls Jack whose jealousy of Jill approaches paranoia. Jack persistently refused to infer from Jill's behavior toward him, however loving, that she "really" loved him. He believed instead that, despite the evidence, she loved Tom, Dick, or Harry. A curious feature of Jack's tendency to attribute to Jill a lack of love for him and a love for Tom, Dick, or Harry was the more she said she loved him, the less he tended to believe her.

Like someone who commits the fallacy of poisoning the well (although Laing himself does not identify it as such), Jack reasoned to himself as follows: Look at all the things she's doing to show me that she loves me. If she really loved me, she wouldn't be so obvious about it and try so hard. The fact that she is trying so hard proves she is pretending. She must be trying to cover up her feelings—her true feelings. She probably loves Tom.

Like one whose well has been poisoned, Jill found herself in a "double bind": If she tried to act even more loving, she would further confirm Jack's assumption that she was pretending. If, on the other hand, she pretended to act less loving and more aloof, then she would confirm his suspicions that she did not love him. He could then say: "See, I told you, she really doesn't love me. Look at how aloof she has become."

At this point the relationship could become truly interesting and truly perverse. Jack might try to pretend that he did think she loved him, so that, in his view of her, she would think she had fooled him. He would then mount evidence (she had exchanged glances with a man, had smiled at a man, had walked in a provocative way, and so on) that seemed to him to substantiate his secretly held view that she did not love him.

But as his suspicion mounted, he might discover that the evidence he had accumulated suddenly looked very thin. Instead of abandoning his belief like a sane and logical person, he would probably take another course, saying to himself: "Well, she's really more clever than I thought she was!

She saw through my plan and so avoided being caught. I haven't been smart enough. She realizes that I am suspicious, so she is not giving anything away. I had better bluff her by pretending to some suspicions that I do not feel, so that she will think I'm on the wrong track." So he might pretend to her that he thought she was having an affair with Tom, when he "knew" that she was having an affair with Dick!

The similarity between the logical fallacy of poisoning the well and the psychological bind Laing describes seems striking. Whether learning to untie the logical knots is by itself sufficient to relieve a patient of his or her parallel psychological confusions is still an open question. In the eyes of a growing number of psychotherapists, however, such knowledge very often contributes considerably in effecting, if not a cure, then certainly a deeper insight (on the part of both therapist and patient) of the psychological condition. In a way, what is nowadays being discovered is an insight that the great seventeenth-century philosopher Baruch Spinoza was perhaps the first to state clearly. In his major work, many chapters of which are devoted to what we would now call psychology rather than philosophy, Spinoza put it as follows: "An emotion which is a passion ceases to be a passion once we form a clear and distinct idea of it." If we should find ourselves in the grip of an overwhelming passion to which we have become enslaved, Spinoza is saying, we can succeed in freeing ourselves by trying to gain some understanding of it. That is, perhaps, the method and aim of much present-day psychotherapy.

19

The World Is Flat
(Class of 1491)

The fallacy that most of us fall prey to at one time or another is called *appeal to authority*—although the word *misappeal* would be more accurate. It arises whenever we try to justify or validate an idea or proposal by quoting some authority in its support. If the idea lies within the particular authority's competence, then, of course, no fallacy is involved. We often find ourselves in need of expert opinion, and we know where to go to get it. We do not, however, consult a barber regarding a tax problem, nor an accountant regarding a medical problem. Authorities remain authorities only within their areas of competence. A person may know all there is to know about one subject and yet be a complete ignoramus about everything else.

The English philosopher John Locke gave this fallacy its Latin name: *argumentum ad verecundiam*. The name is appropriate, for *verecundia* means "modesty," and the fallacy or appeal is an attempt to overawe ("shame") an opponent into accepting something by playing on his or her natural reluctance (sense of modesty or shame) to challenge noted or respected authorities—or even time-honored customs and traditions.

Only too obviously, when a person's competence is, say, physics or mathematics, that does not automatically make him or her an expert in education or politics. Yet so awed are some people by authority that they will sometimes be heard to say this sort of thing:

> No federal aid should be provided for public schools. My banker, my dentist, my doctor, my minister, and all my business associates are opposed to it.

Bankers, doctors, and ministers all possess a certain kind of knowledge and can be called authorities, but unless they have taken the trouble to study the matter of federal aid for public schools, their opinions on the subject may be no better than the barber's or cab driver's. On the other hand, if they have taken the trouble to look into the question and have become knowledgeable about it, then it might be worthwhile consulting them. But then we should be doing so not because they happen to be bankers, dentists, doctors, or ministers, but because they have knowledge of the matter. Genuine experts or authorities are consulted for precisely that reason.

For genuine experts or authorities do not claim that their advice or opinions are to be accepted or that they are true because they say so. The opinions are true, or are to be accepted, because of the evidence in support of them—evidence that these people have taken the trouble to gather and investigate and that anyone with the proper training could similarly obtain. Even authorities, in short, do not expect to be taken simply on their word.

The human race, and science in particular, has sometimes paid a steep price for this reverence for authority that seems ingrained in us. The following argument favoring Ptolemy's theory that the earth was the immovable center of the solar system over Copernicus's theory that the earth and other planets moved around the sun is one among many examples to be found in the history of science:

> One may doubt whether it would be preferable to follow Ptolemy or Copernicus. For both are in agreement with the observed phenomena. But Copernicus's principles contain a great many assertions which are absurd. He assumed, for instance, that the earth is moving with a triple motion, which I cannot understand. For according to the philosophers a simple body like the earth can have only a simple motion. . . . Therefore it seems to me that Ptolemy's geocentric doctrine must be preferred to Copernicus's doctrine [Clavius, 1581].

But the Copernican theory survived, while Ptolemy's did not. Phrases such as "according to the philosophers" appeared often in the writings of even the best scientists during the Renaissance, bearing witness to the struggle science had to wage against "authorities." A letter of this period, from the Italian astronomer Galileo to his German colleague Johannes Kepler, suggests the extent of the problem. Galileo had just made use of the telescope for the first time, but the authorities refused to look through it.

> Oh, my dear Kepler, how I wish that we could have one hearty laugh together! Here, at Padua, is the principal professor of philosophy whom I have repeatedly and urgently requested to look at the moon and planets through my glass, which he pertinaciously refuses to do. Why are you not

here? What shouts of laughter we should have at this glorious folly? And to hear the professor of philosophy at Pisa, laboring before the grand duke with logical arguments, as if with magical incantations to charm the new planets out of the sky.

In the face of such stubborn adherence to tradition, it is not surprising that some scientists and institutions came to adopt as their credo: "Authority means nothing."

On the other hand, we must remember that many of those who were so obviously in the wrong held their mistaken views with the greatest sincerity and conviction. The following is a striking example:

> To me truth is precious. . . . I should rather be right and stand alone than to run with the multitude and be wrong. . . . The holding of the views herein set forth has already won for me the scorn and contempt and ridicule of some of my fellowmen. I am looked upon as being odd, strange, peculiar. . . . But truth is truth and though all the world rejects it and turns against me, I will cling to truth still.

These sentences are from the preface to a booklet, published in 1931, by Charles Silvester de Ford, of Fairfield, Washington, in which he sought to prove that the earth is flat.

If modern science has liberated itself to a great extent from irrelevant appeals to authority, some aspects of our society still cling to the notion of expertise. News reports are sprinkled with phrases such as "Official sources hinted" or "An unidentified spokesperson disclosed" without any indication of whether the source is a head of state or a fellow reporter in the next phone booth. A vitamin commercial for something called "Solgar" vitamins is recommended by the "world-renowned nutritionist" Dr. Leonard Passwater, and a hair spray by "world-famous actress Rula Alenska." If you haven't happened to have heard of these world-famous authorities, you must be ignorant. Since no one wants to be suspected of being ignorant, the appeals pass unchallenged.

Contemporary America seems especially prone to the form of the fallacy of appeal to authority known as *argument by consensus* or appeal to the "authority of the many." This out-and-out appeal to numbers is widely used in advertising, where the fact that millions of Americans use a certain product is advanced as a reason for buying it. Here are a few recent examples:

1. Ninety-nine new homeowners out of 100 heat with gas.
2. The kind of car everyone's trying to build.
3. Gordon's Gin. Largest seller in England, America, the world.
4. Eat American lamb. Ten million coyotes can't be wrong.

Such appeals are like saying a book must be good because it is a best seller or that a film that people are lining up to see all over the country must be a great film. The book or film may be successful, but success is irrelevant to the question of merit.

When former Senator George Smathers of Florida made the following accusation, he invoked so many authorities that his argument seems irrefutable at first glance:

> I join two presidents, twenty-seven senators, and eighty-three Congressmen in describing Drew Pearson as an unmitigated liar.

As in all cases of this fallacy, however, the fact that many people agree with a certain conclusion does not make it true.

The consensus form of the fallacy of appeal to authority often shows up when questions of values are being debated. Evidence of the kind accepted by science is often irrelevant in such discussions, so appeals to the "evidence" of sheer numbers are often resorted to, as in this argument:

> In all times and places, in every culture and civilization, people have believed in the existence of some sort of deity. Therefore a supernatural being must exist.

The fact that people everywhere have believed something to be true, of course, does not make it so. After all, the class of 1491 believed the world to be flat.

Just as we should guard against being taken in by an appeal to the authority of a single expert or of many people who think the same way, so we must also be able to recognize appeals to the authority of a select few. Sometimes called "snob appeal," this form of the fallacy of appeal to authority exploits our feeling that we are aristocrats at heart, that we belong not to the mass but to the select few. By falling for this fallacy, we show ourselves to belong very much to that tribe.

The use of glamorous personalities to advertise products trades on snob appeal. Thus Eva Gabor is shown asking the viewer:

> Darling, have you discovered Masterpiece? The most exciting men I know are smoking it.

The ad is probably effective and sells many pipes because so many seem willing to believe that smoking the recommended pipe is crucial to being regarded as exciting by someone like Eva Gabor.

Another recent advertisement, again exploiting our snobbishness, is the one for Camel Filters: "They're not for everybody." The message is clear: If you want to be somebody, perhaps you had better switch to Camel

Filters. In some ways an advertisement like this one might be risky and could even backfire. A thoughtful person might reason, "If they're not for everybody, maybe they're not for me either." Still, the approach is widely used nowadays, as in the following man's cologne ad:

> Guerlain is pleased to announce that only one man in ten thousand wears Imperiale.

"Oh yeah?" we might be tempted to say. "If only one in ten thousand uses it, the product can't be a best seller—so, why take the risk?"

Despite the risks, this sort of appeal to prestige and our sense of snobbery has a long history. The following is from an anti-Prohibition leaflet:

> Is it not strange that wet England produced Shakespeare, wet Germany produced Schiller, wet America produced Lincoln, while dry Turkey has produced no great men since the wine-drinking Mahomet?

The argument is saying in a rather simplistic way that countries that permit the sale of liquor have produced great people, and countries that do not permit liquor have no such people of distinction. The argument, therefore, tries to trade on or exploit the halo that rests over the names of famous people and that mere mention of their names tends to evoke.

But snob appeal goes back even further than Prohibition. An old British chronicle notes:

> If the proposal be sound, would the Saxon have passed it by? Would the Dane have ignored it? Would it have escaped the wisdom of the Norman?

Here too an attempt is made to trade on the glamor evoked by names—this time not of famous people but of famous races.

This form of the appeal to authority seems the reverse of name calling, discussed in a previous chapter. Snob appeal is a case of someone trying to exploit our feeling that we are *somebody;* in the case of name calling, what is exploited is our desire to disassociate ourselves from *nobodies.* "Name dropping" may, in fact, be a rather good label for snob appeal. That is in essence what advertisers do when they resort to the device.

We need to remember, however, that the authority appealed to in such advertisements is that conferred by prestige or exclusivity. These qualities would not be irrelevant if the ads had set out simply to prove that the products in question were prestigious, but their aim is something else—not to prove this point but to get people to buy.

The appeal to authority can take still another form, and this is an appeal to custom or tradition, as in this argument:

> The institution of marriage is as old as human history and thus must be considered sacred.

To this we might reply that so is prostitution. Is it to be regarded as sacred too?

The appeal to custom or tradition has not been overlooked by advertisers. For example, one liqueur advertisement carries the headline:

> Drink Irish Mist, Ireland's legendary liqueur.

Essentially, that is the same appeal as the one made by advertisers who tout their products as "old-fashioned" and "like grandma used to make."

As in the case of many of the other fallacies we have been looking at, this one too has had far-reaching effects on occasion. It is not simply a matter of someone, say, trying to justify a religion by saying, "It's the old-time religion and so it's good enough for me." Arguments in science, which sometimes raged for decades, often rested on assumptions that were at heart appeals to tradition. Let us look at an example that at first may appear much more subtle and technical than it really is, although it deals with a most difficult and subtle problem—the nature of space and time.

In the course of history, a number of classic theories regarding space and time have been worked out. Newton and Leibniz are responsible for two of these theories. Since the two thinkers were also rivals, it is not surprising, perhaps, that they were fiercely opposed in their ideas regarding these matters too.

Newton held that space is absolute, and logically prior to matter—a kind of box in which things are placed. According to him, there could be space without anything in it; but there could not be matter without it being in space. Space is prior to matter. According to Leibniz, however, space is not absolute but relative—that is, rather than being prior to matter, it arises with the creation of matter. For him, without matter, there would be no space.

Leibniz carried on a long and heated debate with Newton regarding the true nature of space. But one particular argument by Leibniz against Newton was especially telling, for our purposes. We must remember that both were God-fearing men. This point is not important as far as the argument itself is concerned, but it is crucial to illustrating how tradition affects even such neutral-seeming matters as the nature of space and time.

To fully understand Leibniz's argument, it is important to keep in mind a certain principle that he thought indisputable and that most of us would regard as such as well. It is called the "principle of sufficient reason" and means simply that no rational being does anything without having a good reason for doing so—that, for example, in choosing something a rational being always chooses what seems at the time to be the best choice open to him or her, all things considered. This is especially true of God, of course, who is purely rational. We ourselves are not always completely rational, and so we sometimes make irrational choices.

Leibniz's argument against Newton involved this principle. If Newton's theory of space and time were true, he argued, then in creating the universe God could have created the universe in this or that or some other portion of empty space. However, then God would have had no reason for preferring to create it in this region rather than in another. But without such a sufficient reason, He would not have created the universe (since He is purely rational and cannot act without reason). Since the universe clearly exists, we know He did create it. Therefore, He was not faced with an empty space to fill, as Newton had claimed.

That, of course, is interesting. And it is especially interesting to us, for it shows us again the powerful influence that tradition—in this case, the belief in God—can exert on us.

A more recent and striking example of this perverse force of tradition involves the current dispute among Freudians concerning the Oedipus complex. It appears that Freud's original idea about the genesis of adult psychoses was that they originated in childhood as a result of adult seduction of children. The thought was, however, abhorrent to Freud and so he substituted the famous Oedipus complex—the seduction takes place not in reality but in the child's mind. Freud's change of mind on this question—induced by the weight and force of tradition—had the unfortunate effect, some of his disciples are now saying, that child molestation didn't get an airing until our own day.

20

The Elephants of Thailand

A medieval legend about a weeping statue illustrates the fallacy we will deal with in this chapter. According to this legend, on Good Friday of each year, while the congregation at a certain church bowed in prayer, the statue on the altar would kneel and shed tears. But if even one member of the congregation looked up from prayer in order to see the tears, the miracle would not occur. To cynics who might say the statue did not really weep, defenders could reply that no proof could be offered for that. For the fact that the statue did not weep while someone was looking was no proof that it didn't do so when no one was looking.

The legend is a good example of the *fallacy of appeal to ignorance*—an argument that uses an opponent's inability to disprove a conclusion as proof of the conclusion's correctness. In effect, the argument shifts the burden of proof outside the argument onto the person hearing the argument. But this is an invalid maneuver, for the inability to disprove a conclusion cannot by itself be regarded as proof that the conclusion is true.

Arguments based on this maneuver are common enough. Some people, for example, claim that there must be life on other planets because no one has ever proved it doesn't exist. This is fallacious reasoning meant to appeal to the emotions since those who propose it wish to place opponents on the defensive. If belief in the argument resulted, it would be irrational, stemming from a feeling of intimidation. In logical arguments, the obligation of providing proof always rests with those who propose a conclusion.

Arguments about weeping statues and little green men from outer space are harmless enough, but the fallacy of appeal to ignorance can crop up in disputes where the stakes are much larger. Chiropractic medicine, for example, has been vilified as having no scientific basis because that basis has never been shown. But the fact that chiropractors have failed so far to prove that their concepts have a scientific foundation is no proof that they lack such a base, which may yet be established.

More serious still are those occasions on which allegations are made concerning conspiracies. In 1950, for example, Senator Joseph McCarthy touched off a witch hunt for communists by saying he had found case histories of persons in the State Department whom he considered communists. He admitted, however, that in some of these cases he did not have much information but said the FBI had assured him there was nothing in its files to disprove their communist connections. The lack of disproof was taken as proof—a clear instance of an appeal to ignorance, one with tragic consequences for many.

Sometimes the lack of evidence in a conspiracy case is cited as proof that the conspiracy not only exists but is also devilishly clever. This is not unlike the case of the hidden elephant where a traveler boasts to a friend, "There are elephants in Thailand so intelligent that they have learned how to hide in trees." The friend replies, "But I once spent a whole year in Thailand and *I* didn't see them!" To which the traveler smugly replies, "I *told* you those elephants are smart!"

Note that this mode of argument is not fallacious in a court of law, where, if the defense can legitimately claim that the prosecutor has not established guilt, then a verdict of not guilty is warranted. Although the claim to such a verdict may seem to commit the fallacy of appeal to ignorance, it does not really do so. The relevant legal principle is that a person is presumed innocent until proven guilty. We do not say that defendants *are* innocent until proven guilty, but only that they are presumed to be so. Clearly, not every person whose guilt has not been proven is innocent; some, in fact, are later proven to be guilty. But until that is done, individuals are regarded as legally innocent, whether they are actually innocent or not. Practice in court is therefore not really an exception to our rule.

Outside a court of law, someone making use of an appeal to ignorance will frequently try to strengthen a case with question-begging epithets.

> I have never once heard an argument for price controls that any sensible person would accept. Therefore price controls are obviously a bad idea.

This argument is objectionable not only because it bases its proof on ignorance but also because its use of the epithet "sensible" condemns out of hand any arguments for price control that we might be ready to offer. Notice the question-begging epithets in these fallacious arguments as well:

1. No responsible scientist has proved that the strontium 90 in nuclear fallout causes leukemia. Therefore we can disregard the alarmists and continue testing nuclear weapons with a clear conscience.

2. If there were any real evidence for these so-called flying saucers, it would be reported in our reputable scientific journals. No such report has been made; therefore there is no real evidence for them.

The terms "responsible scientist" and "alarmist" in the first argument and "real" and "reputable" in the second argument render us virtually incapable of responding without being labeled as alarmist or disreputable. The arguments are being conducted not on logical but on other grounds.

Sometimes the appeal to ignorance will be found combined with the fallacy of complex question. The question, "What reason could anyone have for forging these documents?" implies, for example, that, since we don't know, the documents must therefore be genuine. This is a complex question because it assumes that no one could have had a reason to forge the papers in question. In addition, it is an appeal to ignorance because it makes ignorance of the reason proof that they are not forgeries. However, lack of knowledge about the motive of a forgery is no proof that a reason does not exist (which *others* may very well know about).

Another example of the fallacy in this form is the complex question, "How could the world have had no beginning?" Here it is implied that, since we do not know, therefore the world had a beginning.

Studies of the appeal to ignorance sometimes point out that the language of some marriage ceremonies seems to commit this fallacy when the person officiating asks whether anyone present can show just cause why the bride and groom should not be married. Yet, in stating that anyone who can show such cause should now come forward or forever after be silent, the official is not making an argument but only offering a simple statement. He does not attempt to prove that, if no one can show cause why the marriage should not take place, then no such cause exists. He says only that if no one objects to the marriage, then the marriage will proceed.

One further observation: In some cases, it can safely be assumed that, if a certain event occurred, evidence of it could be discovered by those qualified to do so; in those cases it is indeed reasonable to assume, in the absence of such proof, that the particular thing or event did not occur. Thus if an intensive police investigation fails to find evidence that a certain person is a criminal, it would be reasonable to assume that the person in question is probably *not* one. We would not say that such proof is based on ignorance, but rather we would regard it as based on our knowledge that, if the person were a criminal, the fact would not have escaped detection.

21

If You Have Tears, Prepare to Shed Them Now

Strange things happen to people in crowds. Crowds are anonymous and anonymity breeds irresponsibility. We have given crowds some very nasty names to remind us of this. The two most familiar are "mob" and "rabble," with rabble-rousers and mob appeal identifying those whose goal is to stir up such crowds and the methods they employ.

All rabble-rousers have a great deal in common both in their goals (usually greed and power) and in their methods (which generally consist of appeals to our basest instincts, including violence). The language of mob appeal tends to be strongly biased and makes use of many of the linguistic devices we have examined previously in this book.

Living in these chaotic times, we have become all too familiar with the typical concoction designed to sway people *en masse:*

1. "The U.S. is Enemy No. 1 of humanity"—Iranian radio broadcast.
2. "Kill the American dogs"—Muslim mobs in Islamabad
3. "It is a struggle between Islam and the infidels"—Khomeini speech

Nor are we lacking in citizens all too ready to reply in kind. A letter writer avers:

In answer to Louis Archer who states we should send our troops overseas to capture Arab oil fields and that he, for one, is "ready to go." It seems the war-hungry are now developing an unholy thirst for oil. To him and others of his ilk, let me say, your thirsts will never be quenched—nor your gas tanks filled—with my sons' blood.

To blast away with such explosive words as "war-hungry," "unholy thirst," "ilk," and "my sons' blood" is to substitute feelings for clear thinking and make oneself and others vulnerable to the devastation of authoritarianism.

Logicians regard mob appeals as fallacies because such arguments rest on strong feelings of absolute rightness stirred up in an audience, and certitude is no proof of certainty. The fact that we feel strongly about something is no proof (even when the feeling is sincere) that we are therefore right. Consider this outburst:

> My candidate should be elected. Or should we be governed by a political opportunist who has cleverly ridden into office after deliberately arousing a mass hysterical reaction?

This tirade is itself an example of the very thing it vehemently denounces. The same is true of the following pieces of rhetoric:

1. Mr. Jones is a military-minded reactionary. His platform has sold the little man down the river.
2. This radical plot has been hatched by un-American agitators.

Even if the speakers were sincere, we should not let ourselves be carried away by this display of emotion and high-mindedness. We should try to temper this sort of high-mindedness with a dash of cold reason. Our allegiance is too important to be given lightly at the flashing of a sign or the ringing of a familiar bell. We should always remember that such attempts to raise the emotional temperature are usually undertaken in order to pass something off on an audience. For, as all propagandists know, when emotions are deeply stirred, almost anything can be put over.

The same may be said for the use of mob appeal in advertising. Note the exploitation of the emotion invested by us in the word and symbol "America" and of our love of country in the following advertisements:

1. It's America's Whiskey.
2. One American custom that has never changed: a friendly social drink.
3. Great American Soup. About as close as you can get to homemade without making it yourself.

The second example is especially interesting. It was put out by the Licensed Beverage Industries and we can sympathize with their dilemma: How does one push a product that is the cause of so much universal misery? What does one say? Well, as we see, one can stress that it is an old "American custom" (and there certainly can't be anything wrong with that). Furthermore, who would be against friendliness? So do go ahead, keep it up America; in doing so, you're only showing what the whole world admires in you—your good-natured fun and friendliness.

The dilemma that the Licensed Beverage Industries faced, however, was nothing like that confronting the Seagram company after Ray Milland won an Oscar for his portrayal of Don Biram in the movie version of Charles Jackson's novel *The Lost Weekend* (1944). This was one of the first novels (and movies) to deal compassionately and realistically with the problem of alcoholism. Seagram solved it, however, brilliantly. Whole page advertisements declared:

> The House of Seagram congratulates Ray Milland
> on his magnificent performance
> in
> *The Lost Weekend*

If you can't beat them, join them.

More recently, Seagram ads have become even more subtle. One showing a hand covering a nearly empty glass and captioned "Your guest is trying to tell you something. Please listen," is designed to convey their social concern for the problem caused by this product. It goes on further to make some fine observations:

- The good host serves more than food and drink. He serves his guest.
- By giving him his attention. By making him feel comfortable. By listening to what he wants . . . and doesn't want.
- Next time your guest decides he's had enough, be a good enough host to take him at his word . . . or his sign. He'll think better of you for it.

At the bottom of the page, printed in small, elegant characters is the name Seagram, and below it, in even smaller letters, Distillers Company. So the final message is: See, we're really good guys, concerned about you, but if you need a drink, remember the name Seagram.

In addition to appealing to such typical authoritarian ploys as pride in country, in tradition, in custom, those engaging in mob appeal may pretend to fall in with the passions of the crowd they are addressing, passions that they are far from feeling themselves.

Although the methods exploited by authoritarians are often ancient, they continue to be effective and each age has therefore to build its defenses anew. Not to do so will mean facing results that can be dismaying. Some are already in: The New Right Senator from North Carolina, Jesse Helms, won his first Senate race in 1971 against his moderate Democrat opponent, Nick Galifianakis, with the slogan: "Jesse Helms: He's one of us."

Mark Antony's famous funeral oration over the body of Caesar in William Shakespeare's *Julius Caesar* (Act 3, sc. 2) is a brilliant example of this. It is also a brilliant example of mob appeal as a whole. The oration repays study, for the techniques it uses are still the stock in trade of propagandists and hate merchants. Antony has been called upon to give the funeral oration because Caesar's assassins believe he will speak sympathetically of the murder. The crowd is addressed first by Brutus, who, fearing that Caesar was preparing to become Rome's dictator, had killed him in a conspiracy with others. Brutus convinces the crowd that he slew Caesar for the good of Rome, and the crowd murmurs that Brutus should be the next Caesar. But Brutus silences them and urges them to hear Antony praise the dead ruler. Antony instead uses the opportunity to incite the mob against Brutus and his fellow conspirators, doing so with such skill that in an incredibly short time he turns the mob into slaves ready to do his bidding. After breaking them down emotionally ("If you have tears prepare to shed them now"), he so inflames them that they rush out, deranged, seeking the assassins. Antony, who is left behind, is heard muttering to himself:

> Now let it work. Mischief thou art afoot.
> Take thou what course thou wilt!

These last two lines are terribly significant and for this reason: It wouldn't be so bad if such people who set out to win over a mob, to arouse and move it, were themselves somehow caught up in the emotions they were trying to evoke in the crowd. But all too often such people are very much out of it. They do not feel those emotions and passions at all; on the contrary, inside they are cold and calculating and indifferent to feeling. Of course, these outbursts of passion appear as if they arose spontaneously; but we know, as Shakespeare shows here, that often it is the result of the most careful artifice. And that is what is so evil about it. Such rabble-rousers use the mob for their own purposes. Their object is to master the passions of the mob—to shape and transform those passions for their own purposes. For people like that, language is a weapon that they have learned to use with great skill and ingenuity. They know precisely what will accomplish what. They know how to use flattery and irony, how to exploit sarcasm and innuendo; and they know the wonders that repetition and the technique of the big lie can accomplish (a lie so big that no one would believe anyone could say such a thing unless it were true).

And they are not averse to using divisiveness—the tactic of us against them, knowing full well that nothing will unite people as quickly as a sense of being besieged from outside. And so the banners continue flying:

- "We will close these spy nests."
- "America is the mother of corruption."
- "It is a struggle between Islam and the infidels."

22

Should an 8-Year-Old Have to Worry About Cholesterol?

A letter received recently (addressed "Dear Friend") opened with these words:

> Streaks of pain etching his youthful face, the boy drags his withered legs along the sidewalk, two crutches biting into the pavement one short step ahead. The minutes seem like hours, but the thinly built boy finally makes it to his destination, hangs up his coat and prepares for his day's activities. When a handicapped boy pains himself by walking grueling distances on hard wooden crutches, it proves that the handicapped will go out of their way to improve their lives. Now we ask you to go a little out of your way to help the handicapped.
>
> Chairperson, Contributions Committee

Without seeming to be unfeeling, we must recognize that rather than being told how our donations will be used (and what percentage will actually reach those they are designed to help), an attempt is made to open our hearts and with it our pocketbooks by depicting the courage and determination of this crippled boy making his lonely way down the hard pavement. From a psychological point of view, this is masterful, but it is logically objectionable and devious, making use of a further ploy called *appeal to pity*.

The device is very common. It is also very ancient, as we know from a reference to it in Plato's *Apology*, describing the trial in 399 B.C. of Plato's teacher, Socrates. Speaking to his judges, Socrates says:

> Perhaps there may be some one who is offended at me, when he calls to mind how he, himself, on a similar or even less serious occasion, prayed and entreated the judges with many tears, and how he produced his children in court, which was a moving spectacle, together with a host of relations and friends; whereas I, who am probably in danger of my life, will do none of these things.

Despite Socrates' stated refusal to employ an appeal to pity, he goes on to make explicit use of it.

> The contrast may occur to his mind, and he may be set against me, and vote in anger because he is displeased at me on this account. Now if there be such a person among you,—mind, I do not say that there is,—to him I may fairly reply: My friend, I am a man, and like other men, a creature of flesh and blood, and not "of wood or stone," as Homer says; and I have a family, yes, and sons, O Athenians, three in number, one almost a man, and two others who are still young; and yet I will not bring any of them hither in order to petition you for an acquittal.

Socrates' use of the appeal to pity here is subtle. A more straightforward example would be this statement to a jury by the renowned criminal lawyer Clarence Darrow:

> I appeal to you not for Thomas Kidd, but I appeal to you for the long line—the long, long line reaching back through the ages and forward to the years to come—the long line of despoiled and downtrodden people of the earth. I appeal to you for those men who rise in the morning before daylight comes and who go home at night when the light has faded from the sky and give their life, their strength, their toil to make others rich and great. I appeal to you in the name of those women who are offering up their lives to this modern god of gold, and I appeal to you in the name of those little children, the living and the unborn.

Darrow was an expert at manipulating what has become an important tool of many lawyers—playing on the sympathy of jurors. Though both the prosecution and defense make use of the appeal to pity, defense lawyers are especially prone to use it, as in this summing up:

> My client is the sole support of his aged parents. If he is sent to prison, it will break their hearts, and they will be left homeless and penniless. You surely cannot find it in your hearts to reach any other verdict than "not guilty."

The trouble with such appeals is that, however moving they may be, they usually are irrelevant to the issues and therefore should carry no weight with us. As in all such cases, we need to be clear about the question. Thus it is fallacious for the defense attorney just cited to offer evidence about his client's position as sole support of his aged parents as a reason why the court should find him innocent of a crime of which he stands accused. It would not be fallacious, however, for the attorney to offer such evidence as a reason for treating the accused with leniency.

Like many of the authoritarian ploys we have examined here, this one too has been exploited by advertisers. One of the most blatant examples ever was a full-page advertisement placed by a group of television dealers in 1950, when television was beginning to be mass-produced.

THERE ARE SOME THINGS
A SON OR DAUGHTER WON'T TELL YOU!

"Aw gee, Pop, why can't we get a television set?" You've heard that. But there's more you won't hear. Do you expect a seven-year-old to find words for the deep loneliness he's feeling?

He may complain—"The kids were mean and wouldn't play with me!" Do you expect him to blurt out the truth—that he's really ashamed to be with the gang—that he feels left out because he doesn't see the television shows they see, know the things they know?

You can tell someone about a bruised finger. How can a little girl describe a bruise deep inside? No, your daughter won't ever tell you the humiliation she's felt in begging those precious hours of television from a neighbor.

You give your child's *body* all the sunshine and fresh air and vitamins you can. How about sunshine for his morale? How about vitamins for his mind? Educators agree—television is all that and more for a growing child.

When television means so much more to a child than entertainment alone, can you deny it to your family any longer?

Many people found this advertisement in bad taste, and it was soon withdrawn. Today advertisers are somewhat more subtle, but they still persist in making irrelevant appeals to sympathy, as in the successful slogan for Avis Rent-a-Car: "We're number two," in Ford Mustang's ad "Life passes you by so fast, the least you can do is enjoy the trip," and in the ad for Boeing Airplanes showing a photograph of an elderly, homey couple standing in the doorway together with a little mutt, all looking very lonely and captioned: "Swing by home on your next business trip." This last ad is clearly designed to kindle recollections of family and home. We are made to feel sorry for the elderly couple, whom we identify with our parents, and so come to feel we ought to fly home—on a Boeing, of course—and cheer them up.

Nor is the absurd always avoided. A corn oil margarine advertisement asks us: "Should an 8-year-old have to worry about cholesterol?"

It would be wrong to think that only "bad guys" or out-and-out "villains" make use of such appeals. The "good guys" cannot always resist using them as well. William Jennings Bryan provided a classic and memorable example in his famous Cross of Gold speech. The speech was delivered in Chicago to the 1896 Democratic Convention. Bryan's address opposed gold as a monetary standard and favored bimetalism. It ended with these rousing words:

> Having behind us the producing masses of this nation and the world, supported by the commercial interests, the laboring interests and the toilers everywhere, we will answer their demand for a gold standard by saying to them: You shall not press down upon the brow of labor this crown of thorns, you shall not crucify mankind upon a cross of gold.

At the final words, Bryan cast his arms straight out as if nailed to a cross. He then dropped his arms and took one step back. For several seconds there was no sound from the transfixed audience. Then pandemonium broke loose, and a tremendous ovation began to swell. Bryan's supporters hoisted the 36-year-old congressman to their shoulders and paraded him about the hall. A band struck up a Sousa march. The following day the convention nominated Bryan for president.

That is the power contained in a symbol.

Yet there is, fortunately, a kind of wisdom in people, for Byran went on to lose the election. He was nominated again in 1900, and then once more in 1908—losing both times. Of course, he had some very outspoken opponents as well. One of them described him at the time as "a mouthing, slobbering demagogue, whose patriotism is all in his jawbone." Still, he was able to hold masses of people spellbound with his oratory. Part of this power came from a magnificent voice, but part of it also came from his ability to exploit our tendency to be powerfully stirred by symbols—regardless, as here, of how appropriate their use in a particular context may be.

For what, after all, does the crucifixion and the crown of thorns have to do with bimetalism? Nothing, of course. But a clever speaker can forge that connection for us, rousing our sympathy in the process. This is not to suggest that the use of symbols is always objectionable and should always be condemned. On the contrary, on occasion it is perfectly justified and enables us to create a moment and express a thought possible in no other way.

Richard II is not the most popular of Shakespeare's plays, but there are many memorable moments in it and it provides much scope for imaginative direction. Richard, believing that he rules by divine right and that therefore he can do no wrong, plays favorites, alienates friends and family, and makes a shambles of his rule. His cousin, Bolingbroke, rises against him and has him imprisoned. In his cell, awaiting trial, Richard, in a long and moving soliloquy, bemoans his present state. As the cell darkens, assassins enter and stab him to death. Although the play could end here, it usually does not. Very often directors have the lights turned up a bit and let the audience see—this is their last glimpse of the play and players—the murdered Richard resting in the arms of the other members of the cast in the pose of Michelangelo's Pietà. This is a very moving ending and dramatically correct, for Richard sees himself, as do all the others, as a partly divine being, ruling by divine right and, therefore, like Christ, God's emissary.

Another way in which some directors try to convey to the audience this idea is to have Richard speak his final soliloquy standing and looking out the window of his cell. His hands are stretched out and rest on the frame of the window, whose bars form a cross. When the assassins stab him, he clutches the bars of the window, as if crucified. This ending, too, is often deeply moving.

Novelist Chaim Potok made use of that same symbol in one of his early works, *My Name is Asher Lev,* with powerful effect. The book tells the story of a young boy, born into a highly religious, orthodox, Jewish Hassidic family, who finds himself drawn to painting for which he has a great gift. The family finds it difficult to adjust to a son with such a gift, for the commandment against making graven images has through the centuries discouraged orthodox Jews from engaging in, to say nothing of valuing, this art. All, therefore, suffer terribly from this, especially the boy's mother who loves him deeply, but who has to protect him continually from his father, whom she also loves but who regards this gift as the work of the devil. The boy is not insensitive to her deep suffering and to the pain that his own obsession with developing this gift causes her. On more than one occasion, he has spied her waiting at the window of their living room, worriedly looking for him to return. He has seen her watching and waiting this way for his father as well, whose work as the Rebbe's representative frequently takes him away on distant journeys. Now when, after much trial and suffering, the boys grows into a man and comes to paint his masterpiece, what he paints, of course, is this picture of his mother at the window, whose frame is shaped in the form of a cross and whose arms and hands seem to have become entangled in the ropes of the Venetian blinds. The painting is an immediate sensation. The family and the small Jewish community is, however, stunned and outraged by it. For them it is an act of sacrilege and impiety. Psychologically and artistically, however, the choice of this particular symbol feels correct, for as Chaim Potok makes clear in his novel, what the protagonist needed and what his own tradition could not supply was a symbol as expressive of his deep anguish and sorrow as this one.

But it is not only religious symbols that have this powerful impact on us and whose potential for harm and distortion we have to guard ourselves against continually. Each country and nation over the course of time has come to develop and crystallize its experiences in its own inconography, creating in the process a kind of mythology of enormous potential power—

both for good and ill. Although we are a comparatively young country and nation, we too have not failed to create such a mythology for ourselves; nor have we been spared the spectacle of its gross exploitation. A dramatic, as well as politically and spiritually costly example, as later events proved, was Nixon's Checkers speech, with its masterful exploitation of such bits of American mythology as the sacrificing wife (cloth coat), the faithful dog (Checkers), the adoring daughters, the devoted husband—all to cover up possible corruption.

> My family was one of modest circumstances and most of my early life was spent in a store out in East Whittier. It was a grocery store—one of those family enterprises. I worked my way through college and to a great extent law school.
> The only reason we were able to make it go was because my mother and dad have five boys and we all worked in the store.
> Why do I feel so deeply? Why do I feel that in spite of the smears, the mis-understanding, the necessity for a man to come up here and bare his soul as I have? And I want to tell you why. Because you see, I love my country.

In Nixon's case, unlike William Jennings Bryan's, this pulling of the heart-strings led eventually to the presidency—with what subsequent results it is needless to repeat.

23

You Are
in a Strange Town

The final fallacy we will consider—called the *appeal to fear*—is sometimes also referred to as "swinging the big stick." Relying as it does on the threat of harm to advance a conclusion, it is, unfortunately, all too effective in many cases. By arousing sufficient fear, it succeeds in making us believe things that we would reject as false in calmer moments.

The appeal to fear should be distinguished from an all-out threat. If someone should hold a gun to your back and say, "Your money or your life," it would not do to reply, "Ah ha! That's a fallacy!" It is not a fallacy because it is not an argument. Although the holder of the gun is appealing to your sense of fear and even offering a reason why you should do as you are told, he or she is not offering evidence in support of the truth of some statement. The robber is not arguing with you but simply ordering you. The same would be true of threats such as, "If you don't keep that dog out of my yard, I'll shoot it," or "You get back into bed or I'll spank you."

In contrast to such examples, the attorney who says to a jury, "If you do not convict this murderer, one of you may be her next victim" is actually making a fallacious argument. A reason is advanced for an action being advocated, namely, the conviction of a defendant. But the issue of fear that is raised is irrelevant to the real issue, which is not conviction but guilt. The argument might be expressed more fully in this way:

> You must believe with me that this woman is guilty of the crime of which she is accused, for if you do not find her guilty of it, she will be released and you may end up being her next victim.

Put this way, the argument is clearly fallacious, for what a defendant might do in the future is not relevant to—and in no way proves either his or her innocence or guilt of—a crime committed in the past. The fear stirred up by the attorney deceives us into thinking that the argument is relevant.

An appeal to fear therefore offers fallacious evidence. It is not difficult to find illustrations from history of the use of the ploy. The defense of religious dogma has often involved such appeals. An elegant and terrifying example is the document of excommunication drawn up and read to the young Spinoza at his trial.

Spinoza had been born in Amsterdam in 1632, the son of a Jewish family who a generation earlier had fled to Holland from Portugal in order to escape the Inquisition. Holland was a haven for religious dissenters, and the Jewish community prospered there. Having a sceptical turn of mind, which was reinforced by his studies, Spinoza gradually became estranged from the tenets of Judaism. He discovered severe discrepancies in the Bible, and in his probing and questioning of these discrepancies and contradictions he began what came to be known as "higher criticism" of the Bible. It was not that the discrepancies Spinoza pointed out were completely unknown to others. For example, the story about God making the sun stand still—which involves the assumption that it moves—was an obvious difficulty known for some time to other critical readers of the Bible. But Spinoza, unlike others before him, tried to get to the root of the contradictions he found, doing so in devastating detail. The Jewish community became alarmed at this probing and questioning, fearing that their Christian hosts would be offended. They tried to bribe Spinoza to keep his opinions to himself. When this failed, they threatened him with excommunication, a rite that had so disgraced at least one other faced with it that he had committed suicide.

The ceremony of excommunication took place when Spinoza was 24 years old. The document containing the formula of excommunication read in part:

> Let him be cursed by the mouths of the Seven Angels who preside over the seven days of the week, and by the mouths of the angels who follow them and fight under their banners. Let him be cursed by the Four Angels who preside over the four seasons of the year, and by the mouths of all the angels who follow them and fight under their banners. . . . Let God never forgive him his sins. Let the wrath and indignation of the Lord surround him and smoke forever on his head. Let all the curses contained in the book of the Law fall upon him. . . . And we warn you, that none may speak with him by word of mouth nor by writing, nor show any favor to him, nor be under one roof with him, nor come within four cubits of him, nor read any paper composed by him.

Spinoza continued to live in Amsterdam for a while but eventually moved away, never to return. The excommunication did not succeed in stifling his criticism, but it didn't exactly encourage the free flow of ideas either. And although Spinoza went on to become one of the great thinkers of all time, it took the world a hundred years to come to realize it.

In our own day threats and scare tactics are still with us, though we are more likely to encounter them in language like the following:

1. Don't argue with me, young man. Remember who pays your salary.
2. Desegregation of labor unions is not desirable, and any official who thinks it is will discover his error at the next election.

These arguments are crude forms of the fallacy. They are explicit about the threats being issued.

The fallacy also lends itself to somewhat more veiled threats, however:

> Mr. Editor, I hope you will agree that this little escapade by my son has no real news value. I know you'll agree that my firm buys thousands of dollars worth of advertising space in your paper every year.

Logically speaking, this argument should be rejected, for the value of a firm's ad to a newspaper is entirely irrelevant to the question of whether a "little escapade" is or is not newsworthy. Of course, what the man is telling the editor is that, should he print this story about his son, he will take his business elsewhere. So it is, again, simply a threat.

Appeals to fear tend to multiply during periods of stress or conflict. For example, in the 1960s when the battle for civil rights was raging, black leader Malcolm X made this argument:

> It's time for you and me to stop sitting in this country letting some cracker senators, northern senators and southern senators, sit in Washington, D.C., and come to a conclusion in their mind that you and I are supposed to have civil rights. There's no white man that's going to tell me anything about my rights. . . . In 1964 it's the ballot or the bullet.

Here, a direct threat was made to white America: Either the demands for civil rights are met, or there will be violence.

In 1974, the oil-producing countries of the Middle East framed a more subtle threat to segments of this country. They compiled a list of U.S. companies that they judged to favor Israel. This was interpreted as an appeal to fear directed at American firms that might favor Israel in the Arab-Israeli dispute. Similarly, during the period of strongly anti-Communist activities of the John Birch Society in this country, the society issued the following statement, preceding a list of names of advertisers:

> This list of advertisers has been compiled so that members of the Anti-Communist Conservative Movement will have a way of determining those

firms that are standing up to be counted in the fight to preserve our American heritage.

Although the statement went on to point out that there was no suggestion intended that those whose names did not appear were therefore Communists, an implication to that effect was clear nevertheless. For in matters of this sort, saying what is not intended may amount to the same thing as saying it in the first place.

Like the other authoritarian ploys we have discussed, this one has been used to support not just wrong or questionable stands but worthy causes as well. It is especially favored, for example—and understandably so—by the American Cancer Society. In recent years the society has put out posters with captions designed to strike fear in us, such as these:

1. "We'll miss ya, baby."
2. Mark Waters was a chain smoker. Wonder who'll get his office?
3. If you want to die a slow death from cancer, smoke Salems—to be sure.

Similarly an advertisement by the United Cerebral Palsy Society is headed, "The baby we save could be yours" (trying to exploit not only our fear and pity but our guilt as well). One by the American Civil Liberties Union warns: "If the Moral Majority has its way, you'd better start praying."

Nor have commercial advertisers overlooked this device. An advertisement for an insurance retirement policy warned: "Maybe one person in ten will read this ad. The rest may wish they had when they retire." One for new ski bindings asked, "What would you rather do? Spend $90 now for new bindings or $400 later when you break a leg?" Somewhat more interesting is the dishwasher detergent ad that announced: "Spots are never in good taste. So get the Cascade look. . . . virtually spotless." Since no one wants to be a social outcast, stirring up such fears can marvelously increase the sales of the product.

Fear is also the guiding principle behind this advertisement for *Time-Life Family Legal Guide:*

You are in a strange town, strolling aimlessly down a street. You could—if you don't fully understand your rights—wind up in jail for the night.

Consider the events that have to come together for you to benefit from your wisdom in having purchased the volume in question: you have to find yourself in a strange town; you have to be strolling about aimlessly down a street (no doubt in the dead of night); you have to be stopped by a police officer who demands that you explain your presence there; you are unable to do so, which he regards as sufficiently wanting as to jail you. Of course, if you had had the foresight to buy the *Family Legal Guide,* you would have read it from cover to cover, would have remembered the appropriate answers to give or questions to ask when so accosted by a police officer, and would have sufficiently impressed the officer with your knowledge of your rights, as to permit you to continue your aimless strolling down the street at night in this strange town. This is a bit much—even for Madison Avenue.

Conclusion

If we have learned one thing from the journey we have just concluded, it is the importance of becoming wordwise. To survive in this twentieth-century world—to say nothing of thriving in it—requires that we become smart in the ways in which words are used to deceive, dominate, and impoverish us.

Learning to protect ourselves involves both the need to understand the way words really work and to abandon the naive notion that language is solely the *instrument* of thought. Instead, we must realize that language is what makes thought possible in the first place, and that that is what makes language not only so very important but also so potentially dangerous.

One such danger inheres in language's capacity to bare our souls and reveal us as we are. This applies not only to such subtleties of language as intonation and inflection, but even to spelling and grammar. As Richard Mitchell observed, "When you have lunch with a man who eats his lasagna with his fingers, you have reason to suspect that he may have one or two other social deficiencies." Similarly, it does not take an expert in English grammar and composition or a social psychologist to recognize verbal deficiencies or to guess how the person in question became saddled with them. I leave it to the reader to analyze the kinds of self-revelation contained in this note that a student gave to her instructor, accompanied by a book she wanted him to look at: "Please brief yourself with chapter's 1-3-2-6-9-14-16-19-18. I've read some of this book, and I would like to know your opinion of this book's validity. I hold your opinion in good thought."

In this book we have explored this feature of language in order to recognize when such self-revelations take place and how we might avoid them ourselves. Language being a minefield, it would be useless to hope for too much. If someone as shrewd as Richard Nixon could not resist telling us he is not a crook, it is unlikely that the rest of us will always be successful in escaping the traps that lie in wait for us. But we can nevertheless hope to be more successful than we are now, and for this, only two things are required. The first is a working knowledge of the principal ways in which language transmits messages we never wanted sent. And the second—even more important—consists in developing the habit of paying closer attention to what we say and write. This heightened self-awareness, incidentally, is certainly not meant to stifle all spontaneity. What it should do is to help us confine spontaneous expression only to those occasions and contexts where it is appropriate (which are rather less common than some people seem to think).

But gaining mastery over the verbal message we send out to the world is only half the battle. What about the incoming messages? Will they be deliberate lies, deceptions, or manipulations? Will they contain honest (though nevertheless dangerously misleading) errors of fact or logic?

Unravelling such confusions has become more and more difficult. The reason is not just the highly rarefied atmosphere in which they now generally take place but also the complicated factual matter with which they now more frequently tend to be intertwined. Not much background or information is ordinarily required to unravel the confusion involved in the argument that hunting is not cruel because it gives a lot of employment to a lot of people and a lot of pleasure. The same objection applies to the argument that vegetarianism is an injurious and unhealthy practice because if all people were vegetarians, the economy would be seriously affected and many people would be thrown out of work. Most readers would instantly recognize that both are silly and fallacious arguments, for in the former case the question is not whether people find hunting fun but whether animals do. In the latter, the question is whether subsisting on a diet of vegetables is harmful to vegetarians, not to the economy.

Consider, however, the 1981 press conference conducted by President Reagan. When asked about the nation's 8.9-percent unemployment rate, Reagan claimed that, "comparing this to the beginning of our term, there are a million more people working than there were in 1980." How many people realized that Reagan's reply, a matter of comparing apples and oranges, was totally beside the point. In addition, how many were aware that Reagan could hardly have taken much comfort in this particular evasion since the total number of people employed was also beginning to decrease significantly, with about 100,000 fewer people working in December of 1981, than were twelve months earlier? And when President Reagan was asked about the unemployment rate of Blacks, then at 17 percent, he referred job seekers to the previous Sunday's Wasington *Post*. "There were 24 full pages of classified ads," he said. "What we need is to make more people qualified to go and apply for those jobs." But how many of those listening were aware that many, if not most, of those pages were filled, as such papers are in most major cities, with ads for such occupations as cellular immunologists, computer operators, psychiatric nurses, and other jobs demanding skills far beyond those of most unemployed workers. In addition, how many would have recalled that his administration had only recently scuttled about one-third of federal job-training programs that might have helped some of these unemployed acquire the skills necessary to qualify for some of these jobs?

My purpose in citing these examples is not to single out either President Reagan or his party as being especially guilty of mishandling truth or logic. Democrats—and, indeed, politicians everywhere—are equally capable of similar finagles, as are newspaper columnists, advertisers, businesspeople, school teachers, and so on, ad infinitum. If the President's lapses have any special significance, it is that *because* he is President we unreasonably tend to give more weight and credence to his words than we might to less exalted persons. That this may be more our fault than his is precisely the point.

The better we become at spotting defective logic, emotion-charged irrelevancies, evasions masquerading as proofs, and all the other booby traps that lie hidden in language, the more valuable we shall be as citizens and the safer we shall be as individuals. To be sure, all our skills cannot absolutely protect us against outright lies, especially when we do not, or cannot, know the facts. But since liars can seldom resist playing other, more easily identified manipulative games with language, we can learn how and when to be wary, as well as when to suspend our belief in an assertion of fact until we can be assured that it really is fact. And this may be especially important to do when the assertion comes from a so-called authority.

Although the benefits of this sort of questioning are obviously considerable, it is not a habit of mind natural to us. It needs to be encouraged, cultivated, and nourished—how much so we saw only too clearly from the chilling results of Stanley Milgram's experiment on how people react to authority. The kind of authoritarianism uncovered by Milgram is, unfortunately, very much a feature of our times and growing in strength. Nor does it look as if it is going to go away very soon. On the contrary, the increasing intellectualism so characteristic of our time, has had the effect of making many of us feel insecure and inadequate and thus more than ever prone to authoritarianism's appeal.

How strangely vulnerable we have all become was dramatically and comically shown in a memorable segment of *Candid Camera* some years ago when Allen Funt caused havoc in the state of Delaware by simply positioning a large sign over one of its major expressways. It read:

DELAWARE CLOSED

Cars and trucks screeched to a halt. Vans pulled off the highway. Motorists left their vehicles, confused and bewildered. One hapless driver approached Funt, who stood beneath the sign as hidden movie cameras recorded the event, and asked: "When do you think it'll reopen? I live there and my family is in there."

Such is the power of authority and the depth of our vulnerability.

It has been said that language is the breath of civilization. Let us take care that it never becomes civilization's undoing.

Index

A CATALOG OF SELECTED DOVER BOOKS IN ALL FIELDS OF INTEREST

100 BEST-LOVED POEMS, Edited by Philip Smith. "The Passionate Shepherd to His Love," "Shall I compare thee to a summer's day?" "Death, be not proud," "The Raven," "The Road Not Taken," plus works by Blake, Wordsworth, Byron, Shelley, Keats, many others. 96pp. 5³⁄₁₆ x 8¼. 0-486-28553-7

100 SMALL HOUSES OF THE THIRTIES, Brown-Blodgett Company. Exterior photographs and floor plans for 100 charming structures. Illustrations of models accompanied by descriptions of interiors, color schemes, closet space, and other amenities. 200 illustrations. 112pp. 8⅜ x 11. 0-486-44131-8

1000 TURN-OF-THE-CENTURY HOUSES: With Illustrations and Floor Plans, Herbert C. Chivers. Reproduced from a rare edition, this showcase of homes ranges from cottages and bungalows to sprawling mansions. Each house is meticulously illustrated and accompanied by complete floor plans. 256pp. 9⅜ x 12¼. 0-486-45596-3

101 GREAT AMERICAN POEMS, Edited by The American Poetry & Literacy Project. Rich treasury of verse from the 19th and 20th centuries includes works by Edgar Allan Poe, Robert Frost, Walt Whitman, Langston Hughes, Emily Dickinson, T. S. Eliot, other notables. 96pp. 5³⁄₁₆ x 8¼. 0-486-40158-8

101 GREAT SAMURAI PRINTS, Utagawa Kuniyoshi. Kuniyoshi was a master of the warrior woodblock print — and these 18th-century illustrations represent the pinnacle of his craft. Full-color portraits of renowned Japanese samurais pulse with movement, passion, and remarkably fine detail. 112pp. 8⅜ x 11. 0-486-46523-3

ABC OF BALLET, Janet Grosser. Clearly worded, abundantly illustrated little guide defines basic ballet-related terms: arabesque, battement, pas de chat, relevé, sissonne, many others. Pronunciation guide included. Excellent primer. 48pp. 4³⁄₁₆ x 5¾. 0-486-40871-X

ACCESSORIES OF DRESS: An Illustrated Encyclopedia, Katherine Lester and Bess Viola Oerke. Illustrations of hats, veils, wigs, cravats, shawls, shoes, gloves, and other accessories enhance an engaging commentary that reveals the humor and charm of the many-sided story of accessorized apparel. 644 figures and 59 plates. 608pp. 6 ⅛ x 9¼. 0-486-43378-1

ADVENTURES OF HUCKLEBERRY FINN, Mark Twain. Join Huck and Jim as their boyhood adventures along the Mississippi River lead them into a world of excitement, danger, and self-discovery. Humorous narrative, lyrical descriptions of the Mississippi valley, and memorable characters. 224pp. 5³⁄₁₆ x 8¼. 0-486-28061-6

ALICE STARMORE'S BOOK OF FAIR ISLE KNITTING, Alice Starmore. A noted designer from the region of Scotland's Fair Isle explores the history and techniques of this distinctive, stranded-color knitting style and provides copious illustrated instructions for 14 original knitwear designs. 208pp. 8⅜ x 10⅞. 0-486-47218-3

Browse over 9,000 books at www.doverpublications.com

CATALOG OF DOVER BOOKS

ALICE'S ADVENTURES IN WONDERLAND, Lewis Carroll. Beloved classic about a little girl lost in a topsy-turvy land and her encounters with the White Rabbit, March Hare, Mad Hatter, Cheshire Cat, and other delightfully improbable characters. 42 illustrations by Sir John Tenniel. 96pp. 5³⁄₁₆ x 8¼.   0-486-27543-4

AMERICA'S LIGHTHOUSES: An Illustrated History, Francis Ross Holland. Profusely illustrated fact-filled survey of American lighthouses since 1716. Over 200 stations — East, Gulf, and West coasts, Great Lakes, Hawaii, Alaska, Puerto Rico, the Virgin Islands, and the Mississippi and St. Lawrence Rivers. 240pp. 8 x 10¾.
0-486-25576-X

AN ENCYCLOPEDIA OF THE VIOLIN, Alberto Bachmann. Translated by Frederick H. Martens. Introduction by Eugene Ysaye. First published in 1925, this renowned reference remains unsurpassed as a source of essential information, from construction and evolution to repertoire and technique. Includes a glossary and 73 illustrations. 496pp. 6½ x 9¼.   0-486-46618-3

ANIMALS: 1,419 Copyright-Free Illustrations of Mammals, Birds, Fish, Insects, etc., Selected by Jim Harter. Selected for its visual impact and ease of use, this outstanding collection of wood engravings presents over 1,000 species of animals in extremely lifelike poses. Includes mammals, birds, reptiles, amphibians, fish, insects, and other invertebrates. 284pp. 9 x 12.   0-486-23766-4

THE ANNALS, Tacitus. Translated by Alfred John Church and William Jackson Brodribb. This vital chronicle of Imperial Rome, written by the era's great historian, spans A.D. 14-68 and paints incisive psychological portraits of major figures, from Tiberius to Nero. 416pp. 5³⁄₁₆ x 8¼.   0-486-45236-0

ANTIGONE, Sophocles. Filled with passionate speeches and sensitive probing of moral and philosophical issues, this powerful and often-performed Greek drama reveals the grim fate that befalls the children of Oedipus. Footnotes. 64pp. 5³⁄₁₆ x 8 ¼.   0-486-27804-2

ART DECO DECORATIVE PATTERNS IN FULL COLOR, Christian Stoll. Reprinted from a rare 1910 portfolio, 160 sensuous and exotic images depict a breathtaking array of florals, geometrics, and abstracts — all elegant in their stark simplicity. 64pp. 8⅜ x 11.   0-486-44862-2

THE ARTHUR RACKHAM TREASURY: 86 Full-Color Illustrations, Arthur Rackham. Selected and Edited by Jeff A. Menges. A stunning treasury of 86 full-page plates span the famed English artist's career, from Rip Van Winkle (1905) to masterworks such as Undine, A Midsummer Night's Dream, and Wind in the Willows (1939). 96pp. 8⅜ x 11.
0-486-44685-9

THE AUTHENTIC GILBERT & SULLIVAN SONGBOOK, W. S. Gilbert and A. S. Sullivan. The most comprehensive collection available, this songbook includes selections from every one of Gilbert and Sullivan's light operas. Ninety-two numbers are presented uncut and unedited, and in their original keys. 410pp. 9 x 12.
0-486-23482-7

THE AWAKENING, Kate Chopin. First published in 1899, this controversial novel of a New Orleans wife's search for love outside a stifling marriage shocked readers. Today, it remains a first-rate narrative with superb characterization. New introductory Note. 128pp. 5³⁄₁₆ x 8¼.   0-486-27786-0

BASIC DRAWING, Louis Priscilla. Beginning with perspective, this commonsense manual progresses to the figure in movement, light and shade, anatomy, drapery, composition, trees and landscape, and outdoor sketching. Black-and-white illustrations throughout. 128pp. 8⅜ x 11.   0-486-45815-6

Browse over 9,000 books at www.doverpublications.com

THE BATTLES THAT CHANGED HISTORY, Fletcher Pratt. Historian profiles 16 crucial conflicts, ancient to modern, that changed the course of Western civilization. Gripping accounts of battles led by Alexander the Great, Joan of Arc, Ulysses S. Grant, other commanders. 27 maps. 352pp. 5⅜ x 8½. 0-486-41129-X

BEETHOVEN'S LETTERS, Ludwig van Beethoven. Edited by Dr. A. C. Kalischer. Features 457 letters to fellow musicians, friends, greats, patrons, and literary men. Reveals musical thoughts, quirks of personality, insights, and daily events. Includes 15 plates. 410pp. 5⅜ x 8½. 0-486-22769-3

BERNICE BOBS HER HAIR AND OTHER STORIES, F. Scott Fitzgerald. This brilliant anthology includes 6 of Fitzgerald's most popular stories: "The Diamond as Big as the Ritz," the title tale, "The Offshore Pirate," "The Ice Palace," "The Jelly Bean," and "May Day." 176pp. 5⅜ x 8½. 0-486-47049-0

BESLER'S BOOK OF FLOWERS AND PLANTS: 73 Full-Color Plates from Hortus Eystettensis, 1613, Basilius Besler. Here is a selection of magnificent plates from the *Hortus Eystettensis*, which vividly illustrated and identified the plants, flowers, and trees that thrived in the legendary German garden at Eichstätt. 80pp. 8⅜ x 11.
0-486-46005-3

THE BOOK OF KELLS, Edited by Blanche Cirker. Painstakingly reproduced from a rare facsimile edition, this volume contains full-page decorations, portraits, illustrations, plus a sampling of textual leaves with exquisite calligraphy and ornamentation. 32 full-color illustrations. 32pp. 9⅜ x 12¼. 0-486-24345-1

THE BOOK OF THE CROSSBOW: With an Additional Section on Catapults and Other Siege Engines, Ralph Payne-Gallwey. Fascinating study traces history and use of crossbow as military and sporting weapon, from Middle Ages to modern times. Also covers related weapons: balistas, catapults, Turkish bows, more. Over 240 illustrations. 400pp. 7¼ x 10⅛. 0-486-28720-3

THE BUNGALOW BOOK: Floor Plans and Photos of 112 Houses, 1910, Henry L. Wilson. Here are 112 of the most popular and economic blueprints of the early 20th century — plus an illustration or photograph of each completed house. A wonderful time capsule that still offers a wealth of valuable insights. 160pp. 8⅜ x 11.
0-486-45104-6

THE CALL OF THE WILD, Jack London. A classic novel of adventure, drawn from London's own experiences as a Klondike adventurer, relating the story of a heroic dog caught in the brutal life of the Alaska Gold Rush. Note. 64pp. 5³⁄₁₆ x 8¼.
0-486-26472-6

CANDIDE, Voltaire. Edited by Francois-Marie Arouet. One of the world's great satires since its first publication in 1759. Witty, caustic skewering of romance, science, philosophy, religion, government — nearly all human ideals and institutions. 112pp. 5³⁄₁₆ x 8¼. 0-486-26689-3

CELEBRATED IN THEIR TIME: Photographic Portraits from the George Grantham Bain Collection, Edited by Amy Pastan. With an Introduction by Michael Carlebach. Remarkable portrait gallery features 112 rare images of Albert Einstein, Charlie Chaplin, the Wright Brothers, Henry Ford, and other luminaries from the worlds of politics, art, entertainment, and industry. 128pp. 8⅜ x 11. 0-486-46754-6

CHARIOTS FOR APOLLO: The NASA History of Manned Lunar Spacecraft to 1969, Courtney G. Brooks, James M. Grimwood, and Loyd S. Swenson, Jr. This illustrated history by a trio of experts is the definitive reference on the Apollo spacecraft and lunar modules. It traces the vehicles' design, development, and operation in space. More than 100 photographs and illustrations. 576pp. 6¾ x 9¼. 0-486-46756-2

Browse over 9,000 books at www.doverpublications.com

A CHRISTMAS CAROL, Charles Dickens. This engrossing tale relates Ebenezer Scrooge's ghostly journeys through Christmases past, present, and future and his ultimate transformation from a harsh and grasping old miser to a charitable and compassionate human being. 80pp. 5³⁄₁₆ x 8¼. 0-486-26865-9

COMMON SENSE, Thomas Paine. First published in January of 1776, this highly influential landmark document clearly and persuasively argued for American separation from Great Britain and paved the way for the Declaration of Independence. 64pp. 5³⁄₁₆ x 8¼. 0-486-29602-4

THE COMPLETE SHORT STORIES OF OSCAR WILDE, Oscar Wilde. Complete texts of "The Happy Prince and Other Tales," "A House of Pomegranates," "Lord Arthur Savile's Crime and Other Stories," "Poems in Prose," and "The Portrait of Mr. W. H." 208pp. 5³⁄₁₆ x 8¼. 0-486-45216-6

COMPLETE SONNETS, William Shakespeare. Over 150 exquisite poems deal with love, friendship, the tyranny of time, beauty's evanescence, death, and other themes in language of remarkable power, precision, and beauty. Glossary of archaic terms. 80pp. 5³⁄₁₆ x 8¼. 0-486-26686-9

THE COUNT OF MONTE CRISTO: Abridged Edition, Alexandre Dumas. Falsely accused of treason, Edmond Dantès is imprisoned in the bleak Chateau d'If. After a hair-raising escape, he launches an elaborate plot to extract a bitter revenge against those who betrayed him. 448pp. 5³⁄₁₆ x 8¼. 0-486-45643-9

CRAFTSMAN BUNGALOWS: Designs from the Pacific Northwest, Yoho & Merritt. This reprint of a rare catalog, showcasing the charming simplicity and cozy style of Craftsman bungalows, is filled with photos of completed homes, plus floor plans and estimated costs. An indispensable resource for architects, historians, and illustrators. 112pp. 10 x 7. 0-486-46875-5

CRAFTSMAN BUNGALOWS: 59 Homes from "The Craftsman," Edited by Gustav Stickley. Best and most attractive designs from Arts and Crafts Movement publication — 1903–1916 — includes sketches, photographs of homes, floor plans, descriptive text. 128pp. 8¼ x 11. 0-486-25829-7

CRIME AND PUNISHMENT, Fyodor Dostoyevsky. Translated by Constance Garnett. Supreme masterpiece tells the story of Raskolnikov, a student tormented by his own thoughts after he murders an old woman. Overwhelmed by guilt and terror, he confesses and goes to prison. 480pp. 5³⁄₁₆ x 8¼. 0-486-41587-2

THE DECLARATION OF INDEPENDENCE AND OTHER GREAT DOCUMENTS OF AMERICAN HISTORY: 1775-1865, Edited by John Grafton. Thirteen compelling and influential documents: Henry's "Give Me Liberty or Give Me Death," Declaration of Independence, The Constitution, Washington's First Inaugural Address, The Monroe Doctrine, The Emancipation Proclamation, Gettysburg Address, more. 64pp. 5³⁄₁₆ x 8¼. 0-486-41124-9

THE DESERT AND THE SOWN: Travels in Palestine and Syria, Gertrude Bell. "The female Lawrence of Arabia," Gertrude Bell wrote captivating, perceptive accounts of her travels in the Middle East. This intriguing narrative, accompanied by 160 photos, traces her 1905 sojourn in Lebanon, Syria, and Palestine. 368pp. 5⅜ x 8½. 0-486-46876-3

A DOLL'S HOUSE, Henrik Ibsen. Ibsen's best-known play displays his genius for realistic prose drama. An expression of women's rights, the play climaxes when the central character, Nora, rejects a smothering marriage and life in "a doll's house." 80pp. 5³⁄₁₆ x 8¼. 0-486-27062-9

DOOMED SHIPS: Great Ocean Liner Disasters, William H. Miller, Jr. Nearly 200 photographs, many from private collections, highlight tales of some of the vessels whose pleasure cruises ended in catastrophe: the *Morro Castle, Normandie, Andrea Doria, Europa,* and many others. 128pp. 8⅞ x 11¾. 0-486-45366-9

THE DORÉ BIBLE ILLUSTRATIONS, Gustave Doré. Detailed plates from the Bible: the Creation scenes, Adam and Eve, horrifying visions of the Flood, the battle sequences with their monumental crowds, depictions of the life of Jesus, 241 plates in all. 241pp. 9 x 12. 0-486-23004-X

DRAWING DRAPERY FROM HEAD TO TOE, Cliff Young. Expert guidance on how to draw shirts, pants, skirts, gloves, hats, and coats on the human figure, including folds in relation to the body, pull and crush, action folds, creases, more. Over 200 drawings. 48pp. 8¼ x 11. 0-486-45591-2

DUBLINERS, James Joyce. A fine and accessible introduction to the work of one of the 20th century's most influential writers, this collection features 15 tales, including a masterpiece of the short-story genre, "The Dead." 160pp. 5³⁄₁₆ x 8¼. 0-486-26870-5

EASY-TO-MAKE POP-UPS, Joan Irvine. Illustrated by Barbara Reid. Dozens of wonderful ideas for three-dimensional paper fun — from holiday greeting cards with moving parts to a pop-up menagerie. Easy-to-follow, illustrated instructions for more than 30 projects. 299 black-and-white illustrations. 96pp. 8⅜ x 11. 0-486-44622-0

EASY-TO-MAKE STORYBOOK DOLLS: A "Novel" Approach to Cloth Dollmaking, Sherralyn St. Clair. Favorite fictional characters come alive in this unique beginner's dollmaking guide. Includes patterns for Pollyanna, Dorothy from *The Wonderful Wizard of Oz*, Mary of *The Secret Garden*, plus easy-to-follow instructions, 263 black-and-white illustrations, and an 8-page color insert. 112pp. 8¼ x 11. 0-486-47360-0

EINSTEIN'S ESSAYS IN SCIENCE, Albert Einstein. Speeches and essays in accessible, everyday language profile influential physicists such as Niels Bohr and Isaac Newton. They also explore areas of physics to which the author made major contributions. 128pp. 5 x 8. 0-486-47011-3

EL DORADO: Further Adventures of the Scarlet Pimpernel, Baroness Orczy. A popular sequel to *The Scarlet Pimpernel*, this suspenseful story recounts the Pimpernel's attempts to rescue the Dauphin from imprisonment during the French Revolution. An irresistible blend of intrigue, period detail, and vibrant characterizations. 352pp. 5³⁄₁₆ x 8¼. 0-486-44026-5

ELEGANT SMALL HOMES OF THE TWENTIES: 99 Designs from a Competition, Chicago Tribune. Nearly 100 designs for five- and six-room houses feature New England and Southern colonials, Normandy cottages, stately Italianate dwellings, and other fascinating snapshots of American domestic architecture of the 1920s. 112pp. 9 x 12. 0-486-46910-7

THE ELEMENTS OF STYLE: The Original Edition, William Strunk, Jr. This is the book that generations of writers have relied upon for timeless advice on grammar, diction, syntax, and other essentials. In concise terms, it identifies the principal requirements of proper style and common errors. 64pp. 5⅜ x 8½. 0-486-44798-7

THE ELUSIVE PIMPERNEL, Baroness Orczy. Robespierre's revolutionaries find their wicked schemes thwarted by the heroic Pimpernel — Sir Percival Blakeney. In this thrilling sequel, Chauvelin devises a plot to eliminate the Pimpernel and his wife. 272pp. 5³⁄₁₆ x 8¼. 0-486-45464-9

AN ENCYCLOPEDIA OF BATTLES: Accounts of Over 1,560 Battles from 1479 B.C. to the Present, David Eggenberger. Essential details of every major battle in recorded history from the first battle of Megiddo in 1479 B.C. to Grenada in 1984. List of battle maps. 99 illustrations. 544pp. 6½ x 9¼. 0-486-24913-1

ENCYCLOPEDIA OF EMBROIDERY STITCHES, INCLUDING CREWEL, Marion Nichols. Precise explanations and instructions, clearly illustrated, on how to work chain, back, cross, knotted, woven stitches, and many more — 178 in all, including Cable Outline, Whipped Satin, and Eyelet Buttonhole. Over 1400 illustrations. 219pp. 8⅜ x 11¼. 0-486-22929-7

ENTER JEEVES: 15 Early Stories, P. G. Wodehouse. Splendid collection contains first 8 stories featuring Bertie Wooster, the deliciously dim aristocrat and Jeeves, his brainy, imperturbable manservant. Also, the complete Reggie Pepper (Bertie's prototype) series. 288pp. 5⅜ x 8½. 0-486-29717-9

ERIC SLOANE'S AMERICA: Paintings in Oil, Michael Wigley. With a Foreword by Mimi Sloane. Eric Sloane's evocative oils of America's landscape and material culture shimmer with immense historical and nostalgic appeal. This original hardcover collection gathers nearly a hundred of his finest paintings, with subjects ranging from New England to the American Southwest. 128pp. 10⅝ x 9.
0-486-46525-X

ETHAN FROME, Edith Wharton. Classic story of wasted lives, set against a bleak New England background. Superbly delineated characters in a hauntingly grim tale of thwarted love. Considered by many to be Wharton's masterpiece. 96pp. 5³⁄₁₆ x 8 ¼.
0-486-26690-7

THE EVERLASTING MAN, G. K. Chesterton. Chesterton's view of Christianity — as a blend of philosophy and mythology, satisfying intellect and spirit — applies to his brilliant book, which appeals to readers' heads as well as their hearts. 288pp. 5⅜ x 8½.
0-486-46036-3

THE FIELD AND FOREST HANDY BOOK, Daniel Beard. Written by a co-founder of the Boy Scouts, this appealing guide offers illustrated instructions for building kites, birdhouses, boats, igloos, and other fun projects, plus numerous helpful tips for campers. 448pp. 5³⁄₁₆ x 8¼. 0-486-46191-2

FINDING YOUR WAY WITHOUT MAP OR COMPASS, Harold Gatty. Useful, instructive manual shows would-be explorers, hikers, bikers, scouts, sailors, and survivalists how to find their way outdoors by observing animals, weather patterns, shifting sands, and other elements of nature. 288pp. 5⅜ x 8½. 0-486-40613-X

FIRST FRENCH READER: A Beginner's Dual-Language Book, Edited and Translated by Stanley Appelbaum. This anthology introduces 50 legendary writers — Voltaire, Balzac, Baudelaire, Proust, more — through passages from *The Red and the Black, Les Misérables, Madame Bovary,* and other classics. Original French text plus English translation on facing pages. 240pp. 5⅜ x 8½. 0-486-46178-5

FIRST GERMAN READER: A Beginner's Dual-Language Book, Edited by Harry Steinhauer. Specially chosen for their power to evoke German life and culture, these short, simple readings include poems, stories, essays, and anecdotes by Goethe, Hesse, Heine, Schiller, and others. 224pp. 5⅜ x 8½. 0-486-46179-3

FIRST SPANISH READER: A Beginner's Dual-Language Book, Angel Flores. Delightful stories, other material based on works of Don Juan Manuel, Luis Taboada, Ricardo Palma, other noted writers. Complete faithful English translations on facing pages. Exercises. 176pp. 5⅜ x 8½. 0-486-25810-6

FIVE ACRES AND INDEPENDENCE, Maurice G. Kains. Great back-to-the-land classic explains basics of self-sufficient farming. The one book to get. 95 illustrations. 397pp. 5⅜ x 8½. 0-486-20974-1

FLAGG'S SMALL HOUSES: Their Economic Design and Construction, 1922, Ernest Flagg. Although most famous for his skyscrapers, Flagg was also a proponent of the well-designed single-family dwelling. His classic treatise features innovations that save space, materials, and cost. 526 illustrations. 160pp. 9⅜ x 12¼. 0-486-45197-6

FLATLAND: A Romance of Many Dimensions, Edwin A. Abbott. Classic of science (and mathematical) fiction — charmingly illustrated by the author — describes the adventures of A. Square, a resident of Flatland, in Spaceland (three dimensions), Lineland (one dimension), and Pointland (no dimensions). 96pp. 5$\frac{3}{16}$ x 8¼. 0-486-27263-X

FRANKENSTEIN, Mary Shelley. The story of Victor Frankenstein's monstrous creation and the havoc it caused has enthralled generations of readers and inspired countless writers of horror and suspense. With the author's own 1831 introduction. 176pp. 5$\frac{3}{16}$ x 8¼. 0-486-28211-2

THE GARGOYLE BOOK: 572 Examples from Gothic Architecture, Lester Burbank Bridaham. Dispelling the conventional wisdom that French Gothic architectural flourishes were born of despair or gloom, Bridaham reveals the whimsical nature of these creations and the ingenious artisans who made them. 572 illustrations. 224pp. 8⅜ x 11. 0-486-44754-5

THE GIFT OF THE MAGI AND OTHER SHORT STORIES, O. Henry. Sixteen captivating stories by one of America's most popular storytellers. Included are such classics as "The Gift of the Magi," "The Last Leaf," and "The Ransom of Red Chief." Publisher's Note. 96pp. 5$\frac{3}{16}$ x 8¼. 0-486-27061-0

THE GOETHE TREASURY: Selected Prose and Poetry, Johann Wolfgang von Goethe. Edited, Selected, and with an Introduction by Thomas Mann. In addition to his lyric poetry, Goethe wrote travel sketches, autobiographical studies, essays, letters, and proverbs in rhyme and prose. This collection presents outstanding examples from each genre. 368pp. 5⅜ x 8½. 0-486-44780-4

GREAT EXPECTATIONS, Charles Dickens. Orphaned Pip is apprenticed to the dirty work of the forge but dreams of becoming a gentleman — and one day finds himself in possession of "great expectations." Dickens' finest novel. 400pp. 5$\frac{3}{16}$ x 8¼. 0-486-41586-4

GREAT WRITERS ON THE ART OF FICTION: From Mark Twain to Joyce Carol Oates, Edited by James Daley. An indispensable source of advice and inspiration, this anthology features essays by Henry James, Kate Chopin, Willa Cather, Sinclair Lewis, Jack London, Raymond Chandler, Raymond Carver, Eudora Welty, and Kurt Vonnegut, Jr. 192pp. 5⅜ x 8½. 0-486-45128-3

HAMLET, William Shakespeare. The quintessential Shakespearean tragedy, whose highly charged confrontations and anguished soliloquies probe depths of human feeling rarely sounded in any art. Reprinted from an authoritative British edition complete with illuminating footnotes. 128pp. 5$\frac{3}{16}$ x 8¼. 0-486-27278-8

THE HAUNTED HOUSE, Charles Dickens. A Yuletide gathering in an eerie country retreat provides the backdrop for Dickens and his friends — including Elizabeth Gaskell and Wilkie Collins — who take turns spinning supernatural yarns. 144pp. 5⅜ x 8½. 0-486-46309-5

CATALOG OF DOVER BOOKS

HEART OF DARKNESS, Joseph Conrad. Dark allegory of a journey up the Congo River and the narrator's encounter with the mysterious Mr. Kurtz. Masterly blend of adventure, character study, psychological penetration. For many, Conrad's finest, most enigmatic story. 80pp. 5³⁄₁₆ x 8¼. 0-486-26464-5

HENSON AT THE NORTH POLE, Matthew A. Henson. This thrilling memoir by the heroic African-American who was Peary's companion through two decades of Arctic exploration recounts a tale of danger, courage, and determination. "Fascinating and exciting." — *Commonweal.* 128pp. 5⅜ x 8½. 0-486-45472-X

HISTORIC COSTUMES AND HOW TO MAKE THEM, Mary Fernald and E. Shenton. Practical, informative guidebook shows how to create everything from short tunics worn by Saxon men in the fifth century to a lady's bustle dress of the late 1800s. 81 illustrations. 176pp. 5⅜ x 8½. 0-486-44906-8

THE HOUND OF THE BASKERVILLES, Arthur Conan Doyle. A deadly curse in the form of a legendary ferocious beast continues to claim its victims from the Baskerville family until Holmes and Watson intervene. Often called the best detective story ever written. 128pp. 5³⁄₁₆ x 8¼. 0-486-28214-7

THE HOUSE BEHIND THE CEDARS, Charles W. Chesnutt. Originally published in 1900, this groundbreaking novel by a distinguished African-American author recounts the drama of a brother and sister who "pass for white" during the dangerous days of Reconstruction. 208pp. 5⅜ x 8½. 0-486-46144-0

THE HUMAN FIGURE IN MOTION, Eadweard Muybridge. The 4,789 photographs in this definitive selection show the human figure — models almost all undraped — engaged in over 160 different types of action: running, climbing stairs, etc. 390pp. 7⅞ x 10⅝. 0-486-20204-6

THE IMPORTANCE OF BEING EARNEST, Oscar Wilde. Wilde's witty and buoyant comedy of manners, filled with some of literature's most famous epigrams, reprinted from an authoritative British edition. Considered Wilde's most perfect work. 64pp. 5³⁄₁₆ x 8¼. 0-486-26478-5

THE INFERNO, Dante Alighieri. Translated and with notes by Henry Wadsworth Longfellow. The first stop on Dante's famous journey from Hell to Purgatory to Paradise, this 14th-century allegorical poem blends vivid and shocking imagery with graceful lyricism. Translated by the beloved 19th-century poet, Henry Wadsworth Longfellow. 256pp. 5³⁄₁₆ x 8¼. 0-486-44288-8

JANE EYRE, Charlotte Brontë. Written in 1847, *Jane Eyre* tells the tale of an orphan girl's progress from the custody of cruel relatives to an oppressive boarding school and its culmination in a troubled career as a governess. 448pp. 5³⁄₁₆ x 8¼.
0-486-42449-9

JAPANESE WOODBLOCK FLOWER PRINTS, Tanigami Kônan. Extraordinary collection of Japanese woodblock prints by a well-known artist features 120 plates in brilliant color. Realistic images from a rare edition include daffodils, tulips, and other familiar and unusual flowers. 128pp. 11 x 8¼. 0-486-46442-3

JEWELRY MAKING AND DESIGN, Augustus F. Rose and Antonio Cirino. Professional secrets of jewelry making are revealed in a thorough, practical guide. Over 200 illustrations. 306pp. 5⅜ x 8½. 0-486-21750-7

JULIUS CAESAR, William Shakespeare. Great tragedy based on Plutarch's account of the lives of Brutus, Julius Caesar and Mark Antony. Evil plotting, ringing oratory, high tragedy with Shakespeare's incomparable insight, dramatic power. Explanatory footnotes. 96pp. 5³⁄₁₆ x 8¼. 0-486-26876-4

Browse over 9,000 books at www.doverpublications.com

THE JUNGLE, Upton Sinclair. 1906 bestseller shockingly reveals intolerable labor practices and working conditions in the Chicago stockyards as it tells the grim story of a Slavic family that emigrates to America full of optimism but soon faces despair. 320pp. 5³⁄₁₆ x 8¼. 0-486-41923-1

THE KINGDOM OF GOD IS WITHIN YOU, Leo Tolstoy. The soul-searching book that inspired Gandhi to embrace the concept of passive resistance, Tolstoy's 1894 polemic clearly outlines a radical, well-reasoned revision of traditional Christian thinking. 352pp. 5³⁄₁₆ x 8¼. 0-486-45138-0

THE LADY OR THE TIGER?: and Other Logic Puzzles, Raymond M. Smullyan. Created by a renowned puzzle master, these whimsically themed challenges involve paradoxes about probability, time, and change; metapuzzles; and self-referentiality. Nineteen chapters advance in difficulty from relatively simple to highly complex. 1982 edition. 240pp. 5⅜ x 8½. 0-486-47027-X

LEAVES OF GRASS: The Original 1855 Edition, Walt Whitman. Whitman's immortal collection includes some of the greatest poems of modern times, including his masterpiece, "Song of Myself." Shattering standard conventions, it stands as an unabashed celebration of body and nature. 128pp. 5³⁄₁₆ x 8¼. 0-486-45676-5

LES MISÉRABLES, Victor Hugo. Translated by Charles E. Wilbour. Abridged by James K. Robinson. A convict's heroic struggle for justice and redemption plays out against a fiery backdrop of the Napoleonic wars. This edition features the excellent original translation and a sensitive abridgment. 304pp. 6⅛ x 9¼.
0-486-45789-3

LILITH: A Romance, George MacDonald. In this novel by the father of fantasy literature, a man travels through time to meet Adam and Eve and to explore humanity's fall from grace and ultimate redemption. 240pp. 5⅜ x 8½.
0-486-46818-6

THE LOST LANGUAGE OF SYMBOLISM, Harold Bayley. This remarkable book reveals the hidden meaning behind familiar images and words, from the origins of Santa Claus to the fleur-de-lys, drawing from mythology, folklore, religious texts, and fairy tales. 1,418 illustrations. 784pp. 5⅜ x 8½. 0-486-44787-1

MACBETH, William Shakespeare. A Scottish nobleman murders the king in order to succeed to the throne. Tortured by his conscience and fearful of discovery, he becomes tangled in a web of treachery and deceit that ultimately spells his doom. 96pp. 5³⁄₁₆ x 8¼. 0-486-27802-6

MAKING AUTHENTIC CRAFTSMAN FURNITURE: Instructions and Plans for 62 Projects, Gustav Stickley. Make authentic reproductions of handsome, functional, durable furniture: tables, chairs, wall cabinets, desks, a hall tree, and more. Construction plans with drawings, schematics, dimensions, and lumber specs reprinted from 1900s The Craftsman magazine. 128pp. 8⅛ x 11. 0-486-25000-8

MATHEMATICS FOR THE NONMATHEMATICIAN, Morris Kline. Erudite and entertaining overview follows development of mathematics from ancient Greeks to present. Topics include logic and mathematics, the fundamental concept, differential calculus, probability theory, much more. Exercises and problems. 641pp. 5⅜ x 8½. 0-486-24823-2

MEMOIRS OF AN ARABIAN PRINCESS FROM ZANZIBAR, Emily Ruete. This 19th-century autobiography offers a rare inside look at the society surrounding a sultan's palace. A real-life princess in exile recalls her vanished world of harems, slave trading, and court intrigues. 288pp. 5⅜ x 8½. 0-486-47121-7

Browse over 9,000 books at www.doverpublications.com

CATALOG OF DOVER BOOKS

THE METAMORPHOSIS AND OTHER STORIES, Franz Kafka. Excellent new English translations of title story (considered by many critics Kafka's most perfect work), plus "The Judgment," "In the Penal Colony," "A Country Doctor," and "A Report to an Academy." Note. 96pp. 5³⁄₁₆ x 8¼. 0-486-29030-1

MICROSCOPIC ART FORMS FROM THE PLANT WORLD, R. Anheisser. From undulating curves to complex geometrics, a world of fascinating images abound in this classic, illustrated survey of microscopic plants. Features 400 detailed illustrations of nature's minute but magnificent handiwork. The accompanying CD-ROM includes all of the images in the book. 128pp. 9 x 9. 0-486-46013-4

A MIDSUMMER NIGHT'S DREAM, William Shakespeare. Among the most popular of Shakespeare's comedies, this enchanting play humorously celebrates the vagaries of love as it focuses upon the intertwined romances of several pairs of lovers. Explanatory footnotes. 80pp. 5³⁄₁₆ x 8¼. 0-486-27067-X

THE MONEY CHANGERS, Upton Sinclair. Originally published in 1908, this cautionary novel from the author of *The Jungle* explores corruption within the American system as a group of power brokers joins forces for personal gain, triggering a crash on Wall Street. 192pp. 5⅜ x 8½. 0-486-46917-4

THE MOST POPULAR HOMES OF THE TWENTIES, William A. Radford. With a New Introduction by Daniel D. Reiff. Based on a rare 1925 catalog, this architectural showcase features floor plans, construction details, and photos of 26 homes, plus articles on entrances, porches, garages, and more. 250 illustrations, 21 color plates. 176pp. 8⅜ x 11. 0-486-47028-8

MY 66 YEARS IN THE BIG LEAGUES, Connie Mack. With a New Introduction by Rich Westcott. A Founding Father of modern baseball, Mack holds the record for most wins — and losses — by a major league manager. Enhanced by 70 photographs, his warmhearted autobiography is populated by many legends of the game. 288pp. 5⅜ x 8½. 0-486-47184-5

NARRATIVE OF THE LIFE OF FREDERICK DOUGLASS, Frederick Douglass. Douglass's graphic depictions of slavery, harrowing escape to freedom, and life as a newspaper editor, eloquent orator, and impassioned abolitionist. 96pp. 5³⁄₁₆ x 8¼. 0-486-28499-9

THE NIGHTLESS CITY: Geisha and Courtesan Life in Old Tokyo, J. E. de Becker. This unsurpassed study from 100 years ago ventured into Tokyo's red-light district to survey geisha and courtesan life and offer meticulous descriptions of training, dress, social hierarchy, and erotic practices. 49 black-and-white illustrations; 2 maps. 496pp. 5⅜ x 8½. 0-486-45563-7

THE ODYSSEY, Homer. Excellent prose translation of ancient epic recounts adventures of the homeward-bound Odysseus. Fantastic cast of gods, giants, cannibals, sirens, other supernatural creatures — true classic of Western literature. 256pp. 5³⁄₁₆ x 8¼. 0-486-40654-7

OEDIPUS REX, Sophocles. Landmark of Western drama concerns the catastrophe that ensues when King Oedipus discovers he has inadvertently killed his father and married his mother. Masterly construction, dramatic irony. Explanatory footnotes. 64pp. 5³⁄₁₆ x 8¼. 0-486-26877-2

ONCE UPON A TIME: The Way America Was, Eric Sloane. Nostalgic text and drawings brim with gentle philosophies and descriptions of how we used to live — self-sufficiently — on the land, in homes, and among the things built by hand. 44 line illustrations. 64pp. 8⅜ x 11. 0-486-44411-2

ONE OF OURS, Willa Cather. The Pulitzer Prize–winning novel about a young Nebraskan looking for something to believe in. Alienated from his parents, rejected by his wife, he finds his destiny on the bloody battlefields of World War I. 352pp. 5³⁄₁₆ x 8¼. 0-486-45599-8

ORIGAMI YOU CAN USE: 27 Practical Projects, Rick Beech. Origami models can be more than decorative, and this unique volume shows how! The 27 practical projects include a CD case, frame, napkin ring, and dish. Easy instructions feature 400 two-color illustrations. 96pp. 8¼ x 11. 0-486-47057-1

OTHELLO, William Shakespeare. Towering tragedy tells the story of a Moorish general who earns the enmity of his ensign Iago when he passes him over for a promotion. Masterly portrait of an archvillain. Explanatory footnotes. 112pp. 5³⁄₁₆ x 8¼.
0-486-29097-2

PARADISE LOST, John Milton. Notes by John A. Himes. First published in 1667, *Paradise Lost* ranks among the greatest of English literature's epic poems. It's a sublime retelling of Adam and Eve's fall from grace and expulsion from Eden. Notes by John A. Himes. 480pp. 5³⁄₁₆ x 8¼. 0-486-44287-X

PASSING, Nella Larsen. Married to a successful physician and prominently ensconced in society, Irene Redfield leads a charmed existence — until a chance encounter with a childhood friend who has been "passing for white." 112pp. 5⅜ x 8½. 0-486-43713-2

PERSPECTIVE DRAWING FOR BEGINNERS, Len A. Doust. Doust carefully explains the roles of lines, boxes, and circles, and shows how visualizing shapes and forms can be used in accurate depictions of perspective. One of the most concise introductions available. 33 illustrations. 64pp. 5⅜ x 8½. 0-486-45149-6

PERSPECTIVE MADE EASY, Ernest R. Norling. Perspective is easy; yet, surprisingly few artists know the simple rules that make it so. Remedy that situation with this simple, step-by-step book, the first devoted entirely to the topic. 256 illustrations. 224pp. 5⅜ x 8½. 0-486-40473-0

THE PICTURE OF DORIAN GRAY, Oscar Wilde. Celebrated novel involves a handsome young Londoner who sinks into a life of depravity. His body retains perfect youth and vigor while his recent portrait reflects the ravages of his crime and sensuality. 176pp. 5³⁄₁₆ x 8¼. 0-486-27807-7

PRIDE AND PREJUDICE, Jane Austen. One of the most universally loved and admired English novels, an effervescent tale of rural romance transformed by Jane Austen's art into a witty, shrewdly observed satire of English country life. 272pp. 5³⁄₁₆ x 8¼.
0-486-28473-5

THE PRINCE, Niccolò Machiavelli. Classic, Renaissance-era guide to acquiring and maintaining political power. Today, nearly 500 years after it was written, this calculating prescription for autocratic rule continues to be much read and studied. 80pp. 5³⁄₁₆ x 8¼. 0-486-27274-5

QUICK SKETCHING, Carl Cheek. A perfect introduction to the technique of "quick sketching." Drawing upon an artist's immediate emotional responses, this is an extremely effective means of capturing the essential form and features of a subject. More than 100 black-and-white illustrations throughout. 48pp. 11 x 8¼.
0-486-46608-6

RANCH LIFE AND THE HUNTING TRAIL, Theodore Roosevelt. Illustrated by Frederic Remington. Beautifully illustrated by Remington, Roosevelt's celebration of the Old West recounts his adventures in the Dakota Badlands of the 1880s, from round-ups to Indian encounters to hunting bighorn sheep. 208pp. 6¼ x 9¼. 0-486-47340-6

THE RED BADGE OF COURAGE, Stephen Crane. Amid the nightmarish chaos of a Civil War battle, a young soldier discovers courage, humility, and, perhaps, wisdom. Uncanny re-creation of actual combat. Enduring landmark of American fiction. 112pp. 5³⁄₁₆ x 8¼. 0-486-26465-3

RELATIVITY SIMPLY EXPLAINED, Martin Gardner. One of the subject's clearest, most entertaining introductions offers lucid explanations of special and general theories of relativity, gravity, and spacetime, models of the universe, and more. 100 illustrations. 224pp. 5⅜ x 8½. 0-486-29315-7

REMBRANDT DRAWINGS: 116 Masterpieces in Original Color, Rembrandt van Rijn. This deluxe hardcover edition features drawings from throughout the Dutch master's prolific career. Informative captions accompany these beautifully reproduced landscapes, biblical vignettes, figure studies, animal sketches, and portraits. 128pp. 8⅜ x 11. 0-486-46149-1

THE ROAD NOT TAKEN AND OTHER POEMS, Robert Frost. A treasury of Frost's most expressive verse. In addition to the title poem: "An Old Man's Winter Night," "In the Home Stretch," "Meeting and Passing," "Putting in the Seed," many more. All complete and unabridged. 64pp. 5³⁄₁₆ x 8¼. 0-486-27550-7

ROMEO AND JULIET, William Shakespeare. Tragic tale of star-crossed lovers, feuding families and timeless passion contains some of Shakespeare's most beautiful and lyrical love poetry. Complete, unabridged text with explanatory footnotes. 96pp. 5³⁄₁₆ x 8¼. 0-486-27557-4

SANDITON AND THE WATSONS: Austen's Unfinished Novels, Jane Austen. Two tantalizing incomplete stories revisit Austen's customary milieu of courtship and venture into new territory, amid guests at a seaside resort. Both are worth reading for pleasure and study. 112pp. 5⅜ x 8½. 0-486-45793-1

THE SCARLET LETTER, Nathaniel Hawthorne. With stark power and emotional depth, Hawthorne's masterpiece explores sin, guilt, and redemption in a story of adultery in the early days of the Massachusetts Colony. 192pp. 5³⁄₁₆ x 8¼.
0-486-28048-9

THE SEASONS OF AMERICA PAST, Eric Sloane. Seventy-five illustrations depict cider mills and presses, sleds, pumps, stump-pulling equipment, plows, and other elements of America's rural heritage. A section of old recipes and household hints adds additional color. 160pp. 8⅜ x 11. 0-486-44220-9

SELECTED CANTERBURY TALES, Geoffrey Chaucer. Delightful collection includes the General Prologue plus three of the most popular tales: "The Knight's Tale," "The Miller's Prologue and Tale," and "The Wife of Bath's Prologue and Tale." In modern English. 144pp. 5³⁄₁₆ x 8¼. 0-486-28241-4

SELECTED POEMS, Emily Dickinson. Over 100 best-known, best-loved poems by one of America's foremost poets, reprinted from authoritative early editions. No comparable edition at this price. Index of first lines. 64pp. 5³⁄₁₆ x 8¼. 0-486-26466-1

SIDDHARTHA, Hermann Hesse. Classic novel that has inspired generations of seekers. Blending Eastern mysticism and psychoanalysis, Hesse presents a strikingly original view of man and culture and the arduous process of self-discovery, reconciliation, harmony, and peace. 112pp. 5³⁄₁₆ x 8¼. 0-486-40653-9

SKETCHING OUTDOORS, Leonard Richmond. This guide offers beginners step-by-step demonstrations of how to depict clouds, trees, buildings, and other outdoor sights. Explanations of a variety of techniques include shading and constructional drawing. 48pp. 11 x 8¼. 0-486-46922-0

SMALL HOUSES OF THE FORTIES: With Illustrations and Floor Plans, Harold E. Group. 56 floor plans and elevations of houses that originally cost less than $15,000 to build. Recommended by financial institutions of the era, they range from Colonials to Cape Cods. 144pp. 8⅜ x 11. 0-486-45598-X

SOME CHINESE GHOSTS, Lafcadio Hearn. Rooted in ancient Chinese legends, these richly atmospheric supernatural tales are recounted by an expert in Oriental lore. Their originality, power, and literary charm will captivate readers of all ages. 96pp. 5⅜ x 8½. 0-486-46306-0

SONGS FOR THE OPEN ROAD: Poems of Travel and Adventure, Edited by The American Poetry & Literacy Project. More than 80 poems by 50 American and British masters celebrate real and metaphorical journeys. Poems by Whitman, Byron, Millay, Sandburg, Langston Hughes, Emily Dickinson, Robert Frost, Shelley, Tennyson, Yeats, many others. Note. 80pp. 5³⁄₁₆ x 8¼. 0-486-40646-6

SPOON RIVER ANTHOLOGY, Edgar Lee Masters. An American poetry classic, in which former citizens of a mythical midwestern town speak touchingly from the grave of the thwarted hopes and dreams of their lives. 144pp. 5³⁄₁₆ x 8¼. 0-486-27275-3

STAR LORE: Myths, Legends, and Facts, William Tyler Olcott. Captivating retellings of the origins and histories of ancient star groups include Pegasus, Ursa Major, Pleiades, signs of the zodiac, and other constellations. "Classic." — *Sky & Telescope.* 58 illustrations. 544pp. 5⅜ x 8½. 0-486-43581-4

THE STRANGE CASE OF DR. JEKYLL AND MR. HYDE, Robert Louis Stevenson. This intriguing novel, both fantasy thriller and moral allegory, depicts the struggle of two opposing personalities — one essentially good, the other evil — for the soul of one man. 64pp. 5³⁄₁₆ x 8¼. 0-486-26688-5

SURVIVAL HANDBOOK: The Official U.S. Army Guide, Department of the Army. This special edition of the Army field manual is geared toward civilians. An essential companion for campers and all lovers of the outdoors, it constitutes the most authoritative wilderness guide. 288pp. 5³⁄₁₆ x 8¼. 0-486-46184-X

A TALE OF TWO CITIES, Charles Dickens. Against the backdrop of the French Revolution, Dickens unfolds his masterpiece of drama, adventure, and romance about a man falsely accused of treason. Excitement and derring-do in the shadow of the guillotine. 304pp. 5³⁄₁₆ x 8¼. 0-486-40651-2

TEN PLAYS, Anton Chekhov. *The Sea Gull, Uncle Vanya, The Three Sisters, The Cherry Orchard,* and *Ivanov,* plus 5 one-act comedies: *The Anniversary, An Unwilling Martyr, The Wedding, The Bear,* and *The Proposal.* 336pp. 5³⁄₁₆ x 8¼. 0-486-46560-8

THE FLYING INN, G. K. Chesterton. Hilarious romp in which pub owner Humphrey Hump and friend take to the road in a donkey cart filled with rum and cheese, inveighing against Prohibition and other "oppressive forms of modernity." 320pp. 5⅜ x 8½. 0-486-41910-X

THIRTY YEARS THAT SHOOK PHYSICS: The Story of Quantum Theory, George Gamow. Lucid, accessible introduction to the influential theory of energy and matter features careful explanations of Dirac's anti-particles, Bohr's model of the atom, and much more. Numerous drawings. 1966 edition. 240pp. 5⅜ x 8½. 0-486-24895-X

TREASURE ISLAND, Robert Louis Stevenson. Classic adventure story of a perilous sea journey, a mutiny led by the infamous Long John Silver, and a lethal scramble for buried treasure — seen through the eyes of cabin boy Jim Hawkins. 160pp. 5³⁄₁₆ x 8¼. 0-486-27559-0

Browse over 9,000 books at www.doverpublications.com

THE TRIAL, Franz Kafka. Translated by David Wyllie. From its gripping first sentence onward, this novel exemplifies the term "Kafkaesque." Its darkly humorous narrative recounts a bank clerk's entrapment in a bureaucratic maze, based on an undisclosed charge. 176pp. 5$\frac{3}{16}$ x 8¼. 0-486-47061-X

THE TURN OF THE SCREW, Henry James. Gripping ghost story by great novelist depicts the sinister transformation of 2 innocent children into flagrant liars and hypocrites. An elegantly told tale of unspoken horror and psychological terror. 96pp. 5$\frac{3}{16}$ x 8¼. 0-486-26684-2

UP FROM SLAVERY, Booker T. Washington. Washington (1856-1915) rose to become the most influential spokesman for African-Americans of his day. In this eloquently written book, he describes events in a remarkable life that began in bondage and culminated in worldwide recognition. 160pp. 5$\frac{3}{16}$ x 8¼. 0-486-28738-6

VICTORIAN HOUSE DESIGNS IN AUTHENTIC FULL COLOR: 75 Plates from the "Scientific American – Architects and Builders Edition," 1885-1894, Edited by Blanche Cirker. Exquisitely detailed, exceptionally handsome designs for an enormous variety of attractive city dwellings, spacious suburban and country homes, charming "cottages" and other structures — all accompanied by perspective views and floor plans. 80pp. 9¼ x 12¼. 0-486-29438-2

VILLETTE, Charlotte Brontë. Acclaimed by Virginia Woolf as "Brontë's finest novel," this moving psychological study features a remarkably modern heroine who abandons her native England for a new life as a schoolteacher in Belgium. 480pp. 5$\frac{3}{16}$ x 8¼. 0-486-45557-2

THE VOYAGE OUT, Virginia Woolf. A moving depiction of the thrills and confusion of youth, Woolf's acclaimed first novel traces a shipboard journey to South America for a captivating exploration of a woman's growing self-awareness. 288pp. 5$\frac{3}{16}$ x 8¼. 0-486-45005-8

WALDEN; OR, LIFE IN THE WOODS, Henry David Thoreau. Accounts of Thoreau's daily life on the shores of Walden Pond outside Concord, Massachusetts, are interwoven with musings on the virtues of self-reliance and individual freedom, on society, government, and other topics. 224pp. 5$\frac{3}{16}$ x 8¼. 0-486-28495-6

WILD PILGRIMAGE: A Novel in Woodcuts, Lynd Ward. Through startling engravings shaded in black and red, Ward wordlessly tells the story of a man trapped in an industrial world, struggling between the grim reality around him and the fantasies his imagination creates. 112pp. 6⅛ x 9¼. 0-486-46583-7

WILLY POGÁNY REDISCOVERED, Willy Pogány. Selected and Edited by Jeff A. Menges. More than 100 color and black-and-white Art Nouveau–style illustrations from fairy tales and adventure stories include scenes from Wagner's "Ring" cycle, *The Rime of the Ancient Mariner, Gulliver's Travels,* and *Faust.* 144pp. 8⅜ x 11. 0-486-47046-6

WOOLLY THOUGHTS: Unlock Your Creative Genius with Modular Knitting, Pat Ashforth and Steve Plummer. Here's the revolutionary way to knit — easy, fun, and foolproof! Beginners and experienced knitters need only master a single stitch to create their own designs with patchwork squares. More than 100 illustrations. 128pp. 6½ x 9¼. 0-486-46084-3

WUTHERING HEIGHTS, Emily Brontë. Somber tale of consuming passions and vengeance — played out amid the lonely English moors — recounts the turbulent and tempestuous love story of Cathy and Heathcliff. Poignant and compelling. 256pp. 5$\frac{3}{16}$ x 8¼. 0-486-29256-8

Browse over 9,000 books at www.doverpublications.com